Back to Modern Reason

ARNE JARRICK

Back to Modern Reason

*Johan Hjerpe and other petit bourgeois
in Stockholm in the Age of Enlightenment*

LIVERPOOL UNIVERSITY PRESS

First published in 1992 as
Mot det moderna förnuftet
by Tidens Förlag, Stockholm

This translation first published 1999 by
LIVERPOOL UNIVERSITY PRESS
Liverpool L69 3BX

British Library Cataloguing-in-Publication Data
A British Library CIP record is available

ISBN 0–85323–583–X (hardback)
ISBN 0–85323–593–7 (paperback)
Typeset in 11/12 pt Bembo by
Wilmaset Ltd, Birkenhead, Wirral
Printed by Alden Press, Oxford

Contents

List of Illustrations

(after page 84)

Acknowledgements

This book was written under difficult circumstances, although it was part of my research obligations and received economic support from the Swedish Council for Research in the Humanities and Social Sciences (Humanistisk-samhällsvetenskapliga forskningsrådet, HSFR).[1] I am grateful for this support. Research is lonely work, but I was always surrounded by people who corrected and supported, criticised and encouraged. I am very grateful for this too.

First of all, I would like to thank Herman Schück, for having brought Johan Hjerpe to my attention. I would also like to mention my friends at the Department of Economic History in Stockholm – my workplace since the year dot – and among them, in particular, Rolf Adamson, Sven Fritz, Ulf Jonsson, Anu-Mai Köll, Tomas Lappalainen, Gunilla Peterson, Ronny Pettersson and Johan Söderberg, all of whom were very attentive and saved me from blunders I might otherwise have made. Outside the Department, but within the academic community, Anita Ankarcrona, Gunilla Halldén, Gunilla Sahlin and Per-Johan Ödman, among others, offered many pertinent comments, as did the participants of various seminars held at different places in Sweden: seminars on the history of ideas in Stockholm and Umeå; the history seminars in Stockholm, Gothenburg and Uppsala; and the seminar on the history of education at the Department of Education in Stockholm. Archivists throughout Sweden also deserve my deepest gratitude, particularly the staff at the manuscript department of the Royal Library, and Allan Ranius at the diocesan and regional library in Linköping, who were so helpful. Finally, I would especially like to thank Börje Berfeldt, Solveig Hollari and Samuel Jarrick for helping me extract the information needed.

This book is largely based on material already published, before being re-worked and rearranged. Chapter 1 was published under the title 'Johan Hjerpe and the mobilisation of the artisans for king and war, 27 April 1789' ('Johan Hjerpe och hantverkaruppbådet för kung och krig 27 April 1789') in *Scandia*, Volume 53 (1987). Chapter 2 bears a passable resemblance to 'Ten theses about how we think' ('Tio teser om hur vi tänker'), *Häften för kritiska studier*, Number 1 (1988), while Chapter 3 can be found – albeit in a different form – under the title 'Burghers, Common folk and books in eighteenth-century-Stockholm' ('Borgare, småfolk och böcker i 1700-talets Stockholm', *Historisk tidskrift*, Volume 110 (1990). The fourth chapter was published in

Antropologiska studier (1990) under the title 'New cultural history and old history of mentality: some critical and anti-criticial notes' ('Ny kulturhistoria och gammal mentalitetshistoria: några kritiska och anti-kritiska anmärkningar'). Chapter 5 is based on two different articles. One is 'The world according to Hjerpe or two popular pieces of writing from the time of the Enlightenment' ('Världen enligt Hjerpe eller Två folkliga skriftprov från upplysningstiden'), *Historisk tidskrift*, Volume III (1991); the other is 'A shop assistant under the influence of two revolutions' ('Ett bodbiträde i korstrycket från två revolutioner'), *Kulturrådet*, Number 2 (1989). Chapter 6 is previously unpublished. References to my other works are to be found at the end of the book.

Abbreviations

Bou	Bouptechningar
EBAS	Evangeliska brödraförsamlingens arkiv, Stockholm
ESA	Eskilstuna Stadsarkiv
GLA	Göteborgs Landsarkiv
HSFR	Humanistisk-samhällsvetenskapliga forskningsrådet
JHJ	Johan Hjerpes journal
KB	Kungliga Biblioteket
LSB	Linköpings Stiftsbibliotek
NordMA	Nordiska Museets Arkiv
RA	Riksarkivet
SBA	Svensk Bibliografi 1700–1829
SSA	Stockholms Stadsarkiv
UUB	Uppsala Universitetsbibliotek

Introduction: Johan Hjerpe
and Enlightenment

The Bourgeois

Johan Hjerpe was born in Stockholm in 1765 and died sixty years later. The son of a poor Moravian master tailor, he eventually became a member of the evangelical brotherhood, the Moravian brethren.

In his youth, Johan Hjerpe served in the linen shop of the wholesaler Anders Kjellstedt in the Old Town. Like others he started at the bottom but did better than most, rising in time above his humble beginnings.[2] An industrious and decent man, in 1801 he eventually acquired a small workshop for the production of silk thread and camel hair, by which time he was already thirty-five years old. Alone or with an employee, he ran his little workshop for many years before leaving the capital and moving to the country.

In the parish of Synnerby in Skaraborg county, in south-western Sweden, there is an estate called Myran. It was already quite a large estate when Hjerpe purchased it in the early 1820s. Here he spent the last years of his life, as a well-to-do resident of advancing years. The parish register describes him as a fabriqueur who had migrated from the capital.

Ten years before he moved there, Hjerpe had visited Synnerby in the company of a former employer, his good friend Anders Kjellstedt. Presumably planning the purchase far in advance, the site was chosen with care, for his father had once served there as a farm-hand. Unfortunately, Johan fell ill after only five years in his new home and died of a 'raging fever' at the age of sixty years and five months. Fortunately, he left behind no wife to mourn him and made no children fatherless, for he had never married and had fathered no offspring. He left only inanimate objects – among them, a large collection of books and several bundles of manuscripts written in his own hand.[3]

These inanimate objects bring the man to life. It is Johan Hjerpe's unpublished literary remains that make him interesting, for they open up his world of ideas. He was not just anyone, he was a man of the people and he did not belong to the tiny aristocracy that loved to put its thoughts on paper and which succeeded in attracting the interest of posterity.

It would appear that Johan Hjerpe wrote throughout his entire life – a rather voluminous diary in his youth; historical works about Stockholm and world history later on; an account of an excursion to southern Sweden during which he visited Synnerby; and a book of poems, mostly written by others but possibly including some of his own; in total close to 1,500 quarto pages, all of them written in neat black hand writing.

The manuscripts have survived and can be perused to this day. The volumes in his book collection are still, by and large, accessible, even though many were sold and dispersed, when the collection was auctioned off in the cathedral city of Skara after Hjerpe's death.[4] It is also possible to trace what he read, and even to follow his very act of reading, for in several of the preserved manuscripts he has made a neat note of the documents consulted in his interpretation of the world and of history. His precision is considerable, and the page references are usually correct. It is therefore possible to make penetrating comparisons between text and original, and in this way infer what material Hjerpe made use of, reworked according to his own discretion, rejected or simply skimmed over in the documents he read.[5]

Here, then, is a burgher from Stockholm, who grew up during the reign of Gustavus III, the enlightened despot to whom Voltaire paid tribute, a petit bourgeois with a mind that can be opened by anyone curious about the thoughts of such a man. This could, perhaps, provide an answer to the question of whether the enlightened reason of the time made any impression on Hjerpe, or whether Enlightenment was merely a foreign intellectual trend, too remote to dispel what 'les philosophes' would have considered to be his inner darkness.

Enlightenment

The eighteenth-century Enlightenment movement knew that it was indeed an enlightenment movement – for that is what it called itself – and was not preoccupied only with being there.[6] While its advocates disagreed about both the future and the past, they were in agreement when they declared their own present to be the spiritual pinnacle of history.[7]

The Romantic social thinkers of the 1820s naturally took a different view. To them, Enlightenment represented the starting point for a series of happenings: the Revolution, the Jacobin terror and Napoleon's train of conquest through Europe. It is possible – and perhaps even probable – that the emperor Napoleon was indifferent to French Enlightenment. However, many subsequently associated him with it: he pushed Enlightenment to its terrifying culmination, thereby also hastening its ultimate downfall.[8]

By the 1820s, then, Enlightenment had come and gone. But though it may have gone, it was hardly forgotten, as the hatred that was now turned upon it, born of its repercussions, was to do the harm which continued to be felt by nineteenth-century society.

In 1821 the Swedish journal *Hermes* published an essay entitled 'Teleological reflections on world history' by the Romantic writer Lorenzo Hammarsköld who had submitted it as an entry to a competition announced by the Scientific Society of Lund.[9] The essay won first prize. Because Hammarsköld attempted, among other things, to assess the significance of Enlightenment to societal development, and because the intellectual élite obviously liked the essay, it is also probable that it says something about the relationship of the early Swedish Romantic period to the epoch which had just passed. The essay is rich in content. The following excerpt is typical of the way in which Hammarsköld links revolution and enlightenment:[10]

First here in Sweden, France, Holland, Norway, Poland and now recently in Spain and Naples, by virtue of a properly agreed upon contract between Regent and populace, a more precise constitution, safeguarding the sanctity of the rights of the two elements of the state, has been introduced. In this way, according to the demands of world wisdom, the Monarchy has become a visible image of absolute power, from which all life emanates, regulated and directed, but not more, by the Ideas, which through the realm's free Estates are represented; however, from this form of Governance, expressed on paper and sealed, the spirit has nevertheless not penetrated and refined the opinions of the masses. On the contrary, a child of the empirical Encyclopaedia or the Enlightenment known since the French Revolution by the name of Jacobinism, has, in the course of recent events, flourished, multiplied and spread to all parts, which manifests itself through the essence, emanating entirely from certain concepts abstracted from limited experience; a determined endeavour against all ideas striving beyond the temporal good; an ahistorical hatred of all existing forms and a wrath against the Nobility, of which it is not a part. This giant spectre roams everywhere [. . .] Thus, in France and Spain, a fire still glows beneath the ashes, now and then to burst out in conflagrations; thus the English rabble rages against the Machines which have denied them livelihood and bread [. . .]

It was not only its Romantic critics who associated Enlightenment with the Revolution, even if it was typical of them to do so. Friends of Enlightenment did so as well, as, for example, in 'Comments' on the old saying: 'It is better to believe too much than too little', an anonymous little publication of 1799 dedicated to the friends of the Enlightenment (Anmärkningar vid den gamla Folks-maximen: 'Det är bättre att tro för mycket än för litet', helgade åt Upplysningens vänner). The unknown author makes an obvious connection here between hatred of Enlightenment and hatred of Jacobinism, and these two major social movements are associated with uninhibited freedom of thought and expression, a freedom which the author heatedly defends.

Discussion on Enlightenment continued throughout the entire nineteenth century, and continues to this day. New generations have continually assessed and reassessed its continuing impact, both on eighteenth-century France and on their own times. The Frankfurt philosophers must be included in this category – Theodor Adorno and Max Horkheimer, for example, who, from a radical point of departure, associated Enlightenment with the capitalist industrial system, i.e., with a scientifically regulated order.[11] The heirs of the Frankfurt School are, perhaps, Michel Foucault and Jürgen Habermas, prominent figures in the contemporary debate over the consequences of Enlightenment. While Habermas is more positive in his assessment than his Frankfurt School predecessors, Foucault, in explicit adherence to it, clearly aims his remarks at Enlightenment, even if he almost entirely circumvents the concept of the epoch itself.[12] The year before his death, however, Foucault gave a lecture at the Collège de France explicitly dedicated to Enlightenment, entitled 'Enlightenment, the Revolution and the possibilities of progress' in which, at long last, he confessed his intellectual affinity with the Frankfurt School. 'It is this latter philosophy', he writes 'which from Hegel and up to the Frankfurt School, via Nietzsche and Max Weber, has laid the foundations for a form of reflection in which I have sought to work further.'[13]

With time, the association between Enlightenment and Revolution has become less self-evident than it was to the advocates and opponents of yesteryear, and a number of scholars now doubt or deny that the former was the cause of the latter. Some even question these epoch concepts and reduce them to constructions. Here, too, Foucault has had a finger in the pie. Historians such as Roger Chartier and Lynn Hunt and, to some extent, Robert Darnton, belong to this circle of sceptics, although they vary in their degree of scepticism and are also critical of each other.[14] The Frankfurt philosophers were critical of Enlightenment. Hammarsköld disliked it too, although for him it was the workers' struggle against the industrial-capitalist order and not the order itself that was characteristic of it.

The censure which has been aimed at Enlightenment has been concerned with offences which should be mutually exclusive, and it is naturally impossible to determine whether a movement which has been defined in such a contradictory way was the cause of everything for which it has been customarily blamed. Whatever the case, Enlightenment has in some way probably been important to Western history over the past two hundred years, either directly or as one current in a larger course of events. With Enlightenment, a whole series of intellectual processes was thrown into unusually sharp relief, processes which ever since have left their mark on the development of thinking in the Western part of the world. So while Enlightenment eludes every attempt at definitive assessment, it nevertheless deserves to be described, despite the fact that every new description risks being contradicted by a thousand others.

In my view, Enlightenment can be described as an articulated but informal programme for a new view of knowledge and for a new relationship between man, society and the cosmos.[15] It also formed a distinct epoch in the history of Europe, with its centre in France, culminating somewhere in the mid eighteenth century. Even if this programme is still associated at some times with Locke's empiricism and at others with Kant's rationalism (and sometimes with both at once), it consolidated around the challenging thought that knowledge must be sought without prejudice,[16] and for an unprejudiced search for knowledge to be possible, each individual had to be protected from the expectations of the powerful that certain dogmas should be adhered to, not least those of the church. In his major work on Enlightenment, Peter Gay emphasises secularisation as having been at once fundamental and common to both early and later Enlightenment.[17] The new view of knowledge had much to do with demands for certain inviolable human rights. The belief in the possibilities of a steady growth in knowledge was based on the demand that the truth be sought in a 'scientific' manner, through a stringent distinction between the researching subject and the studied object. This is one aspect of that which Adorno and Horkheimer particularly emphasised. In this way, they argue, Enlightenment tends to undermine itself: the human subject is and remains imperfect; knowledge and thus the growth of knowledge are always uncertain.[18] With enhanced knowledge, both a refinement of human souls and an improvement in material conditions in society could follow. This is not to say, however, that Enlightenment was a thoroughly evolutionary-optimist movement. It was, perhaps, once the norm to believe that, but this notion has now been seriously brought into question.[19]

The petit bourgeois has already been identified, and Enlightenment would now seem to have been established – and they are both well matched for each other. It is quite clear that Hjerpe sought out, or at least allowed himself to become exposed to, literature of Enlightenment. He was an avid reader of *Stockholms Posten*, for example – the leading organ of Enlightenment in Stockholm at that time – and had the relevant volumes in his book collection. The preconditions would seem to be suitable for answering the question: what kind of impression has Enlightenment, or an enlightened mentality, made on a petit bourgeois in the Stockholm of the Gustavusian period?[20]

Finding an answer to this is more difficult than it seems. In the first place, one should be cautious about reducing Enlightenment to a few simple formulae, for its most prominent figures were not united around an elaborated programme to the strict sense of the word. On the contrary, they often defended opposing views, even though it is difficult to discern fixed groupings among their ranks. This was just as much the case in the Swedish periphery as in the centre of the enlightened stage. Where John Locke and the leading men of late Swedish Enlightenment, Johan Henrik Kellgren and Nils Rosén von Rosenstein, asserted an empiricistic theory of knowledge, Immannuel Kant and the revolutionary Thomas Thorild defended a rationalistic one. Kellgren's Enlightenment ideology also lacked the anti-aristocratic features which were so prominent with the leading light of the intelligentsia, Thorild. Where Voltaire and the enlightened historian Sven Lagerbring (and periodically Kellgren) accepted enlightened despotism, with its tolerance of some but not all of their subjects' 'misconceptions', Kant and Thorild (and von Rosenstein, although Thorild denied it) stressed the demand for unconditional intellectual autonomy for every individual. If Kant, Rosenstein and Thorild, each in his own way, wanted to spread knowledge and reason to all people, Voltaire (and perhaps Kellgren) dreaded the consequences of enlightenment spreading to the entire populace.[21]

But certain ideas nevertheless held the Enlightenment programme together. The essence of the movement was now, as I see it, the concerted effort on the part of Enlightenment philosophers to divest authorised ideological and cultural positions of their universal, timeless validity. Knowledge had to be supported by experience, but experience was limited and specific, and the truth thus relative and not absolute. This was the reason (not the cause) for Enlightenment philosophers choosing foreign cultures as vantage points for reflecting on their own. In this way, they were able to cultivate the self-reflective relativism that was the basis for the notion of tolerance they fought for and which was intended to dislodge the values that, until then, had been accepted as eternal. This relativism threatened to invalidate the certainty of insights attained by fragile subjects, and rendered more difficult a belief in the cumulative expansion of knowledge. As already stated, this is a very prominent notion in the study by Adorno and Horkheimer of the dialectic of Enlightenment, even if their view was, at the same time, that continued modernisation could eventually replace subjectivity with some sort of automatism or repressive rationality.[22]

This is very interesting. Apart from the naïve faith in the manipulative possibilities of science with which Enlightenment philosophy now tends to be associated, it also generated, as a consequence of its inexorable logic, fundamental doubts about the possibilities of a cumulative growth in knowledge. It could thus be said that the post-modern critique of scholarship has its basis in Enlightenment just as much as modernistic scientism does.

Of the related themes that grew out of the relativism of Enlightenment, some were more prominent than others: a secularised deism or atheism; an expanded consciousness of the value of foreign cultures; and the revolutionary notion that history never repeats itself. For some, but only for some –

such as Fontenelle, Turgot or Condorcet – this notion was elevated to a faith in progress.

These were ideas which, were they to spread to the public, could entail definite changes in mentality beyond the stratum of thought-generators: a more tolerant view of personal differences and opposing views; a cumulative view of the development of society; and a secularised view of man's place in the cosmos, i.e., a view in which an admittedly lingering God remained, albeit remote from the centre of the world of ideas.

But it is not easy to follow the course the ideas of Enlightenment took in their dissemination: if they are found among ordinary people, it is not at all certain that they trickled down 'from above'; and if they are not to be found, it could be either because they were assessed and rejected or because they were incorporated secretly.

In the second place, Enlightenment has sometimes been associated – indeed identified – with the secular education or modernising process which was set in train with the emergence and consolidation of the newly established centralised nation state. In this way, Enlightenment loses its distinctive character and is seen instead as a phase in a long-term process of change. Its ideal of freedom and faith in reason were really an irresistible temptation for the aristocracy and middle-class élite.[23] This faith in reason was also used as an instrument to discipline the people.[24] Magic and superstition which ruled the populace were considered obstacles to the development of society. The art of printing, for example, and efforts to bring literacy to the entire population were interpreted as the technique of those in power to make people good Christians: among other things, heretical notions would be exterminated in this way.[25] So even before the literacy campaign, folk culture would have given in to external pressure. This struggle culminated in the seventeenth century with the oubreak of the witch trials throughout Europe, with confrontations which conclusively sealed the fate of folk culture.[26]

Now, I do not believe that Enlightenment can be reduced to an innovation in power techniques.[27] A whole series of circumstances makes it difficult to arrive at such an interpretation. For example, one of these innovations, the art of printing, was not an obvious technique for the dissemination of the 'correct' doctrine. Much else could be, and was, thus disseminated, including traditional popular notions of the very sort which were intended to be eradicated through the medium of printing. There was also some reluctance on the part of the secular and clerical élite to bring literacy to the people as a whole.[28] Some scholars have also maintained that the distinction between popular and and élite culture has been exaggerated. One of them, Roger Chartier, has argued that too strict a popular culture/élite culture distinction can easily overlook, at least in part, the fact that the same cultural product is appropriated in different ways by different groups, as well as the fact that the distribution of cultural resources was not necessarily analogous with that of socio-economic ones.[29] One could add that the modernising perspective suffers here from an inner tension: on the one hand, it is claimed that central-isation tendencies effected an élite/popular dichotomy in a culture that had previously been shared; on the other, that a specific popular culture had existed which the élite subsequently crushed.

Nevertheless, a 'modernising perspective' on Enlightenment can help us achieve a deeper and more nuanced understanding of the process; it needs a broader view on issues pertaining to what was entailed by the cultural changes and changes in intellect which took place at that time.

Third, whether Sweden had an Enlightenment at all has been ques-tioned.[30] One of those to have done so is the Swedish science historian, Tore Frängsmyr, who has given such an organised description of Enlightenment that it would appear possible so to categorise only a very few countries and movements in eighteenth-century Europe. Frängsmyr requires of an enlight-enment that it be a movement of struggle with select troops assembled around some sort of a programme. In that programme, it should be possible to find a defence of an unprejudiced search for knowledge, belief in empiri-cally-based knowledge, and an elaborated notion of tolerance together with an explicit critique of religion, or at least Christianity. As I understand it, Frängsmyr considers the encyclopaedia of Diderot and d'Alembert as one of the foremost manifestations of this movement, and that Sweden falls almost beyond the framework of such a definition. Almost, but not entirely, as a weak Enlightenment movement emerged even in Sweden during the last two decades of the eighteenth century, that is when it had already exhausted most of its energy in the cultural capitals of Europe. It was only then that the real spirits of Enlightenment appeared on the domestic public scene in Sweden, chief among them being Johan Henrik Kellgren and Nils von Rosenstein. Inspired by the French encyclopaedists and the English empiri-cists, they drew up challenging programmes for the enlightenment and liberation of humanity, programmes which transformed the public scene to an intellectual battleground on which heated exchanges of views took place. But because Enlightenment came late to Sweden, Frängsmyr maintains that it became an episode there. The Romantic passion for old values soon ushered the young movement into a land of twilight.

As a starting point, Frängsmyr's way of delimiting Swedish Enlighten-ment to the few years in which it was at the centre of domestic debate, would, perhaps, be unprofitable in attempting to study its effect on the bour-geoisie and common folk of Stockholm. If the movement were short-lived, it should not have been able to make a profound and lasting impression on its bourgeois or petit bourgeois exponents.

But Frängsmyr's Enlightenment concept is both narrow and broad, his

Enlightenment definition at the same time stringent and inconsistent. Distinct changes in people's outlooks approaching the realisation of the Enlightenment ideal fall beyond this limit of the definition unless they can be linked to a public debate on a distinct Enlightenment programme. This is what makes it stringent. At times, his Enlightenment concept is so broad that any occurrence of a discussion movement around the programme of Enlightenment would appear to be enough to define the epoch (or episode), i.e., even if this movement had no implications for society beyond itself.[31] The inconsistency in this attempt at delimitation is apparent in several respects. On the one hand, Frängsmyr considers the epoch designation to be simply 'something artificial which the historian constructs';[32] on the other hand, that it is possible to come closer to reality with one given definition than with another.[33] Thus, some definitions appeared more artificial to Frängsmyr than others. It is, moreover, his view that all manner of things in the Swedish intellectual environment have been coherently designated as belonging to 'Enlightenment',[34] but he himself has no problem relegating Rousseau, who professed himself to be an enemy of Enlightenment, to that category.[35] Frängsmyr vacillates here somewhat, however, albeit without making an issue of his vacillation: 'Lamm finds this duplicity in Rousseau, who began his career in the spirit of the Enlightenment but subsequently converted to a more mystical–religious outlook. Therefore, *some* [my italics, AJ] have found it difficult to place Rousseau.'[36] One gets the impression that Frängsmyr measures French Enlightenment by a different yardstick from the one he uses on Swedish Enlightenment. One last word: Frängsmyr maintains that the situation of the struggle must be included in the definition of Enlightenment. This entails the militant men of Enlightenment having been in conflict with established society. He also emphasises that Enlightenment was sometimes encouraged by official society, by the court itself (as in Prussia by Frederick the Great).[37]

Apart from the inner tension in Frängsmyr's definition of Enlightenment (of which there is more than I have mentioned), it is also regrettably narrow, in my view. It should be broadened along the following lines. Should one find in this or that country a movement for tolerance and for an unprejudiced search for knowledge, it is reasonable to liken it to an Enlightenment movement. It need not be expressly associated with those phenomena familiar from French Enlightenment in order to deserve the name, even if the concept – the word of recognition, so to speak – is borrowed from it. To demand, like Frängsmyr, such a similarity would be to deprive oneself of the possibility of seeing the parallelism in mutually independent but similar currents in Europe and America at approximately the same period.

With a broader definition such as this it would be possible to consider, for example, the abolition of the secular censor in Sweden in 1766 as part of this trend, as well as continued attempts in that direction. This is not altered by the fact that retreats continually took place on this front. The thinkers of French Enlightenment, too, were not capable of being consistent in their tolerance: they also fell back, again and again, on 'substantival' positions, wanting to permit what they liked and forbid what they disliked. This fact remains in spite of the leading figures of Swedish Enlightenment – Kellgren and von Rosenstein – having found it very difficult to tolerate the intellectual challenge posed by Emanuel Swedenborg. Their principle-based tolerance went no further than this and they abruptly became unprincipled and intolerant in their attempts to impede the dissemination of Swedenborg's ideas.[38]

Enlightenment can, of course, be defined and its influence in Sweden assessed in different ways. One way would be, like Frängsmyr, to search for references in the Swedish environment to 'les philosophes' and so on. This has a certain legitimacy and is based on his essentially healthy reaction to the tendency to let virtually anything at any time bear the name Enlightenment. Another, equally legitimate, attitude is to look for the presence of specific intellectual trends and attitudes which can be associated with the ideal type 'Enlightenment'. In the former case, the intellectual content plays a subordinate role. In the latter case, it is the references to 'les philosophes' which become inessential, while that which is essential is the very identification of those processes which, in different places and at approximately the same time, led in basically the same direction, although achieving expression in different ways.

As it is precisely the distinct cultural changes which are the subject of my study, Frängsmyr's notion of Enlightenment is not quite suitable, whatever its merits. I want to ascertain whether the traces of an enlightened culture and intellect can be found among the bourgeois and petit bourgeois of late eighteenth-century Stockholm.[39] From this perspective, the philosophy of Enlightenment can be used as a reference point in identifying components of such a culture, even if nothing definite can be said about the connection between them. It does not, then, matter greatly whether this complex of ideas is considered a component of the informal encyclopaedic programme, as part of the spontaneous intellectual and mental changes, or both.

The thinkers of the Enlightenment movement had a greater presence in Sweden than Frängsmyr admits. In the Gustavusian period, the debate about the new ideas then surfacing was aired in a flourishing press which was read by many, well beyond the cultural and administrative centre of the country. The tolerance debate in the Swedish press was quite comprehensive and, in general, the themes of Enlightenment made their presence very much felt, as has been demonstrated by the research on this matter conducted by the intellectual historian, Magnus Nyman.[40] The subsequent changes in legislation of the 1778–79 parliament bear witness to the direct influence of enlightenment thinking on Swedish politics. Among other things, restrictions on the death penalty were introduced and a new infanticide bill came into being under the influence of Montesquieu, Beccaria and Voltaire.[41] It was much the same with the tolerance laws regarding Jews and Catholics.[42] Indeed, Press laws were also introduced under the influence of Voltaire, even if they were 'false' and often entailed more restrictions rather than increased freedom of expression.[43] The fact that these changes emanated from established society should not worry Frängsmyr as long as he includes the contribution of Frederick the Great as part of Enlightenment.

But even before the end of the eighteenth century, obvious traces of the doctrine of Enlightenment can be found in Sweden. There are noticeable traces of the encyclopaedists in the writing of Swedish history of the Period of Liberty, for example. Voltaire's view of history haunts the work of the domestic pioneers of the discipline – Lagerbring, Botin and Dalin,[44] whose contemporary revisions of the retrospective myths of Sweden's Great Power period were, moreover, accessible to the bourgeois public. The historians of the Period of Liberty were not satisfied with mere academic 'discourse', but also wanted to educate the people. Some of them thus reworked their monumental studies of 'The history of the Kingdom of Svea' into popular versions in 'the service of youth' (Lagerbring)[45] or 'for beginners and womenfolk' (af Botin) – works which are to be found in contemporary book collections and in the estate inventories of craftsmen and merchants.

Interestingly enough, the spread of Enlightenment literature began long before Enlightenment in Sweden grew to become what can be considered as a movement. Similarly, just as the law reforms of the late 1770s bear the traces of the influence of 'les philosophes', legal praxis was mitigated and changed in an enlightened direction long before Enlightenment became a clearly defined and visible intellectual trend.[46]

This can be seen as an indication that Enlightenment was preceded by something which we may term a proto-Enlightenment. The incessant accumulation of knowledge that was under-way in society was another essential feature of what came to comprise the basis of Enlightenment. In an initial phase this was, perhaps, capable of strengthening tradition, for example in the form of the fundamentalist reading revival in northern Sweden.[47] But in the long run, the consequence had to be increased differentiation and variety and an increasingly personal attitude to knowledge.

How is one to view this? In several ways: through a literacy process (i.e., the development of the ability to read and write), through the growth in printing output – particularly small format and broadsheets – and through the increased acquisition of books. This development is most apparent in Stockholm, the capital of the Swedish proto-Enlightenment. Here, the growth was greatest at the beginning of the eighteenth century, i.e., long before Enlightenment appeared on the agenda. (Chapter 3 is specifically devoted to this subject.)

Let me make it clear at this point that there was not only an Enlightenment in Sweden, but also a proto-Enlightenment, which autonomously paved the way for the enlightenment movement itself. One could perhaps see the expansion of knowledge as tantamount to the emergence of a sort of Enlightenment infrastructure.

Now, such a proto-Enlightenment was certainly not unique to Sweden. France is also thought to have gone through such a proto-phase, at least with regard to the spread of knowledge. By the same token, it should also be said that Enlightenment which developed in France was as impeded a movement as in Sweden: its dissemination was incomplete and in many ways 'distorted'. If one accepts this, it follows that the differences between French and Swedish Enlightenment could be played down.

It is not possible to provide evidence for such a statement, or to 'measure' the distance between the degree of French and Swedish enlightenment, but a number of examples can be given as illustrations of the hypothesis that there is a certain similarity in their preconditions and results. Literacy in France increased between 1686–90 and 1786–90 from 29 to 47 per cent for men and from 14 to 27 per cent for women. In the early eighteenth century, approximately 13 per cent of the artisan journeymen in France owned books, in 1780, this had increased to 35 per cent. In Paris, the development had come further (as will be familiar from Stockholm and other larger cities).[48] Annik Pardailhé-Galabrun has investigated 2,000 Parisian households and established that 41 per cent of them had books. After 1750, this rose to 51 per cent. Here, too, the 'intellectual' infrastructure seems to have been created before (or on the eve of) the Enlightenment movement's breakthrough. Between the mid seventeenth century and the 1760s, the number of books per capita increased from 17 to 30. However, the uneven social distribution here was not altered by their possession, unlike Stockholm.[49]

Thus the differences between France – where Frängsmyr sees so much enlightenment – and Sweden – where he sees almost none at all – were perhaps not so great after all.

It would seem that Enlightenment existed, in spite of everything – both in France and Sweden – and that it should be possible to describe it. Consequently, it should also be possible to study its distinctive reflection in eighteenth-century Sweden. I will therefore do this later in this book, which is also about several things other than the eighteenth-century enlightenment movement. This can best be seen as a sort of triple diptych.

What is a triple diptych and how is one to be read?

All the chapters in this book, apart from the last (plus the epilogue) have been individually published in some form, albeit within the framework of a single research project on certain aspects of the artisan culture of eighteenth-century Stockholm.[50] For me, the text has thus a fixed and coherent structure that perhaps differs from the pattern the reader discerns. And while the relationship with reading is a free act and can be done in many ways, I would nevertheless like to call attention to three particular ways of relating to this particular text.

The rest of the book is assembled in the form of three diptychs, i.e., as three pairs of chapters, which can be read as paired chapters, individually or together. The first chapter in each diptych is a concrete exposition, followed by a chapter with a theoretical discussion related to that exposition.

Each paired chapter has an internal coherence, but the concrete and the theoretical expositions are also self-contained, which means that the book can be read in several different ways. For the reader who reads it as it is written, it will probably seem like a collection of alternating theoretical and empirical essays on thought in general and on eighteenth-century thought in particular. The reader who turns to the empirical chapters but refrains from reading the theoretical ones gets a monograph about Johan Hjerpe and Enlightenment, and the reader who does the opposite will be reading a treatise on the theoretical and methodological preconditions of intellectual research.

Notes

1. HSFR also funded the translation of this book into English.
2. A number of things indicate that the Hjerpe family home was relatively poor, among them the inventory of his father's (Anders Hjerpe's) estate, which shows a deficit of over 130 riksdaler (rd), and an annotation from 1787 in the protocols of the Tailors' Office which approves the father's petition to be spared the quarterly payment to the guild. *SSA*, the Office of the Governor of Stockholm for taxation matters, estate inventory of Anders Hjerpe, 1971/3: 618, Guild Archives, Tailors' Office protocol 4/4 1787.
3. *EBAS*, the catalogue of the Evangelical Brotherhood in Stockholm for the 1780s and 1790s; *GLA*, the Synnerby parish archives, parish catechetical meeting register 1816–24, moving register 1818–59, Records of Deaths 1825, the estate inventories of Skåning district 1808–30; *RA*, the County Accounts, population register and taxation register for the County of Skaraborg, Skara bailiwick, Skåning district, 1822–27; *SSA*, Parish archives, Nicolai parish: birth and baptismal register 1765, parish catechetical meeting register (emigration register) 1819–21; the archives of the hall and textile court (*Hall- och manufakturrättens arkiv*): the Swedish Board of Commerce's licences 1797–1801; roll of fellows and practising manufacturers (*fabriksidkare*) 1739–1841, factory reports; the taxation matters of the Office of the Governor of Stockholm, population registers for Stockholm 1780–1820; *Förteckning på Johan Hjerpes boksamling*; G. Peterson, *Jordbrukets omvandling i västra Östergötland 1810–1890*, p. 23.

4. *Förteckning på Johan Hjerpes boksamling.*

5. *KB, Kong residensestaden Stockholms historiska merckwärdigheter 1252–1792;* J. Hjerpe, *Berättelse om en lustresa sommartiden 1809, Samlingsbok af Johan Hjerpe . . . för diktavskrifter o d; UUB, Johan Hjerpes journal* (referred to subsequently as 'JHJ'); *Merckwärdige händelser för alla årets dagar . . . samlade af J. Hjerpe.*

6. M. Foucault, 'What is enlightenment?', in *The Foucault Reader* (ed. Rabinow, P.) Harmondsworth 1984, pp. xx–xxi, pp. 43–44, where Foucault goes so far as to ask himself whether Enlightenment was not 'the first epoch which has given itself a name', p. 44.

7. T. Frängsmyr, *Framsteg eller förfall: framtidsbilder och utopier i västerländsk tanketradition,* p. 114; P. Gay, *The Enlightenment: an interpretation 1,* p. 3ff; P. Gay, *The Enlightenment: an interpretation 2,* pp. 92, 97; E. Breisach, *Historiography: ancient, medieval and modern,* pp. 205–06.

8. Napoleon's role was unclear and has been much discussed over the years. See, for example, Breisach, *Historiography,* pp. 228–29, 245–47.

9. Cf. Å. Holmberg, 'Att omvärdera omvärlden–synen på exotiska folk i svenska historieböcker', pp. 100–01; Å. Holmberg, *Världen bortom västerlandet: svensk syn på fjärran länder och folk från 1700-talet till första världskriget,* pp. 92f.

10. L. Hammarsköld, 'Teleologiska betragtelser öfver verlds-historien', pp. 44–45.

11. T. Adorno and M. Horkheimer, *The dialectics of Enlightenment,* p. 30.

12. M. Foucault, *Discipline and punishment: the birth of the prison,* is typical of Foucault's 'implicit' treatment of Enlightenment.

13. See also J. Habermas, 'Mit dem Pfeil ins Herz der Gegenwart: to Foucault's lecture on Kant's What is enlightenment?'; A. Richters, 'Modernity-postmodernity controversies: Habermas and Foucault', p. 616; H. L. Dreyfus and P. Rabinow, 'What is maturity? Habermas and Foucault on "What is Enlightenment?" ', pp. 109–21.

14. On this see Robert Darnton, *The Forbidden Best-Sellers of Pre-Revolutionary France,* pp. 181, 218, 225; Roger Chartier, *The cultural origins of the French revolution,* pp. 17–19; P. N. Furbank, 'Nothing sacred', *New York Review of Books,* number 10, 8/6, 1995.

15. Cf. Gay, *The Enlightenment 1,* pp. 3–8.

16. On Swedish Enlightenment, see S. Lindroth, *Svensk lärdomshistoria: gustavianska tiden,* p. 184.

17. P. Gay, *The Enlightenment* , pp. 8 and 18. This process is one of his major themes (Volume 1, Book 2) and recurs in the title of the book.

18. T. Adorno and M. Horkheimer, *The dialectics of Enlightenment,* pp. xiii and 6–42.

19. See, for example, H. Vyverberg, *Historical pessimism in French Enlightenment.*

20. *Förteckning på Johan Hjerpes boksamling; UUB,* JHJ and *Merckwärdige händelser för alla årets dagar . . .* are filled with references to and/or cuttings from *Stockholms Posten,* among others.

21. S. Arvidson, *Thorild och den franska revolutionen,* pp. 19–22, 73, 120; P. Burke, *Popular Culture in Early Modern Europe,* pp. 251–52; S. Lindroth, *Svensk lärdomshistoria: gustavianska tiden,* pp. 173, 178, 181–93; I. Kant. 'Svar på frågan: Vad är upplysning?', pp. 27ff; T. Thorild, *Om upplysningens princip . . . ;* T. T. Segerstedt, *Nils von Rosenstein: samhällets människa,* pp. 276, 282–307, 347–69.

22. Adorno and Horkheimer, *The dialectics of Enlightenment,* p. 30. It is this automatism which figures as the 'system world' in the work of Habermas, while knowledge relativism makes an appearance here as 'rational communication'. See J. Habermas, *The theory of communicative action 1: reason and the rationalization of society,* pp. 8–42, 144, 343.

23. In the so called Period of Liberty in Sweden, Enlightenment reached the social élite above all, the court circles included. See S. Lindroth, *Svensk lärdomshistoria; frihetstiden,* pp. 501–14.

24. Perhaps especially prominent in the work of Foucault, for example his *The history of sexuality: an introduction* and *Discipline and punishment: the birth of the prison*. He has also inspired the acculturation researchers. See, for example, R. Muchembled, *Popular culture and elite culture in France 1400–1750*, pp. 188, 202, 205, 289 and 294. But the association is already made in M. Bachtin, *Rabelais and His World*, pp. 120–23, presumably under the influence of Adorno and Horkheimer, *The dialectics of Enlightenment*, Chapter 1, p. 36 for example.

25. Burke, 'Popular culture . . .', pp. 252–53; E. Johansson, *The history of literacy in Sweden: in comparison with some other countries*, pp. 18–22; Muchembled, *Popular culture and elite culture . . .*, pp. 262, 270, 282–83, 289, 294–95.

26. Burke, 'Popular culture . . .', especially pp. 252–53; P. Burke, *The historical anthropology of early modern Italy: essays on perception and communication*, pp. 187–90: R. Muchembled, *Popular culture and elite culture . . .* Volume 2, especially Chapter 5. For a concrete description of a witch trial, see G. Henningsen, *The witches' advocate: Basque witchcraft and the Spanish Inquisition (1609–1614)*, and for his argument pertaining to popular culture, pp. 387–93 in particular. For a Swedish contribution with a similar view, see P.-J. Ödman, *Konformismens triumf: utvecklingslinjer i svensk 1600-talspedagogik*, a study which, however, is limited to Sweden in the seventeenth century. N. Elias, *The civilizing process 1–2*, emphasises, as do others, that the civilising tendencies originated with the élite (here, the court in particular) and that the centralisation of power was decisive to the process. But he has, perhaps more than others, stressed the very gradual increase in people's impulse control.

27. On this, see Burke, 'Popular culture . . .', pp. 252–53; Burke, *The historical anthropology of early modern Italy*, pp. 120–31; F. Furet and J. Ozouf, 'Three centuries of cultural cross-fertilization: France', p. 217; R. Chartier, 'Les pratiques de l'écrit', pp. 125–26; N. Davis, *Society and culture in early modern France*, pp. 214–16, 218–20, 225: E. L. Eisenstein, 'Some conjectures about the impact of printing on Western society and thought: a preliminary report', pp. 54f. See, for example, R. Chartier, 'Intellectual history or sociocultural history? The French trajectories', pp. 33–36; R. Chartier, *The culture of print: power and uses of print in early modern Europe*, pp. 169–75.

28. On this, see Burke, 'Popular culture . . .', pp. 252–53; Burke, *The historical anthropology of early modern Italy*, pp. 120–31; Furet and Ozouf, 'Three centuries of cultural cross-fertilization: France', p. 217; R. Chartier, 'Les practiques de l'écrit', pp. 125–26; N. Davis, *Society and culture in early modern France*, pp. 214–16, 218–20, 225; Eisenstein, 'Some conjectures about the impact of printing on Western society and thought: a preliminary report', p. 54.

29. See, for example, Chartier, 'Intellectual history or sociocultural history? The French trajectories', pp. 33–36; R. Chartier, *The culture of print: power and uses of print in early modern Europe*, pp. 169–75.

30. T. Frängsmyr, 'Den svenska upplysningen: fanns den?', pp. 8–14; T. Frängsmyr, *Sökandet efter upplysningen. En essä om 1700-talets svenska kulturdebatt*. See also Lindroth, *Svensk lärdomshistoria: frihetstiden*, pp. 510–14; Lindroth, *Svensk lärdomshistoria: gustavianska tiden*, pp. 166–93; T. T. Segerstedt, *Nils von Rosenstein: samhällets människa*, pp. 263–390, esp. 326ff.

31. Frängsmyr, 'Den svenska upplysningen: fanns den?', pp. 7, 8–11.

32. Frängsmyr, *Sökandet efter upplysningen. En essä om 1700-talets svenska kulturdebatt*, p. 22.

33. Ibid., p. 33, for example.

34. Ibid., pp. 9ff, 83, 164.

35. Ibid., p. 46.

36. Ibid., p. 72.

37. Ibid., pp. 61, 142.
38. H. Lenhammar, *Tolerans och bekännelsetvång. Studier i den svenska swedenborgianismen*, pp. 276–79; Häll, *I Swedenborgs labyrint. Studier i de gustavianska swedenborgarnas liv och tänkande*, pp. 245, 311, 385–88.
39. It is precisely such changes which I would like to call 'changes in mentality'. The concept 'changes in people's outlooks' is used here, moreover, to refer to different sorts of mental changes. Both are to be distinguished from the concept of culture or cultural change. The latter concept is used here to designate attitudes which are embedded in the institutions and ceremonies of society or in routine acts which are linked to these. People can, by executing such routine acts or by participating in such ceremonies, reproduce these institutions and the values which uphold them without thereby necessarily sharing those values. I am very much aware of the fact that the concept of culture is a disputed one and defined very differently by anthropologists and ethnographers, which accords a certain freedom in its use. This is also maintained by B. Ehn and O. Löfgren, *Kulturanalys: ett etnologiskt perpektiv*, pp. 11–15. See also R. M. Keesing, 'Theories of culture', L. Magnusson, *Den bråkiga kulturen: förläggare och smideshantverkare i Eskilstuna 1800–1850*, pp. 62–66; C. Winberg, 'Några anteckningar om historisk antropologi', p. 9.
40. M. Nyman, *Upplysningens spegel. Götheborgs Allehanda om Frankrike och värden 1774–1789*.
41. E. Anners, *Humanitet och rationalism. Studier i upplysningstidens strafflagsreformer-särskilt med hänsyn till Gustav III:s reformlagstiftning*, pp. 167–206.
42. M. Nyman, *Press mot friheten. Opinionsbildning i de svenska tidningarna och åsiktsbrytningar om minoriteter 1772–1786*, Chapter 5.
43. B. Åhlén, *Ord mot ordningen: farliga skrifter, bokbål och häxprocesser i svensk censurhistoria*, p. 116.
44. The encyclopaedia was published for the first time during the years 1751–1765. E. Bollerup, 'Om franska inflytelser på svensk historieskrivning under frihetstiden', pp. 245, 247, 249–50, 258, 263–64, 278, 281–82; N. Eriksson, *Dalin–Botin–Lagerbring: historieskrivning och historieforskning i Sverige 1747–1787*, pp. 9–10, 196–219. French influence also made its way via Denmark and Ludvig Holberg, according to Eriksson; Lindroth, *Svensk lärdomshistoria: frihetstiden*, pp. 664, 677, 685; A. af Botin, *Utkast till svenska folkets historia 1–6*, for example 'Sjette Tidehvarf', pp. 635ff; O. von Dalin, *Svea Rikes historia*, for example pp. 129–33. See also C. A. Hessler, ' "Aristokratfördömandet": en riktning i svensk historieskrivning'.
45. Lagerbring published several résumés of his history of the Kingdom of Svea, several with the subtitle 'In the service of youth', as well as *Mindre Sammandrag af Swea Rikes historia*, E. Bollerup, 'Lagerbrings Svea Rikes historia: tillkomst, utgivning, mottagande', pp. 318–20, in which it is asserted that, among other things, the summary was easier to sell than the original work. The yearbook literature that was widely spread at the time also contained modern reassessments of history. See for example [P. Wargentin], *Stockholm stads (historiske) calender 1761–1762*. It was written by Pehr Wargentin: see N. Östman's introduction in Wargentin, pp. iii–xi. About the editions of the yearbook, see S. Lindroth, *Vetenskapsakademiens historia I.2*, p. 848. See also Lindroth, *Svensk lärdomshistoria: frihetstiden*, pp. 676 and 686. In *SSA*, the Governor's taxation matters, the 1791 estate inventories for merchants, master craftsmen and journeymen, Lagerbring's historical works are taken up on three occasions, which is rather a lot when bearing in mind that the same book is otherwise rarely found more than once. See also A. Ankarcrona, *Bud på böcker: bokauktioner i Stockholm 1782–1801*, pp. 198–203. However, neither Dalin's nor Lagerbring's large original editions are thought to have reached a broad

public: the editions included not more than approximately 500 copies. On this, see E. Bollerup, 'Om franska inflytelser på svensk historieskrivning', p. 245, note 3.

46. On this see A. Jarrick and J. Söderberg, 'En dialog om upplysningen före upplysningen', *Ugglan Number 2*, 1994.
47. T. Ericsson and B. Harnesk, ' "Disputationsmöten och öfningsfält för tankekrafter". Läseriet i övre Norrland i 1800-talets början'; J. Holmgren, *Norrlandsläseriet. Studier till dess förhistoria och historia fram till år 1830*.
48. Chartier, *The cultural origins of the French revolution*, p. 69.
49. Annik Pardailhé-Galabrun, *La naissance de l'intime* . . .
50. The project is entitled 'The psychological-social distinctiveness of the Stockholm artisans in the eighteenth century' ('Stockholmshantverkarnas psykologisk-sociala särart under 1700-talet') and was funded by the Swedish Council for Research in the Humanities and Social Sciences, the HSFR (Humanistisk-samhällsvetenskapliga forskningsrådet).

The artisan uprising and
forms of mentality

Chapter 1
Johan Hjerpe and the artisan uprising in support of the king's war

Introduction

On Monday 27 April 1789, the artisan journeymen of Stockholm demonstrated through the Old Town. They had most likely spent the night, not with their masters as they should have, but in hostelries, drunk and up to no good. At about half past eleven in the morning, they occupied the Riddarhustorget outside the House of the Nobility, where they continued their uproar until four o'clock in the afternoon, 'at which time a heavy downpour, combined with the flexed batons of the police officers, helped to disperse the drunken mob'.[1]

It was the last day on which parliament was in session. The four estates represented in it – the peasants, the middle class, the clergy and the nobility – assembled in different places in the city. The artisan journeymen provided a hostile audience for the heated deliberations of the nobility. The king, the enlightened despot Gustavus III, needed a great deal of money for the war he was waging against Russia and Catherine II. Would the nobility concede to the king's appropriation demand to a coming parliament for the foreseeable future, or refuse to commit itself for more than two years?

The artisan journeymen had gone to the House of the Nobility (Riddarhuset) to frighten the nobles into obeying the king. It is hardly surprising, then, that fearing for their safety, many noblemen had 'under their cloaks hidden sabres and loaded pistols' when they sought to clear a path through the crowd to the meeting.[2] They must have been prepared for the possibility that the artisans might mobilise in support of the king and the war, otherwise they would not have taken the trouble to arm themselves. However, they do appear to have been taken by surprise when, in the midst of their deliberations, the king suddenly entered the hall to the accompaniment of high-spirited cheering from the masses outside.[3] The nobility thus not only had to try and elude the clamorous crowd, it also had to resist Gustavus III's theatrical and autocratic arts of persuasion.

The nobility failed, the king celebrated yet another of his fateful despotic triumphs, and the war could be continued. But what did the outcome mean to the reserves outside? Did they have any independent part in the defeat of the nobility and the victory of the king, or were they just a politically indifferent mob bought for a drink and '24 shillings each'? The fact that the estates had been assembled on a Monday of all days is food for thought, as the journeymen's custom of taking a Monday off was still observed in the late eighteenth century.[4] From a constitutional point of view, parliament had to close on 27 April, as the Act of Parliament dictated that it should be concluded within three months, but Gustavus III was hardly the man to allow himself to be constrained by such trifles.

A number of accounts of the drama on Riddarhustorget have been handed down, as scandal-mongering seems to have been rife. However, none of the clamorous crowd themselves left behind any account of their view of events.[5] The artisan journeymen seem not only to have clamoured in chorus when they arrived, but also to have held their peace together *post festum*.

This silence, so socially typical, is as natural as it is regrettable. The account of only one person who was close to the artisan journeymen has been preserved. It was written by Johan Hjerpe – at the time still a young linen shop assistant – and is contained in the voluminous diary he kept between the years 1788 and 1792.[6] Hjerpe was there on the Square of the House of the Nobility as a sort of participant observer. He shared the enthusiasm of the journeymen for king and war, and, to a considerable degree, their social experience, but not, however, their fellowship. Although he ran with them – curious and exhilarated by what was happening – he seems to have played a rather detached role, something to which I will return later.[7]

However, Hjerpe presumably knew more about what these simple people thought and intended with their mobilisation in support of the king than other witnesses who, from a greater social distance, either attributed to them rebellious royalist intentions or considered them the spineless instruments of powerful behind-the-scenes conspirators. For even if Hjerpe was not really a comrade of his 'class brothers', he nevertheless received ideological inspiration from them and from the petty bourgeois environment in which he grew up. The diary – even its very existence – reveals that Hjerpe was an eccentric among the journeymen and shop assistants, but, at the same time, its contents bear witness to how small the distance between him and these people was. By virtue of this, what Johan Hjerpe had to say about himself also becomes interesting when analysing the attitudes of the artisan journeymen.

I am not, however, solely interested in what the artisan journeymen wanted to achieve on 27 April 1789. Rather, I want to try to construe from these events something about what can have guided the actors morally, i.e., in concrete terms, where they apparently set the limits for their violence against 'the enemy'. Another central issue is whether they acted with or without a strategy, and finally, it would be interesting to attempt to ascertain what needs these people sought to meet that day – needs that do not have to be directly linked to the apparent goals of the action.

Contemporary material does not permit a satisfactory treatment of these questions, so I will use witnesses' accounts of the artisan mobilisation chiefly to illustrate such attitudes as obviously came to light on 27 April – on the part of the journeymen in general and Johan Hjerpe in particular. But the exposition nevertheless alludes to a discussion which I will ultimately take up on the issues I think are most important. The point of departure for that discussion is the interpretative perspective which has dominated research and pre-industrial mass contention in the last 20–30 years,[8] but it entails a proposal for rather new interpretive frameworks for the psycho-social dynamic which exists in activities when many people act in concert.

*

A dramatic course of events with social clashes is filled with unpremeditated acts. Suddenly everyone is in a hurry, and people do not have time to hold themselves back. By studying such events it is, perhaps, possible to catch a glimpse of human needs and traits which are otherwise restrained, needs which can be very fundamental and invariable throughout the dramatic course of events in which they suddenly become apparent. The invariable in such fundamental needs becomes manifest in that different mass uprisings acquire a number of similar external features, in spite of essential differences in articulated goals and in spite of their taking place at very different times.[9]

That the artisan uprising of 27 April 1789 has caught my attention is due to its being an exceptionally dramatic event, in which an unusually large number of people got in each other's way. This event can, in certain respects, be compared with other planned popular uprisings in Stockholm's pre-industrial history, but its dramatic intensity was not nearly as great as in, for example, the Fersen riot of 1810, in which a large mob lynched Maria Antoinette's old follower and lover, Axel von Fersen, because he was suspected of having murdered the heir to the Swedish throne, Crown Prince Karl August. And the uncontrolled popular anarchy was far less extensive than in the Crusenstolpe riots of 1838, when a popular disturbance broke out in support of the Assistant Justice of the Court of Appeal, M. J. Crusenstolpe, who was sentenced to imprisonment for having criticised King Carl XIV Johan and his government.[10]

The late 1780s were very colourful, and I could have chosen another event from that time. During the war against Russia of 1788–90, the lower middle class was mobilised on several occasions, for war and king, against the nobility and 'cowardly' officers. It was a war which Gustavus III instigated so as to assure himself a place among the great 'Gustavuses': Gustavus Vasa, the founder of the realm, and Gustavus II Adolf, the protestants' commander in the Thirty Years' War.[11]

So marked was the activity of the inhabitants of Stockholm that the notorious Chief of Police, Henrik Liljensparre, noted in a letter to the king concerning another riot that 'an event of such a nature, so unusual here in the kingdom, going against the grain of the peaceable disposition of the land known to date, aroused my attention'.[12]

Some political, ideological and social circumstances

I shall attempt a step-by-step reconstruction of the course of events on Riddarhustorget on 27 April 1789. First of all, let me very briefly outline some of the political, ideological and social circumstances surrounding this artisan uprising.[13]

According to the Swedish historian Erik Lönnroth, Gustavus III had played with the idea of a heroic war against Russia since the beginning of the 1780s.[14] Nevertheless, there does not seem to have been any imperative external cause for war, however uncontrollably bellicose flames may have burned in the soul of the king.[15] Indeed, all external motives relating to power politics disappear; what remains is, by and large, only the will of the king himself. In the official war propaganda, however, the threat emanating from Russia, and from the 'treacherous' Swedish nobility, soon became the dominant theme. This theme was particularly apparent from the summer of 1788. The Anjala League[16] – a coalition of Finnish soldiers in the Swedish realm, who opposed the war and the war effort[17] – was formed at that time.

The fact that the Russian threat was, perhaps, a fabrication did not prevent the lower estates from being roused to show their patriotism. It must have been very difficult, not to say impossible, to obtain a true picture of the real situation even for those who read everything they could lay their hands on. News and proclamations were systemically distorted and full of untruths.[18] Anti-aristocracy sentiments were simply far too easily aroused.

The parliament of 1789 was apparently convened for *one* main purpose: to give Gustavus III the means to complete the war plans he had already begun to put into effect.[19] A number of other important civil decisions were, however, taken by parliament, but most of them could be linked to the king's strategy of winning over the lower estates to side with him against the nobility and in support of the war.[20] The most decisive event for the parliament was the sovereign's coup in February, when, through his so-called Act of Association and Security, he drastically altered the balance of power in Swedish society. In conflict with the nobility and constitution, he increased his own power and diminished that of the nobles. Among other things, he gave himself the right to declare war on other countries and abolished the exclusive right of the aristocracy to high office and tax-free land.[21] In this way Gustavus III assured himself of popular support for his despotic exercise of power. But popular support for his enlightened despotism culminated in the artisan uprising and the whole thing ended with the king, once more, getting his way.

Popular anarchy broke out in an ideological climate foisted from above. It is important to bear this in mind when attempting to establish the mentality and motives of those involved. The Stockholm bourgeoisie – and the artisans with it – was of singular importance in political life,[22] because of its geographical proximity to the country's power centre.

But the uproar was not only artificial: political and ideological signals were not emitted in an economic or social vacuum. The attitude of the impoverished or semi-impoverished journeymen and masters must also be taken into consideration with the economic and social situation prevailing in the city.

Stockholm was experiencing a period of protracted economic stagnation, both in relation to other cities and in comparison with the countryside,[23] in which the middle-class occupations in particular (trade, manufacturing, the artisan crafts) were encountering increasing difficulties.[24] The crafts had a difficult time holding their own,[25] as can be seen from Figure 1 below, but the manufacturers were perhaps worst afflicted.[26]

An increasing number of journeymen abandoned any hope of being able to establish themselves as independent, franchised artisan entrepreneurs. Under pressure from the economic and demographic crisis, the frequency of marriages declined in the city as a whole,[27] although among the artisan journeymen the opposite was the case. They married in increasing numbers, for to

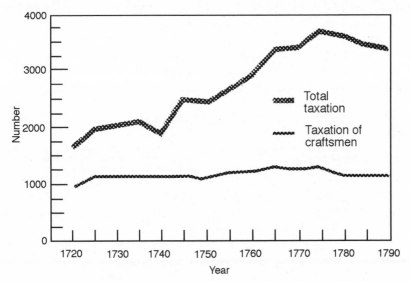

Figure 1. The bourgeois contribution towards ordinary taxation in Stockholm 1720–1790
Source: Boëthius (1943), p. 441; Söderlund (1943), p. 316; Söderlund (1949), p. 86.

delay marriage in anticipation of becoming a master could turn out to be an eternal wait.[28]

According to the economic historian Ernst Söderlund, it was mainly among the guilds in decline or with a great need for capital that the number of journeymen marriages increased. This is complicated, however, by the fact that journeymen's representation among the number of masters did not increase more than within the Stockholm guild system as a whole.[29] The differences in the terms of establishment, which varied from guild to guild, are not enough to explain why, for example, the shoemakers more than other journeymen abandoned the tradition of bachelorhood practised by their contemporaries.

The anti-aristocratic political and ideological signals were coming from a 'favourable' social and economic environment. Among the impoverished masses who were exposed to the flood of propaganda, there was considerable dissatisfaction with both the masters, who put the interests of their guild first, and with the nobility. There was much aggressive energy here seeking an outlet, and which the warmongers sought to exploit and control.

Cast, scene and audience

Cast

Streets, cafés and meeting places echoed to the sound of angry voices. Many were out and about on 27 April, and it is impossible for us to keep track of them all.

Even though it is the attitudes of the artisan journeymen which I am trying to ascertain, the focal point is Johan Hjerpe, the only one of these people who appears to have left behind any observations on the event. Of course, the evidence of others will also be presented, but these people figure, to a great degree, to support Hjerpe's world of ideas more than as the basis for describing how things really happened.

Although there is not much to add about Gustavus III at this stage, he must be included here because he is a continual influence on everyone.

The nobles figure in the account primarily as the opponents of the artisan journeymen and as a foil for their aspirations. The same applies to a few more people: Olof Wallqvist, a leading representative of the clergy; Abraham de Broën, a royalist hotspur who on this – and other – occasions led the way for the city 'rabble'[30] and finally, Henrik Liljensparre – the spider in the police web – is among those whose importance for the artisan journeymen must be discussed if we are to attempt to define the reasons for their attitudes and behaviour.

It would have been good to have been able to include Carl Christopher

Gjörwell as well, a leading royalist who advocated tolerance between people and also maintained good contacts with the city's Moravians. He may have been there on that day, as he had a bookshop on Riddarhustorget, but I have not seen him directly implicated in the preserved accounts, or found anything by his own hand.

Scene

The square called Riddarhustorget is the central scene for the dramatic events of that day, although during the small hours of the morning, the main actors made their preparations elsewhere.

Early in the morning, the king called the faithful to the palace. Some time between ten and eleven o'clock, the lower estates began their separate deliberations:[31] the peasants in the new city hall on Riddarhustorget, the burghers in their 'usual room in the city's bourse', and the clergy in the Cathedral.[32] Couriers were to rush secret notes from His Royal Highness to all of them. At the artisan lodgings, the journeymen were waiting for the signal to rise up, while Johan Hjerpe trotted off to Stortorget, the 'Great Square', to attend to his business in the linen shop. Knights and nobles washed and dressed, secured their weapons under their cloaks and made their way towards the House of the Nobility. One or two may have stopped off at one of the city's many cafés to defer the unpleasant meeting with the restless crowd.

Audience or Witnesses

Popular uprisings can usually be traced in court records, and sometimes also in the periodical and daily press.[33] It has not been possible to do so here, as the artisan uprising had no legal repercussions and the daily newspapers all kept quiet about what happened.[34] Instead, I have mainly resorted to different sorts of personal documents, such as diaries and memoirs. Indeed, such things exist in abundance, as, in retrospect, several contemporary witnesses saw themselves as duty-bound to tell the world their humble thoughts about what had happened. None of those whose accounts have been preserved for posterity saw the event from a neutral vantage point. But, luckily, these observers saw the whole thing from both different ideological points of view and from different sites.[35]

By virtue of his diary, Johan Hjerpe came to be the popular royalist witness.[36] The site for his observations was initially the shop on Stortorget, after which he joined the journeymen in the Old Town. As with other simple folk who have left behind them documents narrating other historical events, Johan Hjerpe was no typical representative of the people,[37] as is apparent not only from the diary, but from other manuscripts he left behind.[38] However, as Hjerpe was closest to the people whose actions he recorded in his writings, he will be treated here as a key witness.

In his memoirs, alderman Rutger Fredrik Hochschild has provided a very detailed account of this uprising and can be viewed as the source material's representative for the minority within the middle class which opposed Gustavus III.[39] He seems to have been very well informed, but I have not been able to determine whether he really was an eye-witness to events or where he got his information from.[40]

Police Chief Henrik Liljensparre was, in the line of duty, practically involved in the efforts to push through the king's plans. He was on a collision course with his aristocratic peers and his retrospective biased petition of 1797 needs to be treated with suspicion.[41]

As far as I know, the peasantry is not represented in the source material, but the clergy are by the Bishop of Växjö, Olof Wallqvist, who left behind him an account of the parliament of 1789, in which several pages are devoted to the commotion at the Riddarhus on 27 April.[42] Wallqvist was a clergyman loyal to Gustavus III, but he tried to convey the impression of only conditional loyalty to the king's ambitious plans. He had difficulty finding credibility in the eyes of the incensed nobility, however, and as far as they were concerned, Wallqvist's word was not to be believed. According to Liljensparre, too, Wallqvist was thought to be 'to the King far too devoted', a view also shared by Gjörwells.[43]

Apart from the king's sister-in-law, Princess Hedvig Elisabeth Charlotta, whose diary will be consulted later,[44] all that remain are the high-placed losers: the nobility. This estate teems with preserved accounts: furious attempts to get even with the king's intriguing as well as more level-headed reflections on the suffering endured. A. L. Hamilton was perhaps the most bitter, displeased with his peers' tractability.[45] Also discontented, but perhaps less indignant, was Fredrik Wilhelm von Ehrenheim.[46] Gudmund Göran Adlerbeth maintained his composure in the face of defeat, giving expression to a sort of realpolitical fatalism in the face of 'the supremacy of the King's might', even if he did also lament the crowd's rowdiness and the king's forcible language.[47] Finally, I will also be making use of an anonymous and unofficial draft protocol of the talks in the hall of the House of the Nobility on that day.[48] This will make it possible to follow the events as seen from within the Hall, both the discussion itself and the tumult outside – the official protocol makes no reference to the commotion in the square.

The course of events

The threat of revolution

For those who knew something of world events, there was an obvious parallel between the agitation on the streets of Stockholm in the 1780s and the pre-revolutionary tumult in progress in Paris.[49] Reports from abroad published by the daily newspapers reached many, including, in the days of rumour, those who could not themselves read.[50]

Johan Hjerpe commented continuously in his diary on what he learned from the press. By June of 1788 he was aware that 'common insurrection' was feared in 'Franckrike',[51] and on the basis of his avid newspaper reading, he predicted that the country was in the throes of a revolutionary transformation.[52] He was almost certainly not alone in his prophecy. Unease among some of the Swedes about developments in France led to apprehension about a growing threat of revolution in Sweden as well. Erik Ruuth wrote to the king in September 1788 about 'much fermentation among the Folk (Allmogen)', for example. He continued:

> Everything points to this, that a revolution would seem to be imminent, which is not to be avoided: the Populace here in Stockholm is said to be, and is, agitated.[53]

Elis Schröderheim also took up the same theme in a letter to Gustavus III.[54] A rumour was circulating to the effect that, with the help of the Dalecarlia regiment, the king was intending to open the banks to obtain funds for the war. Schröderheim embroidered on the theme of alarm among 'the city's inhabitants':[55]

> Man tror, att en del af pöpel med längtan skulle mottaga tillfället till pillage, och att de i små sammankomster af polisen därtill uppmuntras. Den största delen af stadens invånare vänta en revolt utan att veta hvarifrån, och de börja snart att tänka på både försvar och god gömställen för sin egendom.

> One believes that some of the rabble would, with longing, seize the opportunity to pillage, and that they should be encouraged in this by small gatherings of the police. The larger part of the city's inhabitants expect a revolt without knowing from whence it will come, and they will soon begin to think about both defence and good hiding places for their property.

The letter contains at least two noteworthy claims: first, that the police should have encouraged the mob to plunder, and that 'the city's inhabitants' did not know who was intending to start a revolution.

Did the uncertainty of which Schröderheim's letter gives an impression prevail? Quite conceivably, as traces of this fear could be found in all camps. Even Wallqvist was obviously jittery about what he suddenly realised the king meant to undertake; he felt pressurised by his own loyalty to plans, the extent of which he now began to understand for the first time.[56]

To judge from Hjerpe and the others in the chorus of witnesses, the perceived threat of revolution intensified in the spring of 1789, culminating in the days before parliament was dissolved. But who feared whom, or was everybody afraid of everyone else? And how could the plans for revolution have been fomented by the police?

It is quite clear that the charged atmosphere was connected with the imminent confrontation on the matter of appropriation, even though it was also influenced by the recent memory of the king's 'February Revolution'; people thought they knew what Gustavus III was capable of. Many suspected or knew that something was brewing at the prospect of the deliberations between the estates on 27 April. In other respects, the perception of the threat changed depending on the witness consulted. Here – as in France – it was still natural to expect both royal and popular revolutions, and perhaps above all popular royal ones.[57]

According to Hjerpe, a healthy scepticism was needed for all the gossip in circulation: 'Jag stod i Boden på Stortorget och wiste af intet mer än lösa ryckten som dageligen flögo omkring hwilcka man ej kunde rätta sig efter.' ('I stood in my shop on the Great Square and picked up nothing more than the wild rumours which daily flew around, which one cannot be guided by.') Nevertheless, he was unable to restrain his royalist inclination; he was certain that the threat of revolution emanated from the 'dreadful' nobility.[58]

The police chief's recollection of 1797 is questionable when it comes to details (or because of its richness of details).[59] Like Hjerpe, he named – as could be expected – the nobility as the aggressive party, but he also mocked its rapidly waning courage at the sight of his 'reliable and sturdy fellows'.[60]

Von Ehrenheim gave a different version: admittedly he did not deny that the nobles 'by and large went armed to the House of the Nobility' ('till största delen gingo bevärade på Riddarhuset'), but this was in self-defence against an artisan mob which had been egged on by lies to 'Massacre the Nobility'.[61]

Unlike von Ehrenheim who 'went [...] to the House of the Nobility unsure of life or death' ('gick [...] till Riddarehuset oviss om lif eller död'),[62] Adlerbeth was not afraid of 'the rabble, hardly dangerous, without order and without commander' ('den skockade pöbelskaran, föga farlig, utan ordning och utan anförare').[63] He naturally agreed with von Ehrenheim that the nobility were the peaceful party and that it was they who were being threatened, but he was of the view that the threat was posed by more powerful forces which he believed would have 'given the signal for a civil war' ('gifvit tecken till ett inbördes krig') had the estate refused the appropriation.[64] And there is something in the claim that the nobility was politically threatened. Opposition nobles had been under house arrest or in prison since February, and the town watch was the responsibility of the middle-class guard.[65]

Preparations

Many maintained, after the event, that they had known in advance what was in the wind. Only Hjerpe, whose diary notes were contemporaneous with the riot, persevered in a sort of pretentious naïvety and denied that he knew what was going to happen. But in retrospect, he too succumbed to the weakness of allowing hindsight to transform vague premonitions into certain predictions. Not until 1792 at the earliest, did Hjerpe write in his history of Stockholm that 'necessary arrangements were made' ('Nödige anstalter woro tagne') which would have forced the nobles to 'put themselves out' ('beqwäma sig') for the approval of the appropriation.[66] Even if Hjerpe never conceded in his diary that he knew anything in advance, it nevertheless escaped him that the chief of police was present on 27 April – indeed, that it was 'through him that the journeymen came ('genom honom Gesällerna kommo').[67] The credibility of Hjerpe's contemporary ingenuousness is also diminished by Hedvig Elisabeth Charlotta having included shop assistants (!) among those who were initiated into these 'arrangements'.

What were these arrangements? The usual: the chief of police would incite and bribe the mob with money and alcohol, and to rush to the aid of the king.[68] According to several 'witnesses', there were dirty dealings afoot long before the meeting about the appropriation. If the revolution historian George Rudé is to be believed, this accusation would fit into a contemporary European pattern: aristocrats never thought ordinary people capable of their own aspirations. When the masses acted, they were regarded as having been bought by agents or conspirators.[69] More than real testimonies, these charges can only have been a sort of conditioned aristocratic reaction to a typical event.

Hamilton claimed that the Duke of Södermanland, Fredrik, the younger brother of Gustavus III, and even the king 'the entire parliament commanded night patrols' ('hela riksdagen anfört nattpatruller'). Moreover, during the last two nights before the clash, they were supposed to have personally bustled about among 'the worst riff-raff of Stockholm' ('Stockholms största slödder') and handed out money.[70] But Hamilton wrote with a poisoned mind and did not keep real observations separate from his fevered imagination.[71] Indeed, it is generally impossible to determine what it was he really did experience.

However, other testimonies point in the same direction. Hedvig Elisabeth Charlotta's notes state that in 'remote taverns [...] the worst dregs of the journeymen and shop assistants' were gathered together. There they were got drunk and 'urged to make themselves ready'. The princess lamented that the basically good people 'under the influence of the power of gold and temporary enthusiasm' abandoned themselves willingly to acts of violence.[72] Von Ehrenheim used similar terms in his version of what was being planned. Both claimed that the initiative was taken by the king and singled out Liljensparre as his tool, emphasising at the same time, that these high-class conspirators had kept themselves in the background so as not to arouse suspicion.[73] There is no room here for childish fantasies à la Hamilton about a king who ventured out on nocturnal adventures through the streets of Stockholm.

Liljensparre's indirect, and the police force's direct involvement, particularly on the night of Sunday 26 April, recur in several descriptions of events. In Hochschild's account, the journeymen were assembled in their hostelries the entire night because the police had received orders to keep them there.[74] But according to Adlerbeth, they stayed mostly because of the generous flow of strong drink and royal flattery on the lines of 'it was from these his faithful subjects that he [the king] anticipated help against the lords',[75] however that nobleman could be aware this. Naturally, he himself would never have dreamt of setting foot in such a dangerous place. Adlerbeth was probably only extrapolating what had long been a leitmotif in the Gustavusian propaganda.[76] It is likely that the same line was adopted in relation to that night, but that does not prevent it from having taken place within the context of police force as intimated by Hochschild.

It is precisely this special mixture of force and flattery which is interesting as an indication of the fact that the powerful did not – and could not – know whether or not they had won over the journeymen. Everything went smoothly on the Monday, admittedly, but there had, on occasion, been worrying signs that the artisan journeymen were not the homogeneous mass the police liked to think. In Hjerpe's writings, the tailor journeymen figure as the leaders of the royalist crowd. They numbered approximately four hundred, according to his estimate. But the year before, the Office of the Governor of Stockholm had accused them of dragging their heels with the war consignments.[77]

If the uneasy duplicity reflects the attitudes of the authorities, the content of the royal flattery provides clues to understanding the mentality of the artisan journeymen. The emphasis of the royal propaganda on the importance of the journeymen's efforts at a time when that social class was losing its importance may have had a psychological effect, to which I shall return.

The night progressed without the crowd showing any signs of dispersing. If Adlerbeth is to be believed, the drinking continued until morning. Hjerpe appears to be more naïve. He says instead that 'the city's artisan journeymen had on the previous evening been summoned by their Journeymen's Alderman for the next morning' to their lodgings where they were now invited to breakfast 'free of charge'.[79]

What is one to believe? Distinct features recur in most of the accounts. But only the diary entries of Johan Hjerpe and Hedvig Elisabeth Charlotta clearly appear to be contemporary with the dramatic events of 27 April.[80] The other descriptions are all either written several years later, or impossible to date. The social distance between the writers is reflected in how differently they perceive what had transpired. It is precisely in this respect that the agreement between their accounts is interesting: Hedvig Elisabeth Charlotta's claim that the artisan journeymen were gathered together corresponds to Hjerpe's 'naïve' confession that they had been summoned to their lodgings.

The shop assistant and the princess thus shared the view that the artisan journeymen did not act entirely on their own initiative, even if they gave different versions of where outside this circle of people the initiative was taken. Probably these two 'witnesses' drew the correct conclusions. That Wallqvist too – one of the king's foremost propaganda instruments – considered that 'steps were taken'[81] makes this even more credible. However, it is not decisive for the reconstruction of this sequence of events that Hedvig Elisabeth Charlotta's version haunts many others. It is not entirely essential that the princess's journal entries are presumably contemporary with the events to which they related, as the Prince Consort was more of a relater of events than a true witness. What is important in the shop assistant–princess source is partly their independence of each other, and partly that they arrived at the same result from different social and ideological points of departure.

To accept the claim that the artisan journeymen 'did not act entirely on their own initiative' is a euphemism. Were they not quite simply bought by the police? This is easy to believe, especially as Hjerpe also saw Liljensparre among the swarm of workers. The impression is not diminished by the police chief's standard denial of any involvement.[82] His denial should be seen more as a routine defence mechanism against the spread of rumour than as solid evidence of his innocence. It is now beyond all doubt, and was also the common view at the time, that Liljensparre, à la Lenoir, the pre-revolutionary famous or infamous police chief of Paris,[83] maintained a net of informers and did not flinch from bribery when it came to implementing the plans of His Royal Highness.[84]

Even if the journeymen were enticed with alcohol and a little bit of money to participate, they were not, however, simply bought. Influenced, yes, not just by gold as the princess believed, but as a consequence of their hatred of the nobility and because the riot gave them the opportunity to vent the aggressive energy that had been building up. If the initiative behind the action did not come from the journeymen themselves, its powerful instigators nevertheless succeeded in liberating a latent impulse on their part, which was at once royalistic and anarchistic.

While the artisan journeymen began to move towards Riddarhustorget, or perhaps were already in place, a number of other measures and steps were taken. The king called the faithful to the palace. Among others, he sent for Duke Karl and 'informed him of his intention personally to attend the [knights'] assembly'.[85] Secret, virtually identical notes, written in his own hand, went from the king to the three loyal estates telling of the plans to surprise the aristocracy with a personal visit to the House of the Nobility.[86]

The actors take their places

The peasantry did not show the same enthusiasm as the middle class for Gustavus III's bellicose appropriation claim.[87] They were reluctant, but appear at the same time to have felt humble respect for the king.

From the first day of the parliament, the members representing the peasantry were the objects of irritatingly indiscreet attention: they were buttered up with drinks, tobacco and card-games, while at the same time each was shadowed by police spies.[88] Nevertheless, it took a long time before their opposition was entirely overcome. As late as 24 April the 'Peasantry [was] up by H.R.H. and lodged an appeal over the Appropriation' ('Bondeståndet uppe hos k:m: och beswärade sig öfwer Bewillningen'), Hjerpe recounts in his diary. But then Gustavus came out

> och satte sig som en Fader midt ibland sina barn, föreställande dem huru Bevillningen skulle ske & Bönderna gingo därpå glade bort och förbannade Adeln som så narrat dem.

> and sat down like a Father in the midst of his children, picturing for them how the Appropriation should take place & the Peasants did then go from there and cursed the Nobility which had so deceived them.

This is naturally part of Hjerpe's tale, of his romantic fantasy about the 'remarkable Parliament in Stockholm.'[89] Gustavus plays the leading role, the brave and proud journeymen the 'fifth role' and the peasants are the children who have been led astray and who, sitting at the feet of the king with eyes aglow, are gently returned to the fold.

The only thing we know for sure is that Gustavus summoned the estate to him and succeeded in making it yield.[90] Nevertheless, Hjerpe's item is of interest to the analysis of his own views about the difference between the mentality of the peasants and the journeymen, as well as how he positioned himself in social terms. Hjerpe distanced himself, on the one hand, from the peasants through his patronising remarks about them, and on the other hand, in other places in his diary, he emphasised his distance from the aristocracy, not only through his hatred of the nobles, but also by attributing to the journeymen aspirations of their own. Hjerpe's text thus testifies quite clearly as to how close he was to the journeymen and shop assistants of the city, however unsympathetic he may have been as an outsider to their behaviour.

The peasants had capitulated and could thus be initiated into the king's plan for surprising the nobles at the House of the Nobility. This may not

have taken place before the Monday morning, when the peasantry – like the
clergy and burghers – were gathered in session.[91] In any case, Gustavus sent a
note the same morning to the 'Honourable Peasant Estate' (and to the two
other common estates), in which he informed them of his

> Beslut at Skielf gå upp på Riddarhusett at til Sistonee försöka om jag eij
> kan återföra Riderskapet och Adeln til sin sanskyldiga plikt.[92]

> Decision to go up to the House of the Nobility ourself to at last try and see
> whether We cannot bring the Knights and Nobles back to their true duty.

We do not know how the peasant members of parliament reacted to the
news of what the king was about to do. But according to the minutes of the
meeting of the middle class, the speaker lyrically agreed with Gustavus's note
and 'many of the representatives expressed themselves in the most moving
terms' ('flere des ledamöter hade de mäst rörande uttryck').[93] Within the
middle class there was a critical minority, however, which raised the same
sort of objection as the nobles to the unrestricted appropriation.[94]

Among the assembled clergy there broke out – according to Bishop
Wallqvist – something approaching panic when the king's message was
received.[95] When the clerical parliamentarians got word of the mob which
'murmured and made noise' on Riddarhustorget, they were overcome with

> ångesten [. . .] sådant insteg i synnerhet hos Talmannen, at han svettades,
> kunde sjelf tänka på ingenting, uphörde med all vidare föredragning, och
> lemnade ståndet åt syssellöshet.[96]

> anxiety [. . .] gained such a hold particularly with the Speaker, making him
> sweat, so he could himself think of nothing, ceased with all further dis-
> course, and left the estate to idleness.

The clergy feared that the king was intending to place himself above the law,
and they wanted no part of that. According to Wallqvist, it was he himself
who finally succeeded in gathering the estate 'to declare in writing [. . .]
trouble the King' ('at skriftligen anmäla [. . .] bekymmer hos Konungen').[97]

Wallqvist was speaking for himself, and it is impossible to determine what
turmoil Gustavus's note achieved among those servants of the Lord, or what
role Wallqvist himself played in this context. The minutes of the clergy's
meeting on 27 April say nothing on this matter, but 'anxiety' and paralysis
could have been natural reactions among them precisely because, at that
moment, they could have felt it impossible and necessary to heed their temporal lord at the same time. A certain scepticism is intimated, nevertheless, in
that the clergy stressed their satisfaction over the fact that the appropriation
decision was not to set a precedent, a reservation pushed through by the
nobility.[98]

The members of parliament from the loyal estates had, then, taken their places and were in on the king's next move. Some time during the course of the morning, the artisan journeymen decamped from their lodgings. Hjerpe stood in the shop on Stortorget, busy with his daily duties, when the tailor journeymen marched past. Seemingly unsuspecting, he was nevertheless able to give detailed information about the episode: four hundred tailor journeymen had come at 'exactly half eleven'.[99] But now he could no longer contain himself, and 'ran out [...] and followed along to see where the multitude would go' ('sprang ut [...] och fölgde med at få se hwaräst det skulle bära med denna hop').[100]

Hjerpe was now a part of the surging crowd which other people watched – terrified, enraged or encouraged. It was naturally impossible for these onlookers to see that he continued to consider himself merely an independent observer; as far as Hedvig Elisabeth Charlotta was concerned, he was simply one of 'the dregs of [...] the shop assistants' (dräggen av [...] bodbiträden').

This mass of people flowed from all the lodging houses into the square outside the Riddarhus, intoxicated and noisy, as well as being bribed with 24 shillings each, according to Hochschild. Hedvig Elisabeth Charlotta's diary relates that the king distributed 'a half plåt per man' which, after the coin devaluation of the 1770s, amounted to the same thing. Thus, half a riksdaler was equal to a half plåt which was equal to 24 shillings.[101]

It is difficult to determine how many they were and who it was that made up the crowd. According to Hjerpe, 'several thousand' ('flere 1000de') had been assembled.[102] Hedvig Elisabeth Charlotta put the figure at 3,000,[103] while Hamilton counted not less than 'a 10,000-man rabble' ('10,000 man pöbel'). What are we to believe?

In Stockholm at that time there cannot have been more than 3,000 artisan journeymen organised in guilds,[104] but it is also certain that many apprentices and some masters joined in that day. In the 1780s there were between five and six thousand workers in the industries of the city, workers who, apart from the guild journeymen, could easily have comprised a recruitment base for the royalist demonstration, particularly as the workshops were in gradual decline. It would not seem at all impossible for several thousand artisans to have poured into Riddarhustorget that morning. It is probable that a significant proportion consisted of the corps of craftsmen, even if we cannot be sure whether 'all the riff-raff of the town' ('nästan all stadens Pöbel')[105] was there. We will never know the truth, as none of the witnesses made their estimates from a neutral vantage point; all the parties had an interest in exaggeration rather than underestimation. The task of obtaining a picture of the social composition of the crowd is complicated, moreover, by the fact that the riot had no legal repercussions, unlike the Fersen Riot of 1810 and the Crusenstolpe Disturbances of 1838, for example.[106]

The motley horde of a thousand or even several thousand working people was not alone on Riddarhustorget. According to several people, the police chief himself was there to lead events, together with his police officers.[107] Liljensparre is quiet on this subject, but he confessed that he had secured the services of 'a certain number of reliable and sturdy lads' ('ett visst antal påli- tlige och handfasta karlar') who would not shrink from a set to with the refractory nobles if it proved necessary.[108] Everything points to Liljensparre having been on the square that day, as he had been six months earlier when the burghers gathered in the same place to protest against the 'treacherous' officers who led the way to the tavern, the Malm Cellar (Malmens källare).[109] It was also Hamilton's view that Duke Karl had been ready to step into the breach for the middle-class cavalry, as was his brother, Duke Fredrik, who was on the spot with 'his followers'.[110] Adlerbeth tells us that 'goldsmith Oldenburg's squadron' was gathered together 'by the cavalry of the city' ('man sammandrog "gulddragaren Oldenburgs skqadron av stadens kavalleri" ').[111]

For any nobleman who had still not managed to ensconce himself within the walls of the House of the Nobility, it must have been a poor consolation that, here and there in the threatening and armed alliance of police and rabble, there were a number of 'serving men, armed in the defence of their masters' ('tjänstefolk, beväpnade till sina husbönders försvar').[112] For what use was it when that nobleman, 'at risk of life and limb [...] was to cross over the Square of the House of the Nobility ... full of rabble with their pockets full of stones' ('oviss om ljf eller död [...] skulle passera öfver Riddarehus Torget ... fullt af Pöbel med fickorne fulle af stenar')?[113]

By midday, those involved had taken their places: all the estates had gath- ered in their assemblies at the various places and the crowd in Riddarhustorget was in full cry with its hooting and howling. Only the great leading man of the day was still missing,[114] but when the noise outside the hall suddenly rose to a deafening pitch, the assembled noblemen should have had their suspicions, should have realised that the king was approaching, borne by the cheers of the enthusiastic crowd.[115] They appear to have been caught unawares when he entered unannounced.

The riot reaches its climax and subsides

The nobility began their deliberations at about eleven o'clock.[116] At first the discussions were about a gift to Duke Karl. The matter had not been con- cluded when the king abruptly interrupted their proceedings with his unexpected arrival.[117]

Gustavus III sat down in the country marshall's chair.[118] It was a symbolic act, for in so doing he wanted to demonstrate that he had come to the nobles as an unarmed peer,[119] not as the powerful king. Presumably he wanted the nobles to allow themselves to be persuaded rather than forced to yield to his sabre-rattling. The king obviously had no confidence in his powers of persuasion and in the end the nobles allowed themselves to be subdued rather than duped.[120] The estate gave in to the double pressure exerted by the threatening presence of the mob and an autocratic king who, in reality, was not capable of lowering himself to democratic discussions with the highly respected peers of the realm.[121]

When the appropriation decision was finally taken, a deputation of noblemen was sent to the other estates.[122] The king returned to the palace, probably accompanied by the eagerly cheering masses.[123] The matter had been decided: the artisan journeymen had done their duty to the fatherland and should have returned to their workshops. But the cheerful uproar continued for several hours more, and it was not until about four o'clock in the afternoon that the artisan journeymen were persuaded to leave the Square of the House of the Nobility.[124] By then the police had tired of them and were brandishing their truncheons at the very people whose anarchy they had so recently been happy to encourage, and had perhaps even orchestrated.[125] At about the same time, the nobility concluded the verification of the minutes of the meeting and were able to leave the Riddarhuset, bitterly reflecting on their lamentable defeat.[126]

There is much in this résumé which is uncertain. For example, we do not know what Gustavus III intended by his unctuous performance in the House of the Nobility; nor has it been ascertained whether all the members of parliament representing the clergy allowed themselves to be lulled into the same sense of security as Bishop Wallkvist would have us believe. It is also uncertain whether the artisan journeymen were really forcibly expelled from the square, or whether they finally simply got fed up. But apart from this, it can be said that the various sequences took place very much as they have been reported here. However, I have sidestepped two difficult sets of questions which are important to the analysis of the psychological and moral dynamic of the uprising.

The first question concerns how those taking part viewed each other. What did the journeymen believe to be the effects of their clamour; did they think they were able to frighten the assembled noblemen? And, vice versa: did the nobility credit the howling mob with any real strength, and did it exert any influence on their behaviour in the plenary session apart from providing a worrying backdrop to their deliberations? In short, of those involved; who was afraid and who to be feared?

The other question concerns the relations within the temporary and unholy alliance between the crowd and the police. Even if the initiative behind the mobilisation of the artisan journeymen was presumably taken by the chief of police (and, ultimately, the king), it is far from clear whether he succeeded in retaining it once anarchy had broken out. To what extent did the orchestrators really have control over the crowd? Or vice versa, to what extent did these people succeed in overstepping the bounds of what the powerful conspirators had envisaged? Was there any way they could have transformed the mobilisation for king and war into a movement in which, for a short while, they acted to further their own needs?[127]

In order to shed light on the first question let us start out on the square where Johan Hjerpe found himself, fortuitously, in a central position. He had 'managed to get through by the grating around Gustaf Ericson's image' ('upkranglat [sig] wid galrät af Gustaf Ericsons bild'), i.e., by the statue of Gustavus Vasa, the founder of the modern Swedish nation-state. To his way of thinking, there was no room for doubt. The nobility was shaking with fear in the face of the wrath of the people. The artisan journeymen hated the aristocracy as intensely as their hearts beat nobly for the king. From his vantage point, Hjerpe could see how

Adeln på Riddarhusalen förwånade sprungo up i fensterna somliga med bleka och somliga med röda ansikten [. . .] förskräckte öfwer hwad på färde nu war.

The nobility in the hall of the House of the Nobility, surprised, did spring to the windows, some with pale and some with red faces [. . .] terrified as to that which was now happening.

In Hjerpe's version of events, the journeymen contributed actively to the desired outcome, just by being there. The nobility realised that the battle was lost and hurried 'with ayes and cheering [to conclude] the Appropriation' ('med ja och hurrande [ingå] i Bewillningen'). But Hjerpe 'knew' that the defeat entailed a severe test for many noblemen who sat 'quite pale; indeed many trembled with malice and had to bite their tongues' ('aldeles afbleknad; ja mången skjelfde af onska och måste bita sig i tungan').[128]

Of course he did not know what had been happening inside the hall of the House of the Nobility, but he knew how it ended, and on the basis of that knowledge he invented a black-and-white tale of an unequal struggle between the cowardly authorities and the brave people, led by their noble sovereign.

For a different viewpoint, we must leave Hjerpe by the statue of Gustavus Vasa and go into the House of the Nobility. There's not a lot of room and we have to push to get in, as the stairs are full of people and the crowd is jostling all the way into the doors of the hall.[129] An excited Abraham de Broën is at the front, surrounded by journeymen shoemakers.[130]

Without doubt, the members of parliament representing the nobility were clearly upset by the noise of the crowd, which seemed to intensify and subside on demand.[131] Some of those within the majority who were hostile to the king were soon prepared to 'give in to superior force' ('vika sig för öfvermakten').[132] But here the immediate similarities with Hjerpe's diary entries end, and the picture becomes more opaque.

To begin with, it is unlikely that the nobility gave in solely to the superior force of the artisan journeymen. No doubt they felt uneasy when faced with their stones and general hostility, and in spite of the fact that the crowd was commanded by the police force, it was thought far too weak and disorganised to constitute a real danger in itself. Hochschild thought that these poor folk 'could easily have been dispersed by a small number of brave people' ('af ett ringa antal modigt folk lätteligen kunnat skingras').[133] Adlerbeth took the same view,[134] and von Rosenstein had even dared to cry out 'Quiet You damned riff-raff' ('Tyst Ert förbannade Pack') without being met by 'a shower of stones' ('ett skur med stenar').[135] A few young blades within the estate even wanted to go out and fight the 'damned riff-raff', but were prevented by their elders.[136]

The danger lay rather in the implications of the artisan mobilisation. As early as February, the king had demonstrated his constitutional wantonness and lack of respect. If he could now sink to mobilising the city's lowest rabble, what could not be expected of him? The nobility yielded under barely constitutional procedures to prevent Gustavus III from declaring himself sovereign with the support of the other three estates. Naturally, it is far from certain that Gustavus III would have met with a refusal under such circumstances, but it is probable that the members of parliament representing the nobility feared such a consequence, especially as they found themselves in the weaker position, with the city guard in the hands of the middle class, among other things.[137]

Even if the nobles had given in this time, they hardly did so with 'ayes and cheering'. The immediate reason was that the estate could find no means of refuting the king's brazen misinterpretation of how the voting had proceeded. Wild uproar apparently prevailed in the hall and it is even possible that a majority shouted 'No!' to the king's question as to whether the appropriation had been consented to. According to both Hamilton and Hochschild, the majority of the assembled noblemen were against the king.[138] Even the 'semi-official' report of the proceedings gives a hint that there was a lack of agreement,[139] and Hedvig Elisabeth Charlotta offers the thought that the king prevailed with the help of officers who had forced themselves into the room and voted unlawfully.[140] When the king finally issued his ultimate threat and declared 'he to be an enemy of the realm who dares to set himself against a decision already made' ('den för rikets fiende, som vågade sätta sig emot det redan fattade beslutet'), it appeared to be the last straw: 'The noise was renewed and lasted a long time' ('Bullret fick åter fart och varade en lång stund'). Nevertheless, the nobility yielded in the end, and became well-behaved extras in the king's grandiose spectacle; when he despatched a deputation to the other estates, only feeble protests were made.[141]

There is also the other question of how well the police controlled the artisan journeymen's uprising. I will touch on this briefly, and return to it in more detail in the next section, but I must carefully emphasise that the remarks which follow are speculative: it is obvious that the empirical basis is not enough for a satisfactory treatment of the event. The discussion – both here and later on – aims instead at revising the traditional interpretive framework in this area of research.

Presumably, these people were less dangerous for the nobility than Hjerpe imagined and more dangerous than the most condescending nobleman wished to believe. Less dangerous because to a large extent, they acted unstrategically, that is to say without a plan of their own as to how they were to get what they wanted from the despised nobles and lacking any distinct, long-term objective behind their actions. More dangerous because their behaviour, precisely as a consequence of its lack of strategy, developed according to a sort of spontaneous riot dynamic. In this mass context, the journeymen lost some of their normal self-control and could drive each other further than under normal conditions in impassioned violence against the aristocracy which a part of them truly and deeply hated.

In comparison with other pre-industrial mass riots, however, the violence was minimal that day. Unlike, for example, the Fersenian Riot of 1810 and the Crusenstolpe disturbances of 1838 – which both ended in fatalities and extensive material destruction – self-restraint was considerable.[142] No one was badly hurt and most people were merely afraid. Nevertheless, there were certain similarities between these three riots as regards the spontaneous dynamic which evolved; that is to say, the situation generated a violence that had only partly to do with the specific objectives of the actions being taken.

In the riot of April 1789, the chief of police probably calculated coldly and consciously – or strategically – the anarchical consequences of gathering many people in such a small area with the detested noble estate within such close reach. But even if Liljensparre succeeded in effecting the artisan mobilisation according to plan, neither he nor any of Gustavus III's other faithful followers had control over the crowd when the tumult was at its height.

For example, Adam Lewenhaupt failed to calm the crowd with a message from the king to the effect that their help was no longer needed. Instead, he was suspected of not being 'truly devoted to the king, when he came with such a message' ('kungen verkligt tillgiven, då han kom med en såden hälsning').[143] Another example is to be found in Hjerpe's diary telling of how one of the king's men ventured out and even set about a journeyman. He immediately had sticks raining down on him, and 'barely managed to escape to Mademoiselle Maja Lisa's coffee house'.[144]

The pattern is familiar from other episodes in Stockholm in the years around 1789, when a series of events took place which, taken together, introduced a measure of insecurity in the conspirators' expectations of the city's artisan journeymen, and which changed the impression of them as the obedient instruments of the police.

According to one witness, the crowd broke up in the afternoon only to assemble again by evening. The party was not over for the city's royalist artisan journeymen, and once again Police Chief Liljensparre gathered together his band – this time near the Royal Theatre – for a postscript to the favourable outcome of the day's events.[145]

A suggestion for a closer interpretation

I shall now discuss what has emerged about the attitudes of those involved, the motives and reactions of the artisan journeymen and Johan Hjerpe and what they thought, believed and wished – or what their normative, cognitive and affective orientation was. A more penetrating psychological analysis will subsequently be attempted. The reader who finds the interpretation difficult to follow would do best to go on to the next chapter – the second part of the diptych.

What I will suggest here as a speculative interpretation of events entails a certain critique or suggested modification of the perspectives which have dominated this research since Eric Hobsbawm, George Rudé and E. P. Thompson began to study pre-industrial mass unrest at the end of the 1950s.[146] By seeking to demonstrate the rationale in such riots, these historians have chosen to free the pre-industrial masses from the disrepute into which they had fallen through early mass psychology in general and its founder, Gustave Le Bon, in particular. For Le Bon, the individuals in a crowd were under mutual hypnosis and governed by primitive and destructive – in short, 'irrational' – instincts.[147] George Rudé in particular has opposed this view. In his riot studies he has – in declared opposition to Le Bon – emphasised that, in most cases, protesting crowds have had clearly defined objectives for their actions, adapted means to those objectives and exerted a selective force that has met its mark and spared the innocent.[148]

Rudé (as well as Hobsbawm and Thompson) now enjoy broad support within research on social history, and Gustave Le Bon has fallen from favour.[149] Recently, however, some criticism, both theoretical and empirical, has been levelled at their studies of pre-industrial mass riots. This criticism has been aimed at both the vagueness of the mass concept (and other, theoretical shortcomings) and to a number of empirical imperfections in the research.[150] For example, Robert Holton, among others, has reacted against Rudé's restriction of mass studies only to social protest.[151]

However, Holton is of the view that Hobsbawm, Rudé and Thompson at times succeed in elucidating how 'social protest can go hand in hand with social loyalty'.[152] Here Holton suggests a pespective which I would like to take somewhat further, even to the point of saying that one and the same mass action cannot only be at once loyal and 'disloyal', but also 'rational' and simultaneously 'irrational'. That is to say that a mass riot need not be understood only as goal-rational, but should also be capable of being analysed in relation to such needs as the action itself can satisfy, but which cannot be directly linked to these declared goals. Possibly one could say that such a way of looking at things lies between the approaches of modern mass riot research and early mass psychology, and I shall now investigate what such a perspective can contribute to the analysis of the artisan uprising of 27 April 1789.[153]

What they thought and believed

Seen in normative terms, the journeymen were keen royalists and adherents of Gustavus III's war efforts – something they had in common with Johan Hjerpe. But more than him, they displayed an open hatred for the opposition of the nobility and their alleged treason, but also because they had been given a golden opportunity to voice their hatred in relative safety. For a short while they had the chance to be both loyal and 'disloyal' to the authorities of society. That they were probably paid to demonstrate their attitudes alters none of this; a series of other events in the years around 1789 rather strengthens the impression that the artisan journeymen thought what they thought, and acted according to their own beliefs.

There were, of course, no arenas in which the opposing views of journeymen and nobility could be pitted in dialogue, and it never occurred to the common people that this might be possible. They condemned the aristocracy and wanted, quite simply, to force it to yield. Apart from the fact that society provided them with no other opportunity to exert their influence, the artisan journeymen's irreconcilable, militant behaviour was in tune with their general mentality.

There were numerous signs that the authorities could not depend on the journeymen, despite the fact that they did manage to exploit great prejudice in the events recounted here. The temptation to make a much more biased statement is great. Measured by their attitude, these people were all prepared to use force to get what they wanted, largely indifferent to anyone or anything that stood in their way. Several times, in the thick of things even in the less boisterous crowds – Henrik Liljensparre had difficulty defending himself in the face of the enraged artisans.[154]

There were, however, clear limits to the militant and semi-coherent 'righteousness' of these people. First of all, they supported the king. This was an enduring feature of their contradictory psychological make-up.[155] Perhaps because of this, through concessions in parliament to the demands of the middle classes for restrictions on freedom of trade, the king dared to risk the support he had built up among the workers of the city. Against the background of the increasing difficulties exerienced by the trades in general, increasing guild restrictions would have led to a deterioration in conditions for the artisan journeymen.

While the powerless masses have so far been thought capable of operating only with militant, implacable and intolerant expedients – or not at all – it is also obvious that something had been changing among the artisan journeymen and others in similar social positions for several decades. The typical journeyman was not tolerant, not conversant with religion, not particularly modern. But it was typical of the times that tolerant, religiously aware, modern people were to be found among those very artisans,[156] or among their peers,[157] all in tune with a progressive evolution on the part of the authorities towards increased tolerance for people's diverging views and beliefs.[158] Finally, it is clear that, for several centuries, the population – and particularly city folk – had been growing more civilised, and that by the mid-eighteenth century very few murders and manslaughters were committed in Stockholm.[159]

In many respects, Johan Hjerpe was largely in agreement with the artisan journeymen: he felt for the king, he waxed lyrical about the war effort and loudly condemned the 'deceitful' nobility. Yet at the same time, he found himself morally distanced from the artisan journeymen whose 'heroic' behaviour he applauded. He was just a simple man who – perhaps by virtue of his birth[160] – had been won over to modern, tolerant Moravianism. The high-spirited violence of the journeymen worried him, while their support for the king calmed him. That was why he yielded to the temptation of joining the flowing crowd, but did not blend into it completely, remaining instead a sort of detached and passive observer.

In another way too, he emerges as an outsider: he demonstrated no personal desire for war whatsoever, and this in spite of the fact that presumably many other shop assistants were voluntarily mobilised, and despite the admiration he felt for those who showed their bravery.[161]

Hjerpe represented in one and the same person the schism between the moralist new and old. The different moral codes did not blend well, but competed for influence over his feelings. This inner conflict distanced him from most other people who were more or less on his social level.[162] As I have already pointed out, however, there was only a modest difference between their respective standpoints, even if it can be said, *en passant*, that this distance would eventually grow apace with his modest but unmistakable successes in society.

Were Hjerpe typical of the entire, noisy crowd, it could be said that the artisan journeymen not only thought that the nobility had to be forced to yield, but also believed in their ability to make them do so. He was not typical. There is, nevertheless, much to suggest that, in certain respects, the journeymen had the same intuitive basis as Hjerpe for their behaviour on this day.

In the first place the journeymen were certainly aware in advance of the role the police wanted them to play, and despite his denial, so probably was Hjerpe. They drew the inevitable conclusion from the contradictory and importunate behaviour of the police that they were needed. In the second place, the crowd was equipped for battle, even if it was armed, in 'mob fashion', with only stones. Finally, the middle classes were misled by the royal war propaganda, in which set-backs were hushed up as efficiently as the nobility were depicted as pitiful and cowardly. Even for as energetic a newspaper-reader as Johan Hjerpe, the failures of the Swedish military remained hidden, although he may have been aware, as were others, of the severe epidemics which followed in the wake of war.[163]

The motivating factors

I am convinced that it is possible to delve more deeply into how the artisan journeymen were roused on 27 April 1789. At this level of analysis, it is a matter, first and foremost, of identifying the wishes of the journeymen, or which of their needs could be satisfied by their participation, and not primarily what they thought – their normative motives. The analysis deviates, in part, from the interpretive perspectives which have dominated research into pre-industrial popular struggles of the last 20–25 years; the speculative discussion which follows aims to establish new (or neo-) interpretive frameworks for the analysis of popular uprisings.

The artisan uprising developed into a sort of royalist anarchy under police control. This historically distinctive 'gestalt' gave the journeymen the chance to discharge pent-up mental energy, particularly as it could do so without fear of reprisal. At the same time, it was an opportunity to experience a sort of narcissistic gratification precisely by being called to assist the king in his hour of need. *From this point of view*, it meant little whether the stated goal of their action was achieved. Had it not been possible to coerce the nobility, the journeymen would nevertheless have achieved some kind of emotional dividend from their fervent demands. This is a timeless theme, which modifies social history's ends–means-rational image of the pre-industrial masses.

The efforts to mobilise the artisan journeymen formed one element in the authorities' strategy to obtain resources for the war. By the same token, these importunate efforts were of strategic importance to the gratification of the journeymen's narcissistic needs. They themselves acted without strategy, in a double sense. First, they lacked a plan for realising the aim of their action, and secondly, there was no long-term objective to their participation. It is not clear whether the journeymen themselves wanted to fight in the war they encouraged, in spite of the fact that this would presumably have been a consequence of their actions being successful.[164]

They had, at best, a very hazy picture of the true causes of the war. Not even the well-informed Hjerpe could find any really good reasons for it, except that by going to war with Russia, Gustavus III was trying to flush out the traitors within the Swedish army![165] Far-fetched and lacking in substance. To the workers of the city, the war may have appeared more as a tempting fantasy, a focus for the desire to seek revenge for all possible economic, social and perceived injustices.[166]

What has been said so far certainly does not mean that the artisan journeymen at that time were generally incapable of acting strategically. On the contrary, recent research on the artisans has shown how the journeymen – struggling to further their immediate economic interests and to safeguard their honour and status – at an early stage, were capable of acting rationally when it came to adapting means to a certain end. They could organise themselves in groups and wait for the most appropriate moment to seek confrontation.[167] Here is a clear correspondence with British research on pre-industrial mass uprisings. But, in the first place, every social conflict – however much it is fought according to plan – can satisfy different sorts of needs; it has a double import which should not be overlooked. In the second place, the struggle of 27 April did not immediately concern the journeymen themselves, even if their continually worsened plight was significant to those needs they sought to satisfy that day. But in what way?

Forms of social intercourse among the artisans had long been strongly ritualised. Customs were both a symbolic manifestation of definite psychological mechanisms and needs and social activities.[168] For example, the dunking ritual at a journeyman's initiation can be seen as a symbolic enactment of basic, existential traumas which must at the same time have filled a function of creating a collective identity. Through the ceremony, the mature apprentice or journeyman candidate was to put aside his old loyalties and take on new ones. He could not, however, do it in his own way, according to his own requirements, but only according to strictly regulated custom. Personal identity was, for precisely this reason, a collective identity, i.e., tied to the journeyman's newly attained social role, and was intended to entail a break with his old one.[169]

But the rites also had something of an anti-social meaning. Take for example, the initiation rites of the tiled-oven-makers. In the scattered manuscripts collections on old craft practices in the Royal Library of Sweden, the following short description was found:[170]

hos Kakelugnsmakare uti samma Rum som sammankomsten var var giordt en upphöjning och det practiserades altid ett embar natten före sammankomstens början. Detta var Dasswatsen ty när någon skulle bli gesäll så skulle han döpas och rakas [. . .] Man alt detta för sig gick alt efter som han hadde uppfört sig under sin lärotid. Hade han många anmärkningar mot sig [. . .] fick [han kanske] hela embarets inneholl öfwer sig vid döpelseachten.

by the tiled-oven-makers out in the same room as the assembly a hoist and a bucket was always prepared the night before the beginning of the assembly. This was water from the privy because when someone was to become a journeyman then he was to be dunked and shaved [. . .] But all this took place according to how he had conducted himself during his apprenticeship. Had he many black marks [. . .] [he perhaps] got the entire contents of the bucket over him during the dunking.

This item conforms to a familiar pattern, even if the privy water was, perhaps, a distinctive feature of the tiled-oven-makers' venerable traditions. Each apprentice who wished to become a journeyman – and thus acknowledged as a man – was compelled to submit to a degrading ceremony, which was often a sort of high-spirited pastiche of the crowning with thorns following the dunking. Only in this way could he be admitted to the community of journeymen and come to enjoy the rights to which they were entitled. Here is a rite which seems to have had a rationally socialising significance: in his travels, the journeyman would, in the future, always have to side with his brothers in the trade and accept his (at best temporary) position in the social hierarchy.

But the rite cannot be reduced to its social objective, since it was also a symbolic enactment of death and rebirth, was both a flattering initiation and degrading dunking, crowning and crowning with thorns at the same time. The ceremony gave the new journeyman responsibilities and rights and thereby made him an adult, but also gave the initiates of the guild a sacred opportunity for collective regression. It was hardly just in order to secure his allegiance that they poured shit on the poor victim in the traditional manner. For a short while, they perhaps also made him into a sort of redeemer of their own infantile traumas. In other words, the ceremony of the tiled-oven-makers was a way of aligning external demands with inner aspirations; it was social and anti-social at the same time.

The ritual forms of communication were socially functional because they forced the journeyman, who often worked alone, into loyalty with his peers. This loyalty was also consensual, i.e., it meant that the journeyman accepted his position in the social hierarchy.[171] But in their late eighteenth-century context, these ceremonies were an old-fashioned and distinctive cultural manifestation. Even if the ceremonies survived for quite some time in some places,[172] they were losing their functional purpose as quickly as the long-term difficulties of guild craftsmanship increased. And this was quite apart from the fact that the secret rites of the guilds had long been opposed by the authorities.[173]

The Danish historian Camillus Nyrop once claimed that the initiation rites of the Danish guilds degenerated into sadism in the eighteenth century.[174] The possibility that the same thing happened in Sweden cannot be excluded: it may have been natural for the journeymen to dwell unthinkingly on their social failures, to take them out on the poor journeyman candidate as their victim. We do not, however, know what happened in Sweden, because the ceremonies of the guilds have still only been sketchily researched.[175] To date there is no systematic evidence that ceremonial sadism increased during the course of the eighteenth century. It seems, on the contrary, to date much further back.[176]

Members of each craft guild built their collective identity on tradition, among other things on the notion that they of all people were particularly indispensible. They were indispensible to the nation in general, and to the king in particular.[177] Moreover, the artisan corps may themselves have had a unique influence over nature's raw materials: they could move from one type of work to another and, unlike the farmer, did not need to wait for nature to take its course. This might explain why artisans often resorted to magic in order to gain power over their enemies or adverse external conditions.[178]

The artisan journeymen of Stockholm, however, were now becoming dispensible. The economic stagnation within the guild trades became a threat to their collective identity; cracks were appearing in their magical self-esteem. It was precisely that situation in which their chance arose to find some form of redress for their wounded narcissism: the royalist rhetoric made them once again indispensible to king and country.

Some of the journeymen seemed to become particularly intoxicated with their rediscovered but temporary importance to the fate of the nation, and their behaviour followed its own inherent dynamic. For most it was also a matter – we can safely assume – of the uproar on Riddarhustorget giving them the chance to get rid of pent-up energy regardless of the political objectives for which they had risen.

Oppressed crowds have repeatedly obstructed the powers-that-be in spite of their struggle being futile and doomed to failure because such actions in themselves gratify basic instincts regardless of the outcome. This contradicts to a large extent the validity of different types of rationalistic, often contract-theoretical explanations of social conflict. Thus, for example, neither the power differential hypothesis of the sociologist Walter Korpi or the contract theory of the historian Barrington Moore Jr would be particularly useful when explaining the mass uprisings of earlier times, or in the analysis of the artisan uprising of 27 April 1789. According to the former's theory, the level of conflict in society is at its highest exactly when the power differential between the parties – or classes – is least. This is so because the less powerful parties understand, on rational grounds, that the struggle is futile when the power differentials are great. This is a theory which inadequately reflects the history of pre-industrial uprisings. The reason for this is that it is far too 'rational' in its assumptions, that is to say it takes no account of the 'irrational' motives for conflict, and only concerns itself with the rational.[179]

Notes

1. R. F. Hochschild, *Memoarer 1*, p. 232.
2. *RA*, Montgomerys samling, Fredrik Wilhelm von Ehrenheim, p. 77.
3. R. F. Hochschild, *Memoarer 1*, p. 232.
4. L. Edgren, *Lärling, gesäll, mästare: hantverk och hantverkare i Malmö 1750–1847*, pp. 253, 261–63.
5. A survey of the material from 12 guilds for the relevant period has yielded nothing. *KB*, Bokbindareämbetets protokoll 1783–1847, huvudräkenskaper 1729–1822, verifikationer 1653–1791, Guldsmedsämbetets räkningar 1743–1800; *NordMA*, Repslagaregesällskapets protokoll och lådräkning 1688–1809, Skomakaregesällskapets protokoll 1780–1813, Snörmakaregesällskapets verifikationer 1748–1883, handlingar 1752–97, Tenngjutaregesällskapets protokoll och lådräkning 1687–1854; *SSA*, Bleckslagareämbetets protokoll 1739–90, Garvareämbetets protokoll 1785–1835, Kammakareämbetets diverse handlingar, Skräddareämbetets protokoll 1777–87 and konceptprotokoll, Synåls- och knappmakareämbetets protokoll 1744–96 and 1703–1822, Sämsk- och handskmakareämbetets protokoll 1775–1845.
6. *UUB*, JHJ (*circa* 650 quarto pages), notation dated 27 April 1789.
7. For a different view, see R. Liljedahl, 'En gustaviansk handelsbetjänt'.
8. E. Hobsbawm, G. Rudé and E. P. Thompson, whose views will be discussed below (pp. 42ff), have led the way.
9. See, for example, R. Karlbom, *Hungerupplopp och strejker 1793–1867: en studie i den svenska arbetarrörelsens uppkomst*.
10. T. Nerman, *Crusenstoles kravaller*.
11. E. Lönnroth, *Den stora rollen: kung Gustaf III spelad av honom själv*, pp. 51ff and 161–66.
12. *UUB*, Brev från Henrik Liljensparre till Gustav III, 5/8 1788, brev från Henrik Liljensparre till Gustav III, 2/8 1788 Jfr; *RA*, Sjöholmssamlingen, Nordins arkiv: brev från C. G. Nordin till J. M. Nordin, 4/8 1788; *Dagligt allehanda*, 2/8 resp 5/8 1788; *Gömdt är icke glömdt: Historiska bidrag 12*, s 36; Nordin C. G., »Dagboksanteckningar för åren 1786–1792«, i *Historiska handlingar 6*, s 58; Rosén von Rosenstein N, *Samlade skrifter 3*, brev till Gustav III 8/8 1788, s 299; Boberg S, *Kunglig krigspropaganda*, s 32 ff; Staf N, *Polisväsendet i Stockholm 1776–1850*, s 133–138.
13. A short résumé of the events of the war can be found in E. Reuterswärd, 'Kungörandet av Gustav III:s ryska krig 1788–1790', pp. 321–24. See also S. Carlson, *Svensk historia 2*, pp. 186–97.
14. Lönnroth, *Den stora rollen*, pp. 51ff., 161–66. See note 12.
15. I find that sort of historiography far too preoccupied with individuals. Lönnroth does not make use of notes in his written work. His arguments can thus not be tested, piece by piece, in relation to the source material. For a more conventionally power-political explanation of Gustavus III's objective with the war, see Carlsson, *Svensk historia 2*, p. 186.

16. On this, see Carlsson, *Svensk historia 2*, pp. 187–90.
17. Boberg, *Gustaviansk krigspropaganda*, pp. 16 and 32ff.
18. E. Reuterswärd, 'Kungörandet av Gustav III:s ryska krig 1788–1790'.
19. Lönnroth, *Den stora rollen*, p. 201.
20. See B. Boëthius, *Magistraten och borgerskapet 1719–1815*, pp. 482–84; S. Carlsson, *Svensk historia 2*, p. 193–97; E. Söderlund, *Hantverkarna 2*, p. 230; E. F. Heckscher, *Sveriges ekonomiska historia från Gustav Vasa 2:1*, p. 557.
21. On this, see Carlsson, *Svensk historia 2*, pp. 193ff.
22. Boëthius, *Magistraten och borgerskapet*, pp. 439–503.
23. J. Söderberg, 'Den stagnerande staden: Stockholms tillväxtproblem 1760–1850 i ett jämförande europeiskt perspektiv', pp. 162–64; Söderberg, 'Real wage trends in urban Europe, 1730–1850: Stockholm in a comparative perspective'.
24. Boëthius, *Magistraten och borgerskapet*, p. 441; Heckscher, *Sveriges ekonomiska historia . . .*, Diagram XXIII and XXXII.
25. For the 1720–1790 period, r_{xy} is − 0.96 for the connection between the artisan proportion of total taxation in middle-class industry and of total taxation. For references, see Figure 1.
26. J. Söderberg, U. Jonsson and C. Persson, *Stagnating metropolis: economy and demography in Stockholm 1750–1850*, p. 5.
27. Söderberg, '*Den stagnerande staden . . .*' p. 162; Söderberg, 'Real wage trends . . .', p. 169.
28. Heckscher, *Sveriges ekonomiska historia . . .*, p. 550; Söderlund, *Stockholms hantverkarklass*, pp. 305 and 310; Söderlund, *Hantverkarna 2*, pp. 384–85.
29. Söderlund, *Hantverkarna 2*, p. 385; Söderlund, *Stockholms hantverkarklass*, pp. 305, 310.
30. Hochschild, *Memoarer 1*, p. 232; Staf, *Polisväsendet i Stockholm*, p. 1 152; B. Boëthius, 'Abraham de Broën'; C. Hallendorf, 'Hedvig Elisabeth Charlotta', pp. 385–92; *UUB*, Brev från Liljensparre till Gustav III, 6/8 1790.
31. *RA*, Riksdagsacta: Borgarståndets protokoll vid riksdagen 1789, Prästeståndets protokoll vid riksdagen 1789.
32. Sveriges riksdag 1:6 (edited by N. Edén), pp. 18–24. Here it is mistakenly stated that, after 1768, the burghers met in the new town hall (p. 21). The citation from *RA*, Riksdagsacta: Borgarståndets protokoll 1789, p. 2 contradicts this. It is clear from *Stockholms byggnader: en bok om arkitektur och byggnader i Stockholm* by H. O. Andersson and F. Bedoire, picture I, that the Exchange building on Stortorget, the 'Great Square' was ready by 1778.
33. This is the case, for example, with Karlbom, *Hungerupplopp och strejker*; A. Booth, 'Popular loyalism and public violence in the north-west of England, 1790–1800'; G. Lewis, 'The white terror of 1815 in the department of the Gard: counter-revolution, continuity and the individual'; C. Tilly, *The contentious French*, pp. 407–13.
34. Cf. Booth, 'Popular loyalism and public violence . . .', p. 301.
35. For shorter versions of the artisan mobilisation, see for example A. H. Barton, *Scandinavia in the revolutionary era 1760–1815*, p. 170; S. Högberg, *Stockholms historia 2*, pp. 30–32.
36. *UUB*, JHJ, 1788–92.
37. See for instance C. Ginzburg, *The cheese and the worms: the cosmos of a sixteenth-century miller*, or E. Le Roy Ladurie, *Montaillou: Village Occitan de 1294 à 1324* (about the shepherd Pierre Maury); N. Davis. *The Return of Martin Guerre*.
38. *KB*, J. Hjerpe, Kong residensestaden Stockholms . . . ; *LSB*, J. Hjerpe, Berättelse om en lustresa sommartiden 1809; *LSB*, Samlingsbok av Johan Hjerpe . . . ; *UUB*, Merckwärdige händelser . . .
39. Hochschild; Boëthius, *Magistraten och borgerskapet*, p. 469; O. Jägerskiöld, 'Rutger Fredrik Hochschild', pp. 173–74. The editor of the memoirs of Hochschild – Henrik

Schück – did not consider him extraordinarily oppositional to the King. On this, see *Memoarer 1*, pp. vff.

40. Henrik Schück believed that he got 'at least a good part of the facts' from the Sparre brothers. R. F. Hochschild, *Memoarer 1*, pp. vii–viii.
41. *Gömdt är icke glömdt: Historiska bidrag 12*.
42. O. Wallqvist, 'Berättelse om riksdagen 1789', pp. 430–33.
43. A. L. Hamilton, 'Anekdoter till svenska historien under Gustaf III:s regering', p. 134. See *UUB*, Brev från Liljensparre till Gustav III, 27 January 1789. See also S. Boberg, *Kunglig krigspropaganda*, pp. 138–40; E. Reuterswärd, 'Kunggörandet av Gustav III:s ryska krig 1788–1790', p. 333. In *Biografiskt lexikon över namnkunnige svenska män 20:1*, pp. 4–5, the picture of Wallqvist is less rigid. Gjörwell takes Liljensparre's line in his defence of Wallqvist, *KB*, Brev till Johan Lidén, 14 June 1789.
44. *Hedvig Elisabeth Charlottas dagbok 3*.
45. A. L. Hamilton, 'Anekdoter til svenska historien under Gustaf III:s regering'.
46. *RA*, Montgomerys samling: F. W. von Ehrenheim.
47. G. G. Adlerbeth, *Historiska anteckningar 1*, p. 162.
48. *RA*, Riksdagsacta: Konceptprotokoll över plenum hos adeln 27/4 1789.
49. Boëthius, *Magistraten och borgerskapet*, p. 471.
50. *UUB*, Brev från H. Liljensparre till Gustav III, 22/7 1788; B. Bergfeldt, 'Utländska myheter från Paris: två stockholmstidningars bevakning av franska revolutionen under perioden 1788–1793'; M. Nyman, 'News from France in a Swedish provincial paper during the years before the French revolution', pp. 6–12.
51. *UUB*, JHJ, 27/6 1788.
52. Ibid., for 1788 27/5, for 1789 3/2 and May (date not clarified).
53. *UUB*, Brev från Erik Ruuth till Gustav III, September 1788.
54. Schröderheim was also loyal to the king. See Å. Nilsson, 'Elis Schröderheim', p. 579.
55. *Från Tredje Gustafs dagar, 1 Elis Schröderheims skrifter till konung Gustaf III:s historia jämte urval ur Schröderheims brefväxling. Brev til Gustav III 17/9*. See also *UUB*, Brev frän Liljensparre till Gustav III, 6/12 1788.
56. O. Wallqvist, 'Berättelse om riksdagen 1789', pp. 431–32. It is clear from this that the notes referred actually to April 1789 and not to February of the same year, which would have been expected.
57. Compare Tilly, *The contentious French*, pp. 227–31.
58. *UUB*, JHJ, April 1789.
59. *Gömdt är icke glömdt 12*, p. 8.
60. Ibid.
61. *RA*, Montgomerys samling: F. W. von Ehrenheim, p. 76.
62. Ibid., p. 77.
63. Adlerbeth, *Historiska anteckningar 1*, p. 162.
64. Adlerbeth, *Historiska anteckningar 1*, p. 162; B. Boëthius, *Magistraten och borgerskapet i Stockholm 1719–1815*, p. 470; Carlsson, *Svensk historia 2*, p. 194; *Protokoller hos högloflige . . . 1789*.
65. B. Boëthius, *Magistraten och borgerskapet i Stockholm 1719–1815*, p. 470; Carlsson, *Svensk historia 2*, p. 194; *Protokoller hos högloflige . . . 1789*.
66. Adlerbeth, *Historiska anteckningar 1*, p. 162.
67. *KB*, J. Hjerpe, Kong residensestaden . . .
68. *UUB*, JHJ, 27/4 1789.
69. G. Rudé, 'The London "mob" of the eighteenth century', pp. 1–2; Rudé, *The crowd in history 1730–1848*, pp. 214–15. See also Booth, 'Popular loyalism and public violence . . .', p. 301.

70. Hamilton, 'Anekdoter till svenska historien . . .', p. 163.
71. Staf, *Polisväsendet i Stockholm* . . . , p. 152.
72. *Hedvig Elisabeth Charlottas dagbok 3*, pp. 97–98.
73. Ibid., *RA*, Montgomerys samling: F. W. von Ehrenheim, p. 77.
74. Hochschild, *Memoarer 1*, p. 232.
75. Adlerbeth, *Historiska anteckningar 1*, p. 156.
76. Boberg, *Kunglig krigspropaganda*, p. 42; Boëthius, *Magistraten och borgerskapet*, pp. 445–50.
77. Reuterswärd, 'Kungörandet av Gustav III:s ryska krig 1788–1790', p. 326; *Offentliga trycket: 1787 och 1788 års förordningar*, Överståthållarämbetets kungörelse 31/5 1788, p. 173. This uncertainty is visible on many occasions. See for example *UUB*, Brev från Liljensparre till Gustav III, 3/2 1792; *Från Tredje Gustafs dagar 1*, Brev från E. Schröderheim till Gustav III 21/3 1789, p. 284.
78. Adlerbeth, *Historiska anteckningar 1*, p. 156.
79. *UUB*, JHJ, 27/4 1789.
80. Concerning the probable contemporaneity of Hedvig Elisabeth Charlotta's diary notes, see Hallendorff, 'Hedvig Elisabeth Charlotta', pp. 383–92.
81. Wallqvist, 'Berättelse om riksdagen 1789', p. 430.
82. *Gömdt är icke glömdt 12*, pp. 10–11; *Hedvig Elisabeth Charlottas dagbok 3*, p. 98.
83. On Lenoir, police commander in pre-revolutionary Paris, see Darnton, *The Literary Underground of the Old Régime*, esp. Chapter 3; Staf, *Polisväsendet i Stockholm* . . . , pp. 198–99.
84. Staf, *Polisväsendet i Stockholm* . . . , Chapter 3; *UUB*, Brev från Liljensparre till Gustavus III, 19/5 1787, 7/6 1787, 17/9 1798, 27/4 1788, 21/1 1789, 27/4 1789, 9/9 1790, 21/12 1790; *UUB*, Brev från von Axelsson till Gustav III, 1774, 'Projekt till polis i Stockholm'.
85. *Hedvig Elisabeth Charlottas dagbok 3*, p. 98.
86. *RA*, Riksdagsacta, Borgarståndets protokoll och handlingar 1789: 'Till dett Redlige Bonde Ståndet . . .', R 1431, pp. 1602ff (transcript) and R 1432, pp. 1169ff (original), respectively, Prästeståndets protokoll och riksdagsacta 1789 R 712, pp. 968f (transcript) and R 959 (original), respectively. See also Wallqvist, pp. 430–31; *UUB*, JHJ, 27/4 1789, where Hjerpe mentions that the communication was also sent to the middle classes.
87. Carlsson, *Svensk historia 2*, p. 196; Lönnroth, *Den stora rollen*, p. 203.
88. Staf, *Polisväsendet i Stockholm* . . . , p. 147. It is also important to emphasise the substantial improvements in their legal status which the peasants achieved in that parliament. See Carlsson, *Svensk historia 2*, pp. 194–95.
89. *KB*, J. Hjerpe, Kong residensestadens . . . , 1789.
90. Carlsson, *Svensk historia 2*, p. 196; Lönnroth, *Den stora rollen*, p. 203.
91. Wallqvist, 'Berättelse om riksdagen 1789', p. 430; *RA*, Riksdagsacta, Borgarståndets protokoll vid riksdagen 1789.
92. *RA*. Riksdagsacta, Konceptprotokoll över plenum hos adeln.
93. *RA*, Riksdagsacta, Borgerkapets protokoll 1789, pp. 1604–05. See also Adlerbeth, p. 156; *UUB*, JHJ, 27/4 1789. *RA*, Riksdagsacta, Borgarståndets handlingar 1789, pp. 1079–82 and 1099–1100.
94. *RA*, Riksdagsacta, Borgarståndets handlingar 1789, pp. 1079–82 and 1099–1100.
95. Wallqvist, 'Berättelse om riksdagen 1789', p. 430.
96. Ibid., p. 431.
97. Ibid., p. 432.
98. *RA*, Riksdagsacta, Prästeståndets protokoll 1789, pp. 972–74.
99. *UUB*, JHJ, 27/4 1789.
100. Ibid.
101. Hochschild, *Memoarer 1*, p. 232. *Hedvig Elisabeth Charlottas dagbok*, pp. 104–05.

102. *UUB*, JHJ, 27/4 1789.

103. *Hedvig Elisabeth Charlottas dagbok 3*, p. 98.

104. E. Söderlund, *Stockholms hantverkarklass 1720–1772*, p. 314, states that the number of artisan journeymen according to the estate statistics of 1769 was 2,867. According to the population registers, p. 310, they did not number more than 1,489 in the same period.

105. *RA*, Montgomerys samling, F. W. von Ehrenheim.

106. Hedman, 'Massan vid det s k fersenska upploppet', pp. 25–66; Nerman, *Crusenstolpes kravaller*, pp. 92–95, 106, 115, 122ff, 184, 198ff, 207, 214ff, 250, 254 and 280; Rudé, *The crowd in history*, pp. 198ff.

107. Adlerbeth, *Historiska anteckningar 1*, p. 157; Hochschild, *Memoarer 1*, p. 239; *RA*, Montgomerys samling F. W. v Ehrenheim, pp. 76–78; *UUB*, JHJ, 27/4 1789.

108. *Gömdt är icke glömdt 12*, p. 8.

109. J. C. Barfod, *Dagens märkvärdigheter 1*, pp. 78ff; *Gömdt är icke glömdt 12*, pp. 36ff; *Hedvig Elisabeth Charlottas dagbok 2*; p. 287; Hochschild, *Memoarer 1*, pp. 142–43; *RA*, Sjöholmssamlingen: Brev från C. G. Nordin till J. M. af Nordin, 4/8 1788; *RA*; Börstorpssamlingen: F. U. von Rosens brev till F. Sparre, 5/8 1788; *UUB*, JHJ, 27/4 1789; *UUB*, Liljensparres brev till Gustav III, 5/8 1788.

110. A. L. Hamilton, 'Anekdoter till svenska historien under Gustaf III:s regering', p. 164.

111. Adlerbeth, *Historiska anteckningar 1*, p. 157.

112. *Hedvig Elisabeth Charlottas dagbok 3*, pp. 104–05.

113. *RA*, Montgomerys samling, F. W. von Ehrenheim.

114. Adlerbeth, *Historiska anteckningar 1*, p. 157; *Hedvig Elisabeth Charlottas dagbok 3*, p. 98. The chronology is reversed in Hochschild, *Memoarer 1*, p. 232: first came the king, and then the journeymen assembled. The order of events is unclear in Hjerpe's version.

115. Adlerbeth, *Historiska anteckningar 1*, p. 157.

116. Ibid., p. 156; *RA*, Riksdagsacta, Konceptprotokoll . . .

117. *RA*, Riksdagsacta, Konceptprotokoll . . . , pp. 1–3; *RA*, Montgomerys samling, F. W. von Ehrenheim, pp. 73ff; Adlerbeth, *Historiska anteckningar 1*, p. 156; Hochschild, *Memoarer 1*, p. 232; *Protokoller hos högloflige . . .* , pp. 935–38.

118. *RA*, Riksdagsacta, Koncepprotokoll . . . , p. 3; *UUB*, JHJ, 27/4 1789; Adlerbeth, *Historiska anteckningar 1*, p. 157; Lönnroth, *Den stora rollen*, p. 203.

119. Adlerbeth, *Historiska anteckningar 1*, p. 157.

120. Ibid., p. 162.

121. *RA*, Riksdagsacta, Konceptprotokoll . . . , pp. 3–5; Lönnroth, *Den stora rollen*, pp. 203ff.

122. *RA*, Riksdagsacta, Konceptprotokoll . . . , p. 4; Hamilton, 'Anekdoter till svenska historien . . .' p. 167; Hochschild, *Memoarer 1*, p. 234.

123. *UUB*, JHJ, 27/4 1789; *Gömdt är icke glömdt 12*, p. 10; *Hedvig Elisabeth Charlottas dagbok 3*, p. 104; Hochschild, *Memoarer 1*, p. 235.

124. *RA*, Riksdagsacta, Konceptprotokoll . . . , p. 5; *Hedvig Elisabeth Charlottas dagbook 3*, pp. 104–05.

125. Hochschild, *Memoarer 1*, pp. 232ff.

126 Ibid.

127. Cp. Rudé, 'The London "Mob" of the eighteenth century', p. 7; Rudé, *The crowd in history . . .* , pp. 146, 217.

128. *UUB*, JHJ, 27/4 1789.

129. *RA*, Riksdagsacta, Konceptprotokoll . . . , p. 5; *RA*, Montgomerys samling, F. W. von Ehrenheim, p. 77; *UUB*, JHJ, 27/4 1789; Adlerbeth, *Historiska anteckningar 1*, p. 157; *Hedvig Elisabeth Charlottas dagbok 3*, pp. 98–99.

130. Hochschild, *Memoarer 1*, p. 232.

131. *RA*, Riksdagsacta, Konceptprotokoll . . . , p. 4.

132. Ibid., pp. 3–4.

133. Hochschild, *Memoarer 1*, p. 236.

134. Adlerbeth, *Historiska anteckningar 1*, p. 162.

135. *RA*, Montgomerys samling, F. W. von Ehrenheim, p. 79; Hamilton, 'Anekdoter till svenska historien', p. 164.

136. *RA*, Montgomerys samling, F. W. von Ehrenheim, p. 79; *RA*, Riksdagsacta, Konceptprotokoll . . . , p. 5; Hochschild, *Memoarer 1*, p. 235–36.

137. For a brief summary, see Barton, pp. 163ff.

138. Hamilton, 'Anekdoter till svenska historien', p. 165; Hochschild, *Memoarer 1*, p. 234.

139. See *Protokoller hos högloflige . . .* pp. 968ff; *RA*, Riksdagsacta, Ridderskapets och adelsn protokoll . . . See also *RA*, Konceptprotokoll. . . .

140. *Hedvig Elisabeth Charlottas dagbok 3*, pp. 101–02.

141. *RA*, Riksdagsacta, Konceptprotokoll . . .

142. Hedman, 'Massan vid det s k fersenska upploppet', pp. 19–23; Nerman, *Crusenstolpes kravaller*, pp. 82, 110–15, 144, 185–96, 211–19, 253, 276, 288.

143. *Hedvig Elisabeth Charlottas dagbok 3*, p. 552, n. 7. About a similar episode, see Staf, *Polisväsendet i Stockholm*, p. 153.

144. *UUB*, JHJ, 27/4 1789.

145. Hochschild, *Memoarer 1*, p. 237.

146. See for instance E. Hobsbawm, *Primitive rebels*; Rudé, 'The London "mob" of the eighteenth century'; Rudé, *The crowd in history*; E. P. Thompson, *The making of the English working class*; Thompson, 'The moral economy of the English crowd in the eighteenth century'.

147. On Le Bon, see R. A. Nye, *The origins of crowd psychology: Gustave Le Bon and the crisis of mass democracy in the Third republic*, pp. 28, 44, 46, 60–62, 66–71, 77; S. Moscovici, *The age of the crowd: a historical treatise on mass psychology II*. See also S. Freud, *Group psychology and the analysis of the ego*, pp. 72–81.

148. Rudé, *The crowd in history*, pp. 3, 9–13, 198–99, 237, 247–57, 266.

149. Moscovici, *The age of the crowd*, p. 49.

150. See for instance Booth, 'Popular loyalism and public violence . . .'; L. Colley, 'Whose nation? Class and national consciousness in Britain 1750–1830'; D. E. Williams, 'Morals, markets and the English crowd in 1766'; R. L. Woods Jr, 'Individuals in a rioting crowd: a new approach'. One example of a revolt that does not fit very well into the analytical framework of Rudé is Lewis, 'The white terror of 1815 . . .'

151. R. J. Holton, 'The crowd in history: some problems of theory and method', pp. 219, 223–24.

152. Ibid., pp. 226–27.

153. Ulf Jonsson of the Department of Economic History at the University of Stockholm drew my attention to how my interpretation could be related to that of European mass riot research.

154. *RA*, Börstorpssamlingen: letter from Isak Askegren to Fredrik Sparre, 23 July 1790. Liljensparre had the same problem in July 1790, when de Broën was at work again. See *UUB*, JHJ, 21 July 1790; *UUB*, letter from Liljensparre to Gustav III, 6 August 1790. See also C. Tilly, *The contentious French*, on Lenoir, p. 225.

155. Crusenstolpe-kravallerna 1838 had in a way the edge directed against the king. See Nerman, *Crusenstolpes kravaller*, pp. 15–24, ,80, 107, 163.

156. A. Jarrick, *Psykologisk socialhistoria*, pp. 106–09; A. Jarrick, *Den himmelske älskaren: herrnhutisk väckelse, vantro och sekularisering i 1700-talets Sverige*, pp. 69–76.

157. Jarrick, *Den himmelske älskaren*, pp. 100–02.

158. Ibid., Introduction.
159. A. Jarrick and J. Söderberg, 'Spontaneous processes of civilization: the Swedish case'.
160. His father, the tailor Anders Hjerpe (1712–91), was a member of the Evangelical Brethren of Stockholm (Stockhoms evangeliska brödraförsamling) from 1760. *SSA*, Nikolai's församlings register över födelse- och dopböcker (the index of Nikolai parish of birth and baptism records), p. 354, and the record of deaths, pp. 447–48; *EBAS*, Personalkataloger: katalog över Ev Brödrasocieteten i Stockholm (Catalogue of Personnel: catalogue of the Evangelical Brethren in Stockholm) 1761–70.
161. *UUB*, JHJ, 13/9 1789; *KB*, Brev från Carl Christopher Gjörwell till Olof Wallqvist, 9/6 1789, Ep G 8.
162. *UUB*, JHJ, 17/5 1789, 27/5 1789 *circa* 31/12 1789 and 21/7 1790.
163. Reuterswärd, 'Kungörandet av Gustav III:s ryska krig 1788–1790', pp. 324–26.
164. *SSA*, Överståthållarämbetets arkiv, Äldre poliskammaren 1789, Diarier (Archive of the Governor of Stockholm, former administrative police authority 1789, diaries) 21/3, 28/3, 1/4–4/4, 7/4, 9/4, 15/4–17/4, 20/4, 23/4 and 29/4 as well as Polissekreteraren, protokoll och registratur (Police secretary, protocols and registries), 28/3, 14/4, 17/4, 24/4 and an undated proclamation.
165. *UUB*, JHJ, 14/8 1790.
166. Rudé, *The crowd in history*, p. 138.
167. Edgren, *Lärling, gesäll, mästare*, pp. 240–58; A. Griessinger, *Das symbolische Kapital der Ehre: Streikbewegungen und kollektive Bewusstsein deutscher Handwerksgesellen in 18. Jahrhundert*, for instance pp. 145ff.
168. Cp. J. S. La Fontaine, *Initiation; ritual drama and secret knowledge across the world*, Chapters 1–2.
169. S. Ambrosiani, *Från det svenska skråämbetets dagar*, pp. 9 and 112–51; G. Berg, 'Behövlingen i Enköpings snickaregesällskap', pp. 201–08; Griessinger, *Das symbolische Kapital* . . . , Chapter 2; S. Hansson, *Skråtidens gesäller*, Chapters 2–3; C. Nyrop, *Nogle gewohnheiter*, pp. 7–44; Nyrop, *Haandwœrksskik i Danmark*, pp. 191–206; G. Upmark, 'En gesällbok från 1700-talet'; N. Wessel, *Svenska typografernas historia*, pp. 29–41. See also *KB*, Skråarkiv, Strödda handlingar till hantverksskrånas historia. For a discussion of social and developmental psychological conditions for collective consensus identity, see J. Schlumbohm, '"Traditional" collectivity and "modern" individuality: some questions and suggestions . . .', pp. 71–89.
170. *KB*, Skåarkiv, Strödda handlingar till hantverksskrånas historia.
171. Edgren, *Lärling, gesäll, mästare*, pp. 240–50; Schlumbohm, pp. 70–83; P. J. Öberg, *Minnen från gesällåren* . . .
172. Edgren, *Lärling, gesäll, mästare*, p. 253; *KB*, Skråarkiv, Strödda handlingar . . . Inventarium över utställning 1849.
173. Ambrosiani, *Från det svenska skråämbetets dagar*, p. 9.
174. Nyrop, *Haandwœrksskik i Danmark*, pp. 219ff.
175. Söderlund, *Stockholms hantverkarklass*, pp. 313–23.
176. Hansson, *Skråtidens gesäller*, pp. 83–84.
177. Nyrop, *Haandwœrksskik i Danmark*, pp. 29 (carpenters), 45 (bookprinters), 69 (smiths); Nyrop, *Nogle gewohnheiter*, p. 14.
178. An example is the moving of signs. See Nyrop, *Haandwœrksskik i Danmark*, pp. 124–56. See also Edgren, *Lärling, gesäll, mästare*, p. 246.
179. W. Korpi, *Arbetarklassen i välfärdskapitalismen: arbete, fackförening och politik i Sverige*; Barrington Moore Jr, *Injustice: the social bases of obedience and revolt*.

Chapter 2
The coherence of the inconsistent self: some reflections on mentality, identity and historiography

Towards the end of the preceding chapter, I attempted to explain what led the artisan journeymen of Stockholm and Johan Hjerpe to take part in Gustavus III's showdown with the nobility in the spring of 1789, an episode worthy of a war novel. Although this was not stated, my interpretation was based on a set of general hypotheses about the human mind. The hypotheses underlay the text as its analytical precondition, which perhaps made the interpretation difficult to follow, and possibly also more provocative than it would otherwise have been. At the same time, fuller explanations would have been even more irritating for those who do not like theories.

But we have now come to the theoretical part of the diptych, and it is appropriate here to unearth what was buried in the preceding part. I shall do so by formulating and developing a number of hypotheses about mentalities and other forms of human thought. The aim is not, however, only to facilitate the reading of the preceding chapter: there are also more general motives behind such a discussion.

One is that I like the concept of mentality while others dislike it. A contested concept must be clarified by whoever wishes to use it, especially if it is considered hazy by others. And this is precisely what it is. During the past decade or so, the concept of mentality as well as the history of mentality has been criticised as much as applied.

A number of scholars, such as Robert Darnton of Princeton, have complained about the vagueness of the concept, although it should be pointed out that Darnton himself has recently begun to express himself in more positive terms about research into mentality, perhaps as a function of his long-standing polemic with Roger Chartier.[1] Among Swedish researchers, the ethnologist Orvar Löfgren can be seen as a representative of the sceptics.[2]

Others such as Carlo Ginzburg, for instance, regard it as being too much of a consensus term, masking the cultural and ideological differences or conflicts between social classes. Consequently, in his empirical studies, he has substituted the concept of mentality for popular culture, which in turn has recently been exchanged for the concept of representation, the new-old catchword.[3]

I can see no reason to discard the concept of mentality because of these objections. First, the history of science is crowded with ambiguous but useful concepts, such as 'big bang', 'economic growth', 'social movement', 'love' and 'continuity', let alone the complex or vague concept of 'class' itself. According to the latter, this is the case not only with theories of class, but also with quite a few attempts to apply the concept empirically. Quite often grouping people along class lines is accomplished by a non-reflective mixture of economic criteria and status criteria. Second, many empirical enquiries into the collective thoughts of past generations have been conducted in which the concept of 'mentality' has been successfully applied, without having been clearly defined.

Furthermore, and as an aside, it should be said that even the most prominent advocates of the concept of mentality have pointed out that a connection need not exist between consensus and mentality. Jacques Le Goff, for instance, has talked about class mentality coexisting with the profound mental attitudes that people have in common.[4] Michel Vovelle, too, the most prominent member of the so-called Jacobinist camp of French students of the French Revolution, has used the concept.[5] In fact, Michel Vovelle is seen by his critics, i.e., by those *Annales* historians who have recently gone over to studies of representation, as one of the most typical representatives of the history of mentalities. Nevertheless, one of the main themes has surely been the conflicting world-views of social classes in pre-revolutionary and revolutionary France. But despite the almost self-evident fact that different classes (however they are defined) harbour different and conflicting attitudes, those same views that have been shared by almost all men and women of a particular generation in a particular socio-cultural milieu are among the essential observations made by the historians of mentalities.

Despite this, even though the vagueness of the concept of mentality has not prevented it from being a viable and fruitful concept, it would be easier to use were it better and less ambiguously defined. In proposing such a definition, I will also try to relate the concept of mentality to other concepts which have also been used to capture the minds of previous generations. From the very outset, however, it must be admitted that the strategic concept of 'thought' will remain undefined throughout the chapter. Likewise, in this chapter, I will refrain from relating and commenting on the critique of research into mentalities which has been formulated from post-structuralist points of departure. I shall, however, return to this in Chapter 4.

In several contexts, Orvar Löfgren has vented his irritation with the aid of a series of disparaging phases: 'a conceptual apparatus which constitutes something of a tinkering about (bricolage)'; 'the mentality box will end up containing a motley collection of cultural forms'; 'mentality flows throughout history like a sluggish sediment'; 'a problem with the mentality concept is its vagueness', and so on.[6]

Finally, all of these concepts and the types of thought they represent will be related to each other in a discussion about the structure of human thought. The question about the quantification of collective attitudes, which is as important as it is difficult, will not be raised in this chapter; it will instead be discussed in Chapter 5.

The hypotheses – or theses as they will be called in what follows, for purposes of effect – are grouped into two main sections. In the first, an attempt is made to distinguish analytically between different types of thought or configurations of thought.[7] The aim is to achieve conceptual clarity and fashion an instrument for the classification of mental products.

In the second section, the configurations of thought are brought together again in a discussion about what is contradictory in human thought.

Naturally, I have no pretensions whatsoever of being able to make any claims as to how the human brain works. The discussion has to do with ideas, not, by any means, functions.[8] The formal framework which is to be constructed is as immaterial (and imperfect) as the human ideas on which it is imposed.

Configurations of thought

My first thesis is that the spiritual products of people's, individual's, minds can be traced to different levels of articulation or consciousness, two concepts which, I must admit, are not interchangeable (a certain degree of ambiguity remains, after all). They can also be traced to what I have chosen to call different dimensions of thought.

There are two components to the thesis: the first has to do with the form of thoughts, the other with their character. Given its character, one and the same thought can take on different forms. This means that a given thought can appear on different levels of consciousness or articulation, and be more or less distinctly elaborated. A well articulated and highly conscious thought will be found on a high level, while the opposite applies to an unarticulated and unconscious thought.

Let us put ourselves inside the head of the thinking subject. Determining the level depends on the extent to which the person who is thinking is clear about his own thoughts, and has nothing to do with how distinctly or indistinctly that subject is able to convey his thoughts to a partner in conversation or to the outside world in general.

I can conceive of four different articulation or consciousness levels (see Figure 2 below, p. 70). This entails the reduction and gradual delimitation of a thought continuum, which in reality, however, is not divided up like the storeys of a building. The reduction serves as an illustration of an argument – it is heuristic, if you like – and constitutes no attempt faithfully to reproduce reality.[9]

Unconscious 'thoughts' are found on the lowest level, and can never be directly observed. Thoughts have been put in quotation marks as a result of some critical remarks. Nevertheless, I think it fundamentally sound to denote mental activity at the unconscious level as thoughts, i.e., as spiritual or immaterial ideas. Examples of unconscious thoughts are dreams in sleep. Dreams unquestionably merit being designated thought processes, but nevertheless often remain beyond our grasp, i.e., are un- or pre-conscious. Most often, we cannot recall what our dreams were about, and we often experience them as if they were presented to us by some unidentified mind other than our own. And yet, we would never 'dream' of denying that we have 'figured' them out ourselves.

Unconscious thoughts are not necessarily 'repressed' in the Freudian sense. Still, from an analytical, if not an empirical, point of view, dreams illustrate that some of our thoughts might be repressed, or at least inaccessible.[10] Let me emphasise that my borrowing of Freudian concepts is heuristic and need not imply a general affiliation with psychoanalysis (something I will return to below).

The unconscious refers to the impulses of individual human beings. The qualification is a distinction in relation to the *Annales* circle's different use of the concept 'unconscious'. For Fernand Braudel, for instance, the historical process is unconscious in that the intended actions of human beings have consequences which are not intended.[11] It is, among other things, a question of how the intentions of individuals collide and lead to results which no one had wished for or predicted.

Conscious but unarticulated attitudes – non-reflective attitudes – are to be found at the level above the 'unconscious'. This is what I mean by the notion of mentality. Here, unexpressed or only vaguely expressed thoughts are to be found. In a Freudian setting, thoughts are unconscious in so far as they are repressed as forbidden thoughts. In contrast to this, attitudes denoted as mentality are dim and indistinct, not because they have been repressed, but because they are considered self-evident, and taken for granted.[12] These thoughts belong to what Jürgen Habermas would call 'background knowledge' and are unproblematic as long as they are not articulated, are not part of the 'discourse'.[13] And these, naturally, are to be found among individual people. To suggest otherwise would be nonsense. Nevertheless, it is often reasonable to assign mentality of this sort to the very category of collective attitudes. The import is quite simply that the unreflecting nature of certain attitudes is secured precisely by their being shared by many individuals simultaneously. But this need not always be the case. Unreflecting and at the same time personally distinctive attitudes are to be found in each and every one of us.

An unarticulated thought is far from being the same as an unconscious one. This does not prevent articulation and consciousness from occurring at the same time. On the other hand, there is no given connection between that which is vaguely thought and that which is vaguely said. It has just as much to do with the recipient's mental preparedness as with the speaker's clarity of mind. But, for the moment, the recipient is not interesting.

On the third level, I include coherent, clearly articulated thoughts and thought-systems or doctrines. These include both scientific theories and political notions about political or moral conditions and the like. The main thing is that, to the thinking subject, these thoughts form a coherent (if not necessarily consistent) system, i.e., that the thought producer himself considers his notions to be coherent in a special way. It is less important whether a listener considers these thoughts to be coherent as well, since determining the level always begins with the thinking subject.

At the highest level are reflective thoughts, i.e., insights about the subjective limitations of each thought. The thinker sees, here, his notions as bound to his own person, not as qualities of the object, and thus considers them as partial and potentially erroneous.[14] The concept has something in common with Jean Piaget's discussion of egocentricity and decentricity. It is not, however, identical with the concept of decentricity as this is part of the analysis of a development-psychological process, which is not at issue here.

Ideas about the relative validity of each thought are reflections on other thoughts, a sort of meta-thinking – hence the designation used here. But if one can trace a reflective element in a doctrine, as it has been formulated, it should also be included in the highest level of articulation, even if the reflection is not explicitly carried out in it. In this case, it would be possible here, paradoxically, to speak of a reflective mentality on the level of doctrine. The main thing is not that this predicament is admitted, but that it is made a topic in itself.

We turn now to the second part of the first thesis. If the content of the thought has just been held constant, what is in order now is to consider the level of articulation or consciousness as a given, and instead allow the character of the thoughts to vary.

A thought on a certain level of articulation or consciousness can – to put it bluntly – be about how the world is actually arranged, about how it should be ordered, or about the desires of the individual in it. In this context, one could, perhaps, speak of thought dimensions. Thoughts about how things are could, in this case, be assigned to the cognitive dimension, how things should be to the normative dimension and desires to the affective dimension.

Every thought can, in theory, be traced to both a particular level and a particular dimension, but it has no content until it is also 'about' something. What it is about is unimportant in this context, as long as it is about something. The purpose of this conceptual attribution in terms of levels and dimensions is to create analytical instruments to capture all possible mental products. Mental products embraced by the theoretical framework which has been sketched here will, in the following discussion, be referred to as thought configurations.

The 'substance' of a given thought is not, then, unambiguously linked to a certain level of articulation or consciousness. By the same token, thoughts on a certain level can have different characteristics, i.e., be localised to different dimensions.[15] Thoughts would seem to move freely, and if research into the intellect is to grasp them, the variety must be reduced and definite thought configurations discerned.

My second thesis is that the 'substance' of a thought on a given level of articulation or consciousness is always intrinsically connected with the corresponding substances on each and every one of the lower levels. It is not a matter here of some sort of parallelism between different levels, but of dependence or – if you like – 'organic' connections.

The thesis has two complementary implications. One and the same thought substance can, in the first place, be more or less articulated by one and the same individual at two different times. A given thought substance in an individual, expressed on a given level of articulation or consciousness, always testifies, in the second place, to related thoughts on lower levels (and sometimes to correspondences on higher ones). What does this mean? Let me clarify things with the help of a short discussion about the relationship between the level of doctrine and the level of mentality.

Doctrines and other well defined systems of thought are usually traced back to their own era, particularly economic and social conditions. I will not go into a discussion about the plausibility of making such connections.[16] But apart from that, such analyses often lack a psychological linkage between change in 'material conditions' and the doctrinal development which is to be explained. One such missing link is mentality.[17] A doctrine may be devised by a lone individual, but it is nevertheless always tied to less reflected attitudes which the creator of the doctrine shares with other people.

Consider, for example, the emergence of the more or less deistic 'physio-theology' of the eighteenth century,[18] and disregard, in this context, the social and economic processes which could explain this spiritual or intellectual innovation. In accordance with the physiotheistic doctrine, the existence of God was proven by the beautiful order which prevailed in nature. Natural processes were no longer considered to be unpredictable consequences of God's active and arbitrary intervention in the world, but as bound by laws. Because the heavenly natural laws had been established once and for all in the beginning of time, the continual presence of God in people's lives was superfluous. Physitheism thus implied a deistic faith.

Physitheism was, without doubt, just such a doctrine, but it can also be seen as a psychological defence against the secularised influence of the rapidly burgeoning natural sciences. This implies an *ad hoc* redefinition of the theological view of God's relation to people and nature, a redefinition to protect religious faith. Viewed in this way, physitheism was also a mentality. Indeed, it was the first instance of a mentality – or perhaps even an unconscious anxiety defence – and only subsequently a doctrine. One could add in passing that, by the same token, as soon as the physitheistic (and deistic) outlook had left its mark on a person's religious thought-world, everything that could not be understood within the framework of natural laws was frightening and threatened faith in God.

A very different example of the hypothesis about the linkage of the doctrines to lower levels of articulation is the spiteful comparison drawn by the American historian J. H. Hexter between Fernand Braudel and Jean-Paul Sartre.[19] Hexter was of the view that Braudel's theory (on the level of doctrine) of *la longue durée* could be traced back to the conditions he experienced as a prisoner during the Second World War: deprived of any possibility of intervening in the dramatic events of the time, he had a personal motive for playing down the importance of action. For Sartre, on the other hand, the adoption of a personal stance and the personal act appeared as decisive to humanity because, as a member of the resistance, he was forced to make a number of decisions about action on a daily basis.

Hexter's interpretation of the personal motives behind the notion of *la longue durée* and existentialism can, naturally, be questioned. For example, Braudel built on ideas of Lucien Febvre and Marc Bloch about the sluggishness of history, thoughts the origin of which cannot be linked to similar personal predicaments for the first generation of the *Annales* school. But this is not the place for such criticism. I have simply referred to his interpretation in an attempt to illustrate the thesis.

In the preceding chapter – in the analysis of the artisan uprising in the spring of 1789 – the notion of the connection between thoughts on different levels of articulation has already been put to use. I shall briefly return to the theme as yet another example of the area in which the thesis can be used, this time leaving aside the journeymen and the external course of events and instead concentrating on Johan Hjerpe's inner struggles.

Hjerpe developed no ideas resembling doctrines, even if he expressed many very fixed views on the political situation at the end of the 1780s and even if he seems to have been very well up on the political events taking place on the continent.

It has already emerged that his stance was clearly royalist. He was an ardent, almost lyrical, adherent of Gustavus III. He enthusiastically supported Gustavus's war efforts against the Russians and was, partially as a consequence of this, bitterly hostile to the nobility. At the same time, he saluted the middle class and the working people of the city because they so eagerly, and at times militantly, rallied around the king.

Hjerpe's attitudes can be described in this way, and he seems to have chosen to present this picture to himself and others. While relatively coherent, his thoughts must nevertheless be relegated to the level of attitudes. But according to the thesis, it should now be possible to find thoughts on a lower level of clarity or consciousness which are related to those attitudes. And I think this can indeed be done.

Under the surface of Hjerpe's attitudes, it is possible to find a distinct (perhaps unconscious) conditionality in his lofty royalism. He gave lively day-to-day accounts of war preparations and mobilisation and of royalist demonstrations by the people, the most spectacular of them being the uprising of the journeymen at the House of the Nobility. But these accounts are interspersed with 'prophetic' items, eventually written with the benefit of hindsight, about the revolutionary development in Paris. Right up until the first peak of the revolution, Hjerpe was severe in his criticism of Louis XVI who, while admittedly 'quite good', was said to have amassed too much power and thus placed the crown in 'frightful debt'. Apart from the differences in his overall assessment of the two kings, there are a suspicious number of details in his account which amount to the two monarchs resembling each other. When Hjerpe learned, through the press, that the victorious revolutionaries had turned increasingly spiteful towards the former sovereign, the people were transformed in his eyes into an increasingly dangerous mob.

There is much more to be extracted about Hjerpe's view of the world from these items about the revolution, and they will also be assembled in a later chapter (Chapter 6). Here, they serve only as an aid in tracing Hjerpe's ambivalent stance towards both the people and to the king and war.

But there is more to uncover, for under the surface of Hjerpe's explicit admiration for the nobly belligerent and royalist artisan journeymen, it is also possible to find a genuine fear of these people. With a horrified fascination, he reported what they set out to do, but always as a witness who stood apart. He told about artisans who voluntarily allowed themselves to be roused, but he himself chose simply to be an onlooker when the soldiers marched through the city or drilled on what was then Skeppsholmen and is now Blasieholmen, along the waterfront across from the palace. He demonstrated no personal inclination for the war whatsoever.

Hjerpe was, in short, an outsider who wanted to admire, from a distance, the simple people who were close to his own social level but from whose community he stood apart. At closer range, they became unpleasant and made his separateness plain. He sought, instead, personal intimate communion with other people among the Moravians of Stockholm, where he belonged to the 'bachelor corps', the unmarried men.

In Kristinehamn, on the way home from the fair in Karlstad in the summer of 1789, a number of merchants and shop assistants gathered. What Hjerpe himself related about this meeting makes his position clear:

> I stora salen ljungade nyheter, tal om Stockholm &c. Bränwin Engelsk öl och win cerverades i 23 g: wärme. jag begärde watten som werckade et allmänt skratt, men blandat med win war wäl angenämt.

> In the great hall, the news flowed, talk of Stockholm, etc. Aquavit, English beer and wine were served in 23° heat. I ordered water to general laughter, but mixed with wine it was very pleasant indeed.

In sum, at the level of attitudes, Hjerpe was unequivocally a royalist and enthusiastic at the prospect of the willingness of the simple people to fight Gustavus III's war with Russia. His attitudes on these issues belonged ambivalently at a lower level of articulation or consciousness. They *belonged* there because, on the level of attitudes, he attempted to overcome the ambivalence he unconsciously (or in any case inarticulately) felt at a lower level.

The third thesis states that a concrete thought on a high level of articulation or consciousness is more time-bound, i.e., more susceptible to short-term influences, than a thought formed on a lower level.

Cultural patterns change over time: highly articulated thoughts can be assumed to be more flexible than unarticulated ones. To move analytically between the different levels is thus like moving between *les événements* and *la longue durée*, between the event and the permanent: the higher one goes, the more ephemerally culturally-dependent the thoughts which become visible.[20] How can this theoretical thesis be justified?

Human beings are both social and asocial creatures.[21] On the one hand, they need confirmation of their identity by other people and reasonable confirmation of their self-esteem.[22] Such acknowledgement by the surroundings is achieved through social adaptation to it, or to certain parts of it (classes, social strata, etc.).[23] On the other hand, every person experiences imperative urges. These urges are asocial partly because they are not generated by contact with other people,[24] even if they seek their object among them, and partly because the satisfaction of these impulses is in itself socially ruthless.

The primary social tendency of human beings finds expression through communication and people's mutual – violent or peaceful – adaptation. Adaptation creates forms of intercourse or cultural patterns which are specific in terms of time. For the purposes of this discussion, it does not matter whether these are hierarchical or non-hierarchical, whether they have to do with class or are 'classless'. But social conflicts probably propel an articulation of cultural patterns. The more worked out these forms of intercourse are, the more conscious the people who use them can be assumed to be, but the greater too is the risk these patterns run of swiftly becoming *passé*. It is not the same with unarticulated drives: they are indifferent to specific cultural patterns and not modified by them until they are transformed into conscious and articulated configurations of thought. At a low level they are thus time-less, but at a high level bound by time.

Once again, the physitheist example can be put into the service of clarifica-tion. If the concrete physitheistic doctrine emerged at one time and disappeared at another, the same type of anxiety reactions as those seen here each time a secure old image of the world threatens to disintegrate are repeated generation after generation. The attempts made by the scientists and theologians of the eighteenth century to explain – or explain away – the continual 'subsiding of the waters' (elevation of the land) which Swedenborg and others thought they had found now looks hopelessly antediluvian, if not comic. But the manner of protecting oneself against a shift in perspectives which must be the consequence of newly won knowledge is familiar.[25]

If we now introduce an imagined partner in conversation – or the outside world in general – an additional justification for the thesis can be given. A conscious and internally well articulated thought can be communicated directly to the rest of the world. It can then also be contradicted, unlike an unconscious or unarticulated thought which can be imparted only indirectly, if at all. Intellectual products on a high level should thus be easier to change than their counterparts on lower levels.

But the discussion becomes problematic at the level of doctrine and also, in part, at the level of intellect. The doctrine is more thought-out than the men-tality and thus also more resistant to potential and perhaps theoretically embodied anomalies. And vice versa, the unarticulated mentality lacks the intellectual preparedness for 'material' disturbances. If the intellect in general is long lasting, it can thus also shift rapidly when such disturbances grow too difficult. The witch trials of seventeenth-century Europe appear, at least on the surface, to be an illustrative example.[26] Here, however, the rapid changes in attitudes would appear to have concerned the authorities more than the lower orders. Because even after the hectic witchcraft furore died down at the beginning of the eighteenth century, ordinary people continued to accuse each other of black magic and other superstitions. But by then, the authorities had lost interest in goblins and witches.[27]

According to the fourth thesis, a thought in the cognitive dimension is more time-bound than a thought in the normative dimension, which in turn is more time-bound than a thought in the affective dimension. This thesis is implicit in the preceding one.

Desires recur in the affective dimension, but the thesis naturally is not valid for all types of desires. Perhaps concrete desires are the most fickle of mental products: the tie you dream about this year is a different one from last year's but already *passé* next year. The thesis does not concern these, but only the mental representations of basic drives, such as libido, aggressive 'desires', and a need for what are referred to as object relations. But these too are time-bound to a greater or lesser degree.[28]

Norms resemble desires in that they are subjective evaluations and are not inter-subjectively testable. The rudiments of norms are also laid early in the lives of each person and are thus difficult to modify. But even if thoughts in the normative dimension are not inter-subjectively testable, they are nevertheless inter-subjective, i.e., social in nature. Norms manifest socialisation, however that has taken place. In this way, they comprise the link between asocial urges and the socialisation demands of the surroundings.[29] Given a certain level of articulation or consciousness, thoughts of a normative nature are thus, in my view, more time-bound than affective ones, but more stable than thoughts of a cognitive nature.

Newly acquired knowledge is assimilated with old perspectives and values.[30] When, for example, 'subsiding of the waters' could not be denied,[31] it could nonetheless be harmonised, in a transitional period, with a fundamentalist belief in the Old Testament: since the Flood, the waters had been continually receding.[32] The new cognitive findings could be reinterpreted in accordance with an inert normative (and partially cognitive) orientation. Thoughts about how things are in the world (and beyond), then, change more rapidly than thoughts of a different nature, once again also because they are inter-subjectively testable, as opposed to normative reinterpretations, for example.

We would seem to have arrived at a paradox: ill-considered and vague thoughts are more enduring than well-thought-out and distinct doctrines. Is this possible? Yes, but only *ceteris paribus*, i.e., if certain conditions are kept constant. In the next section, these conditions will be allowed to vary.

But to continue. The third and fourth theses can now be combined in a fifth thesis, which also applies under *ceteris paribus* conditions: a thought at a high level of articulation or consciousness is most time-bound in the cognitive dimension and least time-bound in the affective. A thought in the affective dimension is most time-bound at a high level and least time-bound at a low level. Because the fifth thesis is simply a logical consequence of the two previous theses, it needs no special justification. However, a number of things must be noted.

The thesis is an attempt to combine two ways of classifying people's various thoughts. The preceding argument implies a scheme with twelve possible configurations of thought, as can be seen from Figure 2. But these twelve formally possible configurations must be reduced to eleven: doctrines cannot be found in the affective dimension. Doctrines can, to be sure, be built on unarticulated thoughts in all dimensions – and undoubtedly often are – but cannot themselves be included there. For example, Fernand Braudel's notion of *la longue durée* cannot be assigned to the affective dimension even if it could be associated with the level of attitudes or the unconscious level. Perhaps the theory emanated from the passivity imposed on Braudel as an inmate of the prison camps during the Second World War, but that does not in itself make it into an affect.[33]

It is not as easy with the reflective thoughts. If thoughts in the affective dimension are more specifically identified as desires, they must also be capable of appearing on the reflective level. But what is a reflective desire? In principle, it is a desire which is relativised by the insight that it could as easily have been about some other concrete object or some other person: perhaps it is not so important whom the violence is aimed at, for example, as long as the timeless, aggressive energy can be discharged. But it is not enough that the desires are relative: there must also be an insight into this effect on the part of the thinker, something which in turn relativises them further. For example, it becomes more difficult for me to continue supporting Djurgårdens IF (one of the most successful football and ice-hockey teams in Sweden) if I reflect, at the same time, that I could just as easily have supported some other team in order to satisfy certain basic needs which do not actually have anything to do with football or ice-hockey.

Here is an example borrowed from the preceding part of the diptych: for Gustavus III, it does not seem to have mattered very much which nations he went to war with and against, as long as in so doing he was able to act out that need for narcissistic grandeur which was at one with his character.[34] But this is not a particularly good example: a desire does not, in fact, become reflective simply because it is conditional. Even if the king redefined his world view every time circumstances forced him to dream up a new scenario and identify a new enemy, it is very uncertain, if not unlikely, that he was, at the same time, aware of the psychological motives which compelled him. And vice versa, had he taken his grandiose plans for what they were, he would not have set about the business with the same conviction, and might even have abandoned it.

Why improbable? The eighteenth century after all, was, generally, a century in which the serious game of taking oneself into introspective consideration was becoming common. This was certainly the case. Nevertheless, I do not think that the reflective element filled people's minds in the way it would later come to do – and not the king's either.

'Fill'? Do not a number of hitherto unforeseen theoretical complications lurk here? Yes, clearly. The expression hints that the levels of articulation could be seen as communicating vessels and the development as a process in which the reflective increases to the same extent that the non-reflective attitudes decrease. And if the move towards increased reflectivity has not necessarily made the thinking more narrowly time-bound, it has in any case contributed to making the bearer of the thought less convincing. And so we are faced with a new paradox: the gradual extension of the reflective thought, or relativism, is one of the most decisive changes in mentality to have taken place in the last three hundred years (see Introduction).

Mentalities change, then, which – very briefly – must be considered, as it is above all their inertia which has been emphasised up to now. I think it is possible to distinguish two principal mechanisms behind lasting changes in mentality. First, people are not prepared for the psychological effects of social or institutional changes which are not perceived as changes. They made decisions in persistent faith that go against their values, and do not notice that they have gradually altered their very basic attitudes through the insidious influence of the gradual effects of the consequences of their own decisions.[35] An example could be the land reform in rural Sweden of the early nineteenth century, the Swedish equivalent to the enclosure system in England. It was a comprehensive agricultural reform which not only put an end to the open field system, but also spelled the end of the old village community.[36] Perhaps those involved did not realise that, through the restructuring of their socio-economic conditions, their mentality would also ultimately move in a more individualised direction.

Second, people are prepared to change their basic attitudes both when faced with reliable promises of a better life and in connection with catastrophes or very 'credible' threats of catastrophes. In the one case, changes in mentality are related to their not being registered as changes, while in the second case, people are prepared to abandon their old patterns of thought because they are confronted either with irresistible temptations or unavoidable challenges.

Now, if it is true that changes in mentality are mainly brought about by gradual changes in habits which are not seen as such, then this fact also calls into question the third and fourth theses. On the one hand, it certainly seems reasonable that unarticulated thoughts are protected from the challenge of pronounced ideas by their very lack of articulation. On the other hand, they are not protected at all, at least not by intellectual means. What seems to bring about mental change is, partly, precisely the inarticulateness of the mentality. This question cannot be settled by logical means, only empirical ones. Perhaps it is insoluble.

My sixth thesis can be seen as a sort of note in the margins of the previous ones. Its point is that a particular configuration of thought is embraced by fewer people the higher the level of articulation or consciousness on which it exists. Or vice versa: the higher the level of a configuration of thought, the more distinctive and comprehensive it is and the fewer the number of individuals who embrace it.[37]

Historians in particular have glimpsed doctrines and thought systems which among other things, precisely concern the originality of these configurations of thought. And vice versa, the extension of certain attitudes to broad groups has made these sorts of configurations of thought indistinct, sometimes tacit and thus invisible to the historian. In this sense, one could thus say that thoughts on the two highest levels of articulation or consciousness are often characteristically individual and that thoughts on the level of mentality are collective.

Furthermore, it can be assumed that an individually formulated doctrine will be less comprehensive and less distinct the more it is spread and as the intellect is incorporated into the minds of successively more and more people. New doctrines – like new empirical findings – tend to be distorted and reworked in accordance with sluggish norms and timeless desires. They are assimilated, as already mentioned.[38] Note that cognitive processes of this sort need not be socially one-sided: individuals from different classes and social strata mutually misunderstand or misconstrue each other. It is more difficult with unconscious thoughts. Urges are, for example, not unexpressed in the same way as attitudes: there is, rather, an inner compulsion to repress them. While the unexpressed in collective attitudes is partly a consequence of people showing mutual social consideration, drives are repressed in the consciousness because they are asocial. This means that, at the same time, they lack the stamp of the individual since – as I have asserted elsewhere[39] – individuality and sociality are inseparably associated with each other.

According to the seventh thesis – which is also a marginal comment and of more historiographical than historical interest – the four levels of articulation or consciousness correspond to both different cognitive theory orientations and to a variety of genres within historical research.

It is difficult to find strong adherents of positivism within the current field of historical research. Naturally, it is possible to find one or two, perhaps especially among American economic historians.[40] It is more the case that one can discern a vague conflict between an empirical or empiricist orientation and a theoretical one. Note that empiricism and positivism are concepts which should not be confused. Even if positivism claims to be based on empiricism, it partly exceeds and invalidates empiricism through its adherence to the covering law model.[41]

The Danish historian Inga Floto has instead described this relationship as a conflict between 'structural history' and narrative history. It is doubtful whether this pair of opposites correspond to each other,[42] but that does not matter here.

On the basis of the preceding discussion, the vaguely empiricist gist could be posited against a vaguely hermeneutic one. The typical empiricist historian would, in that case, devote himself to studies of doctrines and reflective thoughts, while the hermeneutic history researcher would be more interested in mentalities and unconscious thoughts.[43] On the other hand, one should avoid linking this cognitive-theoretical conflict to the futile discussion about quantitative versus qualitative writing of history. Apart from the fact that it is almost as easy to find 'qualitative' empiricists and 'quantitative' hermeneuticists as the opposite, the distinction is, in my view, theoretically meaningless. I will dwell on this in more detail in Chapter 5.

The four levels also correspond to historiographic genres. While the intellectual historian studies both reflective thoughts and doctrines, the historian of intellect concerns himself with less significance-laden stated attitudes among groups of people, and the psychohistorian with the level of unconscious thought,[44] usually in the individual. A distribution of the genres according to thought dimension would not, on the other hand, be produc-

Field of research	Levels of articulation or consciousness	Dimensions of thought			Social level
		cognitive	normative	affective	
History of ideas	Reflective thoughts				Individual
	Doctrines			▓▓▓	Individual
History of mentalities	Unreflected attitudes				Collective
Psychohistory	Unconscious 'thoughts'				?

Figure 2 The historical-psychological field of research

tive, even if the intellectual historian usually tends towards the cognitive direction and the psychohistorian towards the affective. Note that the designations of genres should be seen as ideal types of sorts: they are sorting instruments for a great deal of research that has run wild, which can only sometimes be assigned to one genre exclusively.[45]

The seven theses which were formulated in the first section can now be summarised in a diagram – an exercise – designated 'The historical-psychological field of research'. I would like to emphasise that this is, indeed, an exercise, a heuristic device for reconstructing people's psychical pasts. The entire diagram refers back to the preceding argument and will not be commented on.

Contradictions in thought

I do not think it a coincidence that Hjerpe's lack of ambiguity on the level of attitudes corresponded with ambivalence or a contradictory nature at a lower level. On the contrary, this yields a pattern typical of most people. In general, it is reasonable to assume that the thoughts of an individual are more characterised by contradictions the less premeditated they are. In the unconscious, irreconcilable impulses coexist. This makes itself felt, albeit in a weakened manner, as insufficient coherence in a person's attitudes and perhaps as logical weaknesses in that person's more worked-out ideas.

First I will give some points of departure for the presentation of the three theses which follow, all of which concern the contradictory nature of human thought. An individual cannot entirely take in his own mind. I consider this to be self-evident and assume that each sphere of ideas must be filled with contradictions.

An additional point of departure for the continued discussion is that the contradictory nature varies within the frame of an individual's mind. Such variations cannot, of course, be measured. In general, however, it can be said that the contradictory nature of an individual's mind increases with the number of 'propositions' contradicting each other. The variations deal with what sort of thought configuration they concern. On the other hand, I do not make allowance for the possibility that an individual can change his mind. The argument is thus static on that count.

Up to now, eleven such types of thought configurations have been identified. In order to make the debate easy to grasp, the levels of articulation and consciousness will now be reduced to three, which means that there will also be fewer configurations of thought, which does not matter in this context.

Finally, as the three remaining theses are very closely related, they will be presented together, and their historiographic significance will be discussed together and not thesis-by-thesis.

The eighth thesis: given the thought dimension, a person's thoughts are less contradictory the more distinct and conscious they are, just as the contradiction between the dimensions decreases the higher the level on which the thoughts are formulated.

The ninth thesis is the logical complement of the eighth: given the level of clarity or consciousness, a person's thoughts are less contradictory in the normative than in the affective dimension and least contradictory in the cognitive dimension.

Finally, as if to complete a decade, the tenth thesis: thoughts on a higher level of clarity or consciousness exist in contrast to thoughts on the lower levels.

The theses can be easily justified, but their implications are less evident. With reference to the eighth thesis, it can be said that the more distinct or conscious a person's thoughts are, the more conscious that person is about how he thinks. That is why his thoughts are, in most cases, less contradictory the more distinct they are. In those parts in which the mind of an individual is introspectively illuminated, there is also greater harmony between knowledge, norms and desires than in the darker recesses of the soul. Note that this is not the same as thoughts being more 'true' the higher the level on which they are formulated. Apart from that, their veracity can only be established in one of the dimensions – the cognitive – if inter-subjective testability is its criterion. But the issue is of a fundamental interest and so I will return to it shortly.

One of the theoretical points of departure for the ninth thesis is the so-called structural principle within Freudian psychoanalysis, i.e., the heuristic division of the psyche into three levels: the ego, the superego and the id. In fact, this very standpoint lies behind the preceding division of thought dimensions. The lower the level of clarity or consciousness it is a matter of, and the closer to the affective dimension on which a set of thoughts (configuration of thoughts) is to be found, the closer one also comes to precisely that unconscious psychic activity in which conflicting impulses coexist. This is very fundamental to psychoanalysis,[46] and as I see it, it is also serviceable for historiographic application, entirely regardless of the general view one has of psychoanalysis.

Given a certain level of clarity or consciousness, an individual's cognitive configurations of thought are the least contradictory. Why?

Both inner and outer forces work to rid a person's knowledge of contradictory features. Chaos is only allowed to govern in the unconscious. Should it force its way up to the conscious 'surface', anxiety is created; ultimately, it is untenable that the consciousness both hates and loves, both wants and does not want, both believes and does not believe that things are this or that way.

The inner disorder must therefore be conquered and this takes place, to a great extent, through cognitive efforts.

Externally emanating impulses which disturb the equilibrium are at work in all dimensions.[47] But newly acquired knowledge is assimilated as far as possible with old perspectives and values. Or, in other words, newly grasped cognitive anomalies must be made compatible with old knowledge, once again to avoid anxiety-creating chaos.

Norms are situated here, somehow bound by time, right between cognition and affect. And for the same reason – they comprise the link between external socialising demands and inner asocial ones. Because it is reasonable to assume that consistent thoughts are to be found on a higher level of clarity or consciousness than inconsistent disorder, thoughts on a high level exist in contradiction to thoughts at a low level. Here we thus have the justification for the tenth thesis.

I will now continue with some of the consequences of the three theses. First, theses eight to ten imply a certain modification of theses three and five. A configuration of thought which is not contradictory should, *ceteris paribus*, be more vigorous than a contradictory one. This is more the case the higher the level of clarity or consciousness. If one takes only this standpoint into account, the theses concerned with being bound in time would be turned upside down. But cognition has powerful affective driving forces: the acceptance by an individual of new empirical (cognitive) findings constitutes a sort of buffer for his norms and desires which, for the sake of his peace of mind, must be left alone. But again, there is no binding logical reason for such a conclusion and, empirically, the question is still undecided.

Second, thoughts in the cognitive dimension are, naturally, not without contradictions either. An individual's thoughts about the factual are partly infected by desires and norms, and partly potentially inconsistent as a consequence of the individual's inadequate general overview of his own mind.

Third, thoughts which are free from contradiction need not be 'true' in an empirical sense. This applies in particular to cognitive efforts to impose order on an inner chaos, an inner disorder which creates anxiety. This standpoint can be broadened to embrace scholarly activities as well. It could be the case that a thought which is not disciplined by inescapable observations is tempted to see the world according to aesthetic patterns. Such patterns are often symmetrical. Dissection is probably the simplest of such symmetries, trisection slightly more complicated. The world can also be viewed as a pyramid: here the broad foundation and here the narrow superstructure. Or, it is possible to see it as an arc, with one in the end returning to the point of departure. Evolutionary theories of different sorts are often like this.

A thought which is full of beauty and convincing harmony must be subjected to as severe scrutiny as an 'ugly' and perhaps empirically more well-founded thought. That a person's spiritual microcosm is not a beautifully coherent system is not to say that he is without a personal identity. Nor does this imply that he is irrational, even if I used the term in the previous chapter. It was not, however, a coincidence that it was put in inverted commas. I shall dwell on these two questions at some length. First, that which concerns personal identity.

For a start, the reader may have formed the impression that the preceding discussion must lead to the exclusion of the concept of personal identity. But as I have already hinted above, this is my view. On the contrary, I believe that most people have a truly personal inner chaos, although it is at the same time similar, in fundamental respects, to those of others. This is, however, easier to state than to demonstrate. Obviously, a statement is not internally consistent simply because it declares itself to be so. Needless to say, it has to be supported by arguments which demonstrate the compatibility of the elements included in the statement, which is precisely what I will try to do now.

According to Erik Homburger Erikson, once the leading student of the conditions of personal development throughout the life-cycle, personal identity means considering oneself as a defined person in a particular social setting. This self-conception is based on two mutually reinforcing experiences, the first being the person's feeling of fundamental 'sameness' through time, the second the acknowledgement or recognition by others of this particular sameness. To be preserved, personal identity thus requires, in Erikson's view, continuous social confirmation: it has to be accepted as true or, according to Jürgen Habermas, maybe rather as truthful.[48]

I find this really simple definition of personal identity quite worthwhile. It is almost irresistibly simple. In order to be preserved, personal identity must be shared. You cannot maintain a belief in what you are unless it is continuously confirmed by your social environment. Thus, personal identity is to be looked upon as an ongoing collective enterprise to be carried out every day, in daily life.

However, during the last two decades, few concepts or theoretical models have been attacked as much as that of the unique identity of the individual. The Freudian and romantic conception of a truly personal inner life is now being incessantly scorned. Even among the representatives of the new brand of psychoanalysis, i.e., among those who adhere to the theory of object relations, the concept of identity has been questioned. But the fiercest attacks have been launched by post-modernists, who claim that there are no identities, only differences. Man is understood as a patchwork of borrowed properties, as a palimpsest, and he only appears as a proper individual occasionally and in conditional contrast to others.

What is to be said about this somewhat pessimistic perspective on the human condition? Well, were there no individual properties, then nothing whatsoever would appear when human beings are compared with each other. Contrasts only become evident if there are differences to posit against each other, indicating that something genuinely personal has been found at the core. It should be admitted, however, that personal identity has, to some extent, more to do with what is common about the impression men and women make on others than with what they feel about themselves. This seems, at least, to be the case with individuals frequently changing social context, thereby obscuring their own feeling of sameness through time. However, this does not necessarily mean that identity is only a cultural construct, something that is only ascribed to a person. Rather, it should be interpreted as yet another aspect of the social character of identity.

But most often, identity should primarily be described in emotional terms, as a feeling of sameness. Viewed in this way, it is essentially to be considered a psychical or phenomenological experience and not an objective or inanimate fact. However, as is the case with all beliefs and convictions, this feeling, too, is established and continuously inter-subjectively validated, the only way of confirming beliefs at all. But a phenomenon is no less real because it is a feeling. Should it fail, the communication process of personal identification would – and often does – lead to mental 'breakdown' in the individual, whatever the elements of identity, be they copied from others or ingenuously created.

While most often considered to be extremely subjectivist, the postmodernist's denial of the individual seems, rather, non-phenomenological and objectivist in the negative sense of word. Further, it could, perhaps, be said that the more rigid and one-sided one's identity, the more fragile it is and, vice versa, the more many-sided the more well-integrated. A fragile identity is not, however, illusory. What is illusory is the apparent solidity of such a pronounced identity, a 'fact' that could be associated with my thesis: coherent thoughts are more prone to change than inarticulate attitudes.

According to modern object relations theory, the pre-oedipal experiences of the infant are of profound importance to different designs of identity formation. The yearning for narcissistic affirmation, if met with sensible recognition, is successively transformed into a capacity for social adaptation. If denied, the quest for narcissistic mirroring deteriorates into a constant feeling of humiliation.[49] Parenthetically, according to the secular downward trend of defamation in the court records during the modern period, some progress in civilisational terms in this area of life seems to have occurred.

However, even if the narcissistic wishes of the infant have been affirmed in a reasonable way, the sum total of all experiences nevertheless eventually make his inner life into a battlefield of conflicting wishes and beliefs. The mature individual is capable of facing this as part of his inescapable human condition.

Now, to return to the phrase formulated above claiming the uniqueness of the inner chaos of the lonely man, what is the decisive argument? Where do we find the centre of individual identity? In the case of the relatively healthy (in physical terms) individual, right in the middle of his or her messy mental universe, where a certain theme would seem to be hidden – a certain problem or question, and sometimes a certain solution to this question too. It is as if the mental activity of the mind either evolves around this theme throughout life, or incessantly departs from it only to return again and again. Even when distancing ourselves from this or that particular question or set of questions, our point of departure is particular or personal. For instance, some people spend their lives combating the Marxism they abandoned while still young. I would even venture to say that the driving force which makes a person seemingly self-contradictory is often precisely the fundamental theme to which he is fettered. Whatever the cost, even the cost of inner confusion and of confusing others, you feel obliged to stick to this or that question or view. Such themes are truly personal, partly because they are culturally acquired – i.e., not part of the biological set-up – and partly because this acquisition has occurred very early in life.

To give one example, let me say a few words about Fredrik Böök, the undisputed king of literary criticism in Sweden in the early twentieth century who was eventually, and for good cause, banned because of his support for the Nazis during the Second World War.[50] Throughout his career, he remained loyal to Germany, a loyalty that, from 'within', forced him to switch over from traditional conservatism to Marxism to national socialism and back again. As a matter of fact, this vacillation to and fro shows that he remained true to something. There you have his identity. But of course, in confusing his fellow-being, his personal identity was threatened at the same time. He thereby endangered the second condition for a personal identity, that of social acknowledgement.

So much for personal identity. What interests me most, however, is not the 'timeless' development of personal identity but, on the one hand, the secular process of individualisation and, on the other, collective rather than personal identities, i.e., deeply shared attitudes between people rather than about people.

The emergence of a collective identity – the feeling of sameness or affinity between people – is, I believe, predominantly organised, so to speak, at the level of the mentality, i.e, at the level of inarticulate ideas. Why? Surely, at the lowest level of articulation, that of unconsciousness, thoughts are in a way impersonal, not necessarily connected with culturally specific experiences. However, that also makes them somewhat asocial, not to say anti-social. Doctrines differ from unconscious thoughts in that they are socially addressed to others and open to refutation. They also bring forward highly personal messages, which to a substantial degree disqualify them as organisers of collective identities. However, if the doctrinal level is to be taken in its broad sense, this conclusion can be questioned. Finally, reflective thoughts are more reflective and personal than social, questioning all beliefs that are taken for granted, and thereby representing the antithesis of the mentality.

I shall now turn to the matter of rationality. The notion that human beings are rational permeates the human sciences, although some maintain that man can nevertheless be irrational, even more that he always is. In my view, it is easier to get by without the conceptual pair of rational–irrational. Allow me to explain.

The belief in man's always equally active rationality is not always elaborated into a thesis, instead it often lurks like a hidden assumption under the surface. Nevertheless, at least two simple components can almost always be identified. In one of them, man is rational when he is able to adapt the means to the ends he has set himself.[51] In the other, man is therefore capable of acting without contradiction. In the person who dithers or takes long detours en route to his goal, rationality has been eliminated. Science has, naturally, not overlooked the fact that there are plenty of people who have difficulty making up their minds, but this irrational behaviour is seldom explained with reference to a lack of conformity between goals or unconscious, competing desires. Instead, it is a matter – as the Norwegian philosopher Jon Elster has put it – of perceived crossed signals.[52] It is because of this that the individual does not act according to his own discretion but like an unfree wanton governed by natural laws. That which appears to be irrational can, however, be made partially meaningful without a 'biological' explanation, namely precisely with reference to latent goals. If this is done, the pair of opposites, rational–irrational, also loses much of its meaning.[53]

In this chapter, I have claimed: 1) that it is fruitful (worthwhile) and possible to distinguish between different levels of thought, as well as between different dimensions of thought; 2) that these levels and dimensions are mutually interconnected; 3) that thoughts in different levels have different life spans; 4) that, generally, these levels are in conflict with each other, and that the conflictive interplay between thoughts on different levels and in different dimensions is structured in a certain way; and 5) that people's inner chaos is personal and therefore that the idea of personal identity is compatible with the thesis on inner contradictory nature.

These statements may seem like dubious banalities. However, in view of the practice of current historical research, I think it would be appropriate to adapt more of these simple statements. For instance, it is conventional in intellectual history to demonstrate the presence of certain perspectives, ideologies or theories with reference to what is stated explicitly in this or that text. In the worst cases, all the potential tensions in the texts are ignored. But even when they are not ignored contradictions are often rationalised, or should I say harmonised, into one consistent perspective.

The historian who seeks the traces of our spiritual past must also seek to determine on which level of clarity or consciousness and in which dimension the identified thoughts are to be found. Such a search can then become an instrument for determining the degree of contradictory nature in these thoughts, but also gives the historian the possibility of safeguarding himself against his own efforts to 'put together' people's thoughts into something internally harmonious, coherent, or even consistent.[54] The historian of the mentalities who looks for just these poorly articulated collective attitudes should expect to find a poorly harmonised set of thoughts and not distort the meaning of what is contradictory in them.

If the exercise presented earlier can be used to locate people's configurations of thought, it should, then, also – in the light of this discussion – lead to more definite expectations about different degrees of contradictory nature in the minds of the people who are being studied.

To give an example of what I mean, let me return to Lindroth's presentation of the history of learning in the eighteenth century. He attempts to define the mentality of Enlightenment, even if he is not of the view that Enlightenment had a pronounced impact in Sweden.[55] In spite of the fact that he finds attitudes, typical of their age, which contradicted each other, he does not consider this. Instead, he attempts to harmonise these attitudes, consider them as expressions of one and the same basic stance.[56] On the one hand, we read, mercantilism was supported 'by a deep distrust of human nature'[57] and the individual must serve the common good.[58] A 'multitude of poor people were "the wealth of the country"'.[59] On the other hand, Lindroth also sees the growth of thoughts about natural laws as typical of the eighteenth century,[60] when 'the noble savage' became fashionable.[61]

By and large, the same people seem to have both distrusted and applauded human nature. But instead of emphasising what is contradictory in this mentality, Lindroth conceals it. He thus summarises:

> A new view of humanity was also embraced, typical of a secularised and enlightened epoch. A modern social science took shape during the eighteenth century, an anthropology in which man was now longer the image of God, but was transformed to figures in columns [. . .]

And then comes the harmonising addition: '[. . .] a "crowd" to please'.

That 'the mercantilists' counted the people cannot be easily linked to an effort to make the people happy. But Lindroth does not care about that. Had he, however, been prepared to see the contradictory in human attitudes, his account would presumably have been different.

Granted, Lindroth's history of learning is not primarily about doctrines, not about elaborated systems of thought, and not about people who, in acting, reveal their unarticulated attitudes. But the preceding argumentation is also valid for such intellectual products. In the previous chapter, for example, the hypothesis was formulated that the rioters were acting out different, and conflicting, needs.

Lindroth is a conventional adherent of 'the Enlightenment project', and he hardly questions the notion that eighteenth-century scientific development was humanising and generally liberating. One can thus wonder whether he is particularly representative of current historical research. Is the Lindroth example a particularly good one, in fact?

I think so. Indeed, his evolutionary optimism has very few advocates these days,[62] but he shares with many others the aspiration to discern an unambiguous ideological or mental orientation in a given historical course of events, including such a leading postmodernistic historian as Michel Foucault.[63] The difference is, rather, that Foucault sees an increasingly authoritarian power where Lindroth sees a humanising one, and disciplining where Lindroth discerns liberation. But for both, the development leads in one direction, indeed almost all phenomena 'march in step'. This is the case, for example, with Foucault's analysis of the development of the morality of criminal law in Europe from the seventeenth century onwards. In his account, the aspiration to correct replaces revenge, in time, as the leading principle of criminal law, but this largely takes place without the involvement of any actors, without any ideological conflicts being depicted and without any internally conflicting subjects appearing on the scene. Here, according to Orvar Löfgren, it is really a matter of a one-way 'inert sludge'.[64]

Further, the fact that many treatises use a cover-up design of debate (I call it 'täckargumentation' in Swedish) is also often ignored. I think that even Michel Foucault has overlooked this in his writing on the reforms of the classical period.

Here is just one example of this. Some time in the second half of the eighteenth century, the German scholar Gottfried Less published a treatise on the ethics of suicide. A superficial reading of this study finds the author condemning suicides on page after page.[65] In 1788, the publication of the study in Sweden almost immediately provoked Swedish opponents into raising their voices against the work. One of them was Olof Holmberg, a vicar from northern Sweden. In a pamphlet entitled *Wälmenta anmärkningar* (*Well-meant remarks*) he attacked Less, not because of his severity, but because of his lenient attitude towards suicides[66] – and he was, in fact, able to find such statements in Less's book.

Now, after a superficial reading of the treatise, it would be quite natural to place Less in the conventional camp of eighteenth-century suicide phobists. However, taking into consideration the cultural context – of which Holmberg's attack must be seen as an integral part – it seems clear that he was right in pointing out the seemingly negligible parts of this treatise in which Less is not clear, in which he slides towards leniency.

From an empirical point of view, it might seem safe to deal with only that which is visible. But only if there is nothing but the visible. Now, apart from the question of levels of articulation, everything is never visible in a text. Every text needs to be interpreted, and to interpret a text is to reveal what is not manifest in it.[67] What is not obvious is still there (somewhere), but since it is not obvious it cannot be empirically confirmed, it cannot be easily pointed out beyond doubt. Doubt will remain. However, you are no better off if you mistake the superficial part for the whole.

Furthermore, certain structural features of a text are more easily discerned if compared with related texts. In the history of mentalities, such series of texts are met more often than expected, such as, for instance, in popular love songs, certain kinds of religious autobiographies, peasant diaries, probate inventories, court records, and so on.

On rare occasions, it can be possible to discern mental traits by way of comparison, the way Ginzburg did with his miller Mennochio,[68] or the way in which I attempt to deal with the hand-written manuscripts of Johan Hjerpe in this book.

The main thing in research into mentalities is to discern attitudes that are not conceptualised, or at least not necessarily, but are still discernible. When excavated, such attitudes are conceptualised by us, the historians. That is not to say that they need have been unconscious, only that they were probably not reflected on this or that attitude.

One example can serve as an illustration. About fifteen years ago, I had the good fortune to come across a massive collection of hand-written religious autobiographies, written by members of the Moravian brethren in different parts of eighteenth-century Europe. Out of approximately a thousand lives, one hundred – written by Swedes – were analysed. Making use of an 'interview' form and a scale with numerical (three) scores, I was able to distinguish 'belief profiles' of a sort representing essential intellectual traits of the members of this revivalist movement. Placed against the doctrinal model, the women members of the sect were more typically Moravian than their male co-religionists.

What is interesting here is that what we could call the intellectual structures discerned by the historian were neither planned, conceptualised nor conceived of as such by the agents themselves. It was I who discerned them.[69]

*

It is to be hoped that the preceding example has given an indication of how the theses in the second section could be put to use in historical research. If the historian of mentalities succeeds in locating a thought in one of the 'boxes' presented in the diagram, he or she would be able to relate certain expectations about contradictory nature to that thought, with the guidance of the theses in the second section. The main thing, in that case, would be concretely to identify the configurations of thought, but it would also be a necessary precondition for the analysis of that which is contradictory in human thought, an analysis which could, perhaps, be helped by the theses I have presented here.

Notes

1. Robert Darnton, *The Great Cat Massacre*; Darnton, *The Forbidden Best-Sellers of Pre-Revolutionary France*, p. 178.
2. Orvar Löfgren, 'Mentalitetshistoria och kulturanalys', pp. 15–23; Orvar Löfgren, 'Mentalitet: några reflektioner kring ett problematiskt begrepp', pp. 14–26.
3. Carlo Ginzburg, *The cheese and the worms*, pp. xiii–xxvi; Carlo Ginzburg, 'Représentation: le mot, l'idée, la chose'.
4. Jacques Le Goff, 'Mentalities: a history of ambiguities', p. 176.
5. Michel Vovelle, 'Ideologies and mentalities', p. xx; Michel Vovelle, *La mentalité révolutionnaire: société et mentalité sous la Révolution française*.
6. O. Löfgren, 'Mentalitet: några reflektioner kring ett problematiskt begrep, pp. 14–21. The argument recurs in O. Löfgren, 'Mentalitetshistoria och kulturanalys', pp. 15–23.
7. The concept 'thought figuration' (*tankefigurationer*) has been used by Johan Asplund and commented on in his book *Det sociala livets elementära former*, p. 22. I have borrowed the concept, but use it in a different way. Asplund's 'thought figure' (*tankefigur*) is reminiscent of the concept 'mentality' as it is defined here.
8. I have, however, allowed the most distinguished American brain researcher, Charles Fair, to read and comment on an abbreviated English version of this chapter. Although Fair, like Georg Klein, had some objections, none of them concerned its neurological aspects.
9. There are numerous examples of similar heuristic classifications. The trisection of time by the *Annales* school is one of the best known and most used. Fernand Braudel, who introduced it, was also fully aware of what was heuristic in his reduction of the historical processes of change to just three distinct divisions. He has confessed that a less reductionist classification is entirely conceivable, with additional [time] perspectives being added to his three famous ones. See F. Braudel, 'History and the social sciences: the *Long Durée*', p. 30.
10. For a critique of the Freudian concept of the 'repressed', see Frederick Crews, 'The revenge of the repressed', *New York Review of Books*, 17 November and 1 December 1994.
11. F. Braudel, 'History and the social sciences', p. 39. Braudel joins an old sociological discussion here. On this, see R. K. Merton, 'The unanticipated consequences of purposive social action'; A. Giddens, *The constitution of society*, Chapter 2.
12. I am fully aware of the fact that, within the social sciences, these kinds of attitudes have been analysed several times before, by Emile Durkheim, Johan Asplund, Pierre Bourdieu and Jürgen Habermas, for example. However, the analytical setting has not been the same as mine.
13. J. Habermas, *The theory of communicative action 1: reason and the rationalization of society*, pp. 335–37. See also J. Habermas, *Communication and the evolution of society*,

Chapters 2–3. For a similar argument, see A. Giddens, *The constitution of society*, Chapter 2.

14. See A. Jarrick, *Psykologisk socialhistoria*, pp. 55–60; J. Piaget, *Play, dreams and imitation in childhood*, p. 185; J. Piaget, *Language and Thought of the Child*.

15. See A. Florén and M. Persson, 'Mentalitetshistoria och mentalitetsbegreppet', pp. 189ff, for a similar argument.

16. I have discussed this elsewhere. See A. Jarrick, 'Världen går framåt, tycker jag', pp. 76–77; A. Jarrick and J. Söderberg, 'Aktörsstrukturalismen: ett nytt hugg på humanvetenskapens gordiska knut', pp. 68–70.

17. Asplund, *Det sociala livets elementära former*, p. 22, contains a similar line of argument.

18. Lindroth, *Svensk lärdomshistoria: frihetstiden*, pp. 217–28; J. Turner, *Without God, without creed: the origins of unbelief in America*, pp. 44–47, 51–54 and 59.

19. J. H. Hexter, 'Fernand Braudel and the Monde Braudellien . . .' pp. 509–10. See also I. Floto, *Historie: Nyere og nyeste tid*, pp. 179–80.

20. See R. Darnton, *The Great Cat Massacre and Other Episodes in French Cultural History*, p. 51. In his discussion of the meaning of folktales, he does not see that thoughts on different levels have different degrees of permanence.

21. The following discussion has several sources of inspiration, including psychoanalysis, Piaget's cognitive psychology and the communication theory of Jürgen Habermas. But the social-asocial distinction which is devised in this context has been largely borrowed from D. Wrong, *Skeptical sociology*, pp. 31–54.

22. Here I have freely brought together certain elements of early post-war ego psychology (*jagpsykologi*) with elements of modern psychodynamic object relation theory. The identity concept is borrowed from E. H. Erikson, *Identity and the life cycle*, pp. 23 ff and *Identity, Youth and Crisis*, pp. 40–47. 'Self-estimation' or narcissism are concepts which have been used, among others, by H. Kohut. On this, see Jarrick, *Psykologisk socialhistoria*, p. 54; *The Leader*, pp. 73ff.

23. This is the central point in structural-functionalistic socialisation theory à la Parsons. See Jarrick, *Psykologisk socialhistoria*, pp. 67–70; Wrong, *Skeptical sociology*, p. 35.

24. I deviate here from Asplund, *Det sociala livets elementära former*, who does not acknowledge any primary inner: pp. 40–45, 48 and 106–07, and elsewhere. See also A. Jarrick, 'Världen går framåt, tycker jag', p. 77; A. Jarrick, 'Ur det förflutnas djup–om psykoanalys och historieforskning'.

25. Lindroth, *Svensk lärdomshistoria: frihetstiden*, pp. 283–96.

26. For a shorter overview of the witch trials and research pertaining to them, see J. Klaits, *Servants of Satan: the age of the witch hunts*; P. Levack, *The witch-hunt in early modern Europe*; R. Darnton, *The Great Cat Massacre*, Chapter 2 for another sudden shift in mentality among printer journeymen in eighteenth-century Paris.

27. Klaits, p. 160. See also Burke, *Popular culture. . . .*, p. 241.

28. The exception is, perhaps, the aggressive 'urge', which maybe can be considered to be derived from frustrations about the other two basic urges. If the frustrations vary, aggression must then also do so.

29. Here I deviate from the view which prevails within traditional psychoanalysis, where the ego rather than the super-ego is the reality-adapted compromise-instance between super-ego and the outside world. On this see S. Freud, *Introductory lectures on psychoanalysis*, pp. 391–95; S. Freud, *New introductory lectures on psychoanalysis*, pp. 110–11; A. Jarrick, 'Freud och historien', pp. 111–12; Jarrick, *Psykologisk socialhistoria*, pp. 46–47.

30. The concept use is borrowed from J. Piaget. See Jarrick, *Psykologisk socialhistoria*, pp. 55–56; J. Piaget, *Play, dreams and imitation in childhood*, pp. 213 and 273.

31. With time, it was realised that it was the land which was raised, not the water which

sank, but the notion had not come that far in the eighteenth century. See Lindroth, *Svensk lärdomshistoria: frihetstiden*, pp. 283–96.

32. Ibid., 287.

33. Hexter, 'Fernand Braudel and the Monde Braudellien . . .', pp. 509f; Floto, *Historie . . .*, pp. 179f.

34. See, for example, E. Lönnroth, *Den stora rollen: kung Gustaf III spelad av honom själv*, particularly the chapters entitled 'De Stora Gustaverna', 'Heroica II-Verkligheten' and 'Ett maskspel'. Naturally, there were other reasons for the military alliances of the time having been short-lived: what was of primary importance to the mercantilistic nation-states was to expand, no matter with whose help.

35. See M. Sahlins, *Kapten Cooks död* for an analysis of just such a process.

36. On this see Ronny Pettersson, *Laga skifte i Hallands län 1827–1876*, in which the Swedish enclosure is also related to agricultural reforms throughout Europe. See also Ronny Pettersson, 'Skifte och äganderätt'.

37. Here, one could use the pair of opposites extensive-comprehensive. But I find the concept 'extensive' to be misleading in this context. See J. Asplund, *Sociala egenskapsrymder: en introduktion i formaliseringsteknik för sociologer*, pp. 107–10.

38. For an analysis of such a course of events, see for example Darnton, *The Literary Underground . . .*; C. Ginzburg, *The cheese and the worms*; A. Vucinich, *Social thought in Tsarist Russia*.

39. Jarrick, *Psykologisk socialhistoria*, pp. 63ff.

40. For a general overview, see S. Wentworth, *Marginalizing history: a critique of the cliometric program in economic history*, pp. 134–62. For programmatic contributions by representatives of New economic history, see for example D. N. McCloskey, 'The achievements of the cliometric school', pp. 13–28; D. C. North, 'Comment', pp. 77–80.

41. The designation 'fact positivist' (*faktapossitivister*) for the Weibullians is therefore misleading; they were, quite simply, empiricists. See B. Odén, *Lauritz Weibull och forskarsamhället*, p. 201.

42. Floto, *Historie*, particularly pp. 176ff and 243ff. Floto is not particularly clear. For instance, she mentions Le Roy Ladurie's *Montaillou* as an example of structural history (pp. 189–92), a book with unmistakably narrative qualities. Representatives of a narrative historiography in later years have also been very hazy when it comes to definitions. See for example L. Stone, 'The revival of narrative: reflections on a new old history'; E. J. Hobsbawm, 'The revival of narrative: some comments'.

43. In some inappropriate way, two main orientations are brought together: a vaguely atheoretical hermeneutic with a psychological-theoretical often psychodynamic one. On the distinction between these, see D. Will, 'Psychoanalysis and the new philosophy of science', especially pp. 166–69.

44. For a presentation of psychohistory, see Jarrick, *Psykologisk socialhistoria*, pp. 34–40; A. Jarrick, 'Ur det förflutnas djup: om psykoanalys och historieforskning'. Presentations and discussions about the area appear continually. Among the most recent are P. Gay, *Freud for historians: the leader*, Chapters 4–6; E. R. Wallace, *Historiography and causation in psychoanalysis: an essay on psychoanalytic and historical epistemology*.

45. See for example E. Le Roy Ladurie, *The peasants of Languedoc*, who explicitly moves between different levels of articulation and does not hesitate to analyse the unconscious alongside interpretations of intellect and discussions of the importance of the Calvinist doctrine: pp. 33–35, 136–52, 160–61 and 196ff, among others.

46. S. Freud, *The ego and the id*; Freud, *Introductory lectures on psychoanalysis*, pp. 41 and 46; S. Freud, *The unconscious*, pp. 166–67 and 182–83; Jarrick, 'Freud och historien', p. 102; H. Kohut, *The search for the self: selected writings of Heinz Kohut 1950–1978*, pp. 360–61.

47. Here I have resorted to Piaget's concept of equilibrium. See J. Piaget, *Structuralism*; Jarrick, *Psykologisk socialhistoria*, p. 55.

48. Erikson, *Identity and the life-cycle*, p. 23; Erikson, *Identity, Youth and Crisis*, pp. 45–53; Jürgen Habermas, *Communication and the evolution of society*, Chapters 2 and 3, especially p. 80.

49. Kohut, *The search for the self*.

50. My views on Böök are based on Thomas Forser, *Bööks trettiotal: en studie i ideologi*.

51. This corresponds most closely to Max Weber's notion of goal rationality. But as I see it, Weber's notion of value rationality can, in fact, also be classified under the concept of goal rationality, only with the qualification that the goal here is always to act in order to promote certain values, while a goal-rational act does not concern values.

52. J. Elster, *Vetenskapliga förklaringar*, pp. 72–75.

53. For a more comprehensive discussion of this, see Jarrick, 'Ur det förflutnas djup . . .'.

54. See, for example, Febvre, *The problem of unbelief in the sixteenth century: the religion of Rabelais*, p. 100, in which the author maintains the anachronistic in ascribing effort to logical consistency in the people of all ages.

55. Lindroth, *Svensk lärdomshistoria: frihetstiden*, p. 501. Lindroth does not use the concept of mentality, but it is just that, among other things, which he depicts.

56. See P.-J. Ödman, *Tid av frihet, tid av tvång: utvecklingslinjer i svensk 1700-talspedagogik*, p. 8 for a similar criticism of Lindroth.

57. Lindroth, *Svensk lärdomshistoria: frihetstiden*, p. 96. See also p. 506.

58. Ibid., p. 68.

59. Ibid., p. 100.

60. Ibid., p. 211.

61. Ibid., p. 68.

62. I am, however, myself an adherent of such a perspective, to a certain extent. On this, see A. Jarrick and J. Söderberg, 'Spontaneous processes of civilization: the Swedish case'.

63. See, for example, M. Foucault, *Madness and civilization: a history of insanity in the Age of Reason*; Foucault, *Discipline and punishment*.

64. Foucault, *Discipline and punishment*, for example pp. 89–97, or page 115 where the acting subject is an unspecified 'man'.

65. Gottfried Less, *Om sjelfmord*.

66. Olof Holmberg, *Wälmenta anmärkningar . . .* ; See also Olof Holmberg, *Orsakerna till förtwiflan och sjelfmord*.

67. Paul Ricoeur, *Freud and philosophy*, Chapter 1.

68. Ginzburg, *Osten och maskarna*.

69. A. Jarrick, *Den himmelske älskaren. Herrnhutisk väckelse, vantro och sekularisering i 1700-talets Sverige*.

On Monday 27 April 1789 parliament was about to assemble for the last time that year, which was why Gustavus III was anxious to persuade all four estates to support him on the appropriations for the war against Russia, which were still unsettled. He wrote to the burghers appealing for their continuing support and telling them about his projected visit to the Riddarhuset [House of the Nobility] '(…) finally I have decided to visit the House of the Nobility myself to try and persuade the knights and nobles of their duty, and their own best interests (…)'

The statue of Gustavus Vasa, which Johan Hjerpe climbed when he saw the result of his Majesty's visit to the House of the Nobility. The linen shop were Johan worked as an assistant was near the *Storkyrkobrinken,* the alley leading to the church in the background. (Lithograph, Carl Johan Billmark, mid-eighteenth century, Royal Library of Sweden)

Extract from Johan Hjerpe's diary, '(...) when I came to the Riddarhustorget, crowds of journeymen and other people arrived from the surrounding streets, until there were several thousand. At last they saw the royal coach outside the House of the Nobility, which meant that his majesty was inside. When they heard the shouts and cheers of the crowd, the astonished nobles ran to the windows, some pale-faced, others red with anger (...)'

Gustavus III, the powerful new king and enlightened despot, in the midst of his revolutionary brethren. Note their white armlets. (Historical plate, Royal Library of Sweden)

While he was in office, Henrik Liljensparre, the first police commissioner of Stockholm, used every means to protect the enlightened despotism of Gustavus III. (Contemporary portrait, Royal Library of Sweden)

This is the site of the events of 27 April 1789: the Riddarhustorget with the old Riddarhus bridge in the foreground. The statue of Gustavus Vasa is over the bridge in the centre right. (Gouache by Ferdinand Tollin, 1841, City Museum of Stockholm)

Nils Rosen von Rosenstein. (Cartoon by Johan Tobias Sergel, Royal Library of Sweden)

Johan Henrik Kellgren. (Unsigned contemporary drawing, Royal Library of Sweden)

Rosenstein and Kellgren, the most prominent figures of the Gustavusian enlightenment.

Stockholms Post-Tidningar, no 61, 6 August 1789, with the news of the outbreak of the French revolution in the boxed paragraph on the front page. It usually took three weeks for 'hot' news to reach Stockholm from Paris.

The women's march to Versailles in October 1789, when they confined Louis XVI in the Tuilleries. (Contemporary cartoon, Royal Library of Sweden) In Johan Hjerpe's diary of 14 July he refers to *Stockholms Post-Tidningar*, no 61 'The outbreak of the dreadful French revolution in Paris, when the people, who . . . equipped themselves with weapons, and having bribed the king's soldiers, stormed the infamous prison of the Bastille.'

View of Norrström in 1790 with the Swedish navy, after the war with Catherine II of Russia. (Watercolour, Royal Library of Sweden. A copy after a painting by J. L. Desprez, Musée du Louvre)

The funeral feast of Carl Michael Bellman in 1795, faithful royalist and much valued by Gustavus III. (Royal Library of Sweden)

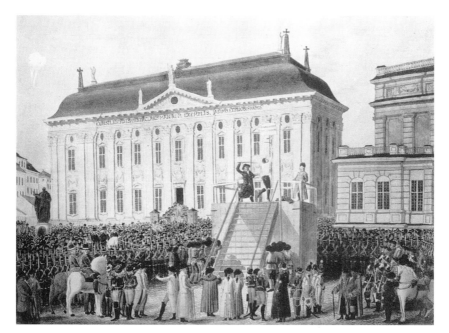

April 1792. Crowds in the Riddarhustorget, as J.J.Anckarström, the assassin of Gustavus III, is about to be scourged on the scaffold before taken to the place of execution at Skanstull, on the southern boundary of Stockholm.

The Crusenstolpe riot in 1838, or 'the rabble-rousers' attack on the city hall, as it was called in the original caption, one of the very few popular riots in the history of pre-industrial Stockholm. (Unsigned lithograph, Royal Library of Sweden)

The old church of Synnerby, about ten miles from the diocesan city of Skara, where Johan Hjerpe lived from the beginning of the 1820s until his death. A new church was built here in 1905. (Royal Library of Sweden)

STOCKHOLMS
HISTORISKE
CALENDER
FÖR ÅR
1761.

INNEHÅLLER
HISTORISKA MÅRKELIGA
HÅNDELSER, SOM SIG I
STOCKHOLM TILDRAGIT,

SAMT

FÖRTEKNING PÅ ÅMBETSMÅN OCH
Betiåning vid de i Stockholm varande
Kongl. Collegier och andra Publika Vårk,
af Civil- och Kyrko-Staterne;

Utgifven,

EFTER KONGL. MAJ:TS NÅDIGSTE
FÖRORDNANDE,

Af

KONGL. VETENSKAPS ACADEMIEN.

TRYCKT UTI KONGL. TRYCKERIET.

Exempl. koftar 1 Dal. 16 öre Kop:mt.

Stockholms Historiske Calender, 1761, a typical small format book of the period. In this almanac Pehr Wargentin, one of Sweden's most influential merchants, started his historical accounts of Stockholm. These were published for some years, and much of Hjerpe's account of the capital was probably based on Wargentin's.

Sammandrag

Af

Swea Rikes

Historia,

Ifrån
De Äldsta til de Nyaste tider.
Til Ungdomens Tjenst upsatt
Af

Swen Lagerbring,

Canc. Råd och Hist. Profeßor i Lund, samt Ledam. af Kgl.
Witterh. Hist. och Antiqv. Acad. och Kgl. Patriot. Sälsk. af
Kgl. Wet. och Witt. Samhället i Götheborg. m. m.

Första Delen,

Som innefattar Rikets Stats-Kunskap,

Med Kongl. Maj:ts Allernådigste Privilegium.

Stockholm,

Tryckt hos Anders Jac. Nordström, 1796.

Title page of Sven Lagerbring's history of Sweden (the abridged edition of 1796). Hjerpe knew this book well. (Royal Library of Sweden)

An illustration from the famous French 'Encyclopaedia' showing the work in a glazier's shop. (Royal Library of Sweden)

A glazier, from a Swedish children's book of 1823. As the working practices and the guild traditions were similar all over Europe, Jacques-Louis Ménétra, the French glazier, would probably have felt at home in this environment. (Royal Library of Sweden)

The pedlar and the bibliophile. Perhaps Voltaire was right in saying that the circulation of books was related to their size. Certainly small books were cheaper and easier to carry around. (Engraving, L.L. Boilly, *c.* 1790)

Book auction at Sotheby's in London. (watercolour, Thomas Rowlandson, *c.* 1790)

Study was done in private, but literacy is an essential part of education and the safeguard of the civilised values. Below a little child is being taught to spell from a life of Jesus. On the table is an edition of Milton in Swedish, probably *Paradise Lost*. (Engravings, school of E. Martin, Royal Library of Sweden)

Isabella Tinkler, a book pedlar in England. (Engraving, G. Gilt, 1794)

The culture of letters
and the measurement of thoughts

Chapter 3
Burghers, common folk and books

Introduction

As there is no easy road to popular culture and mentality, one must take the byways: speeches of welcome, for example, books in the estates left by the poor, broadsheets, biographies and the odd diary. Or, basically, through eyewitness accounts, mementoes and various literary artefacts.

Actions occupied the centre of the preceding diptych. Things will be less eventful here, for I now want to get at the structure of a gradual unfolding of events. First of all, I will try to clarify certain aspects of the change in people's relationship to the printed word, above all during the eighteenth and early nineteenth centuries. That places the *printed word* at the centre of interest both as *material* and *ideal* evidence of popular culture and mentality. A natural point of departure is to assume a link between reading and thought. But unread books can also say something about the intentions of the owner,[1] just as the very act of reading bears on how the material is received.[2,3] A variety of measures are required, for if knowledge of all this is to be acquired, each in itself is insufficient to reach the objective. Together they can capture some of what I am seeking. Much work has already been done by others; what I can contribute will become evident later. I will not consider the periodical press, clearly a limitation, as more people were presumably reached by the ephemeral media than by more enduring publications.

First, the development of literacy will be touched upon briefly, followed by overviews of *book production, trade with books* and *book ownership* by artisans and tradesmen, in that order. Having covered all this ground, I will gradually make my way to the logical conclusion: the content of and very act of reading the publications. But I will pause before that, as it is only through individuals that the act of reading can be followed – individuals such as Johan Hjerpe – the subject of Chapter 6.

A few words on literacy

The Judaeo-Christian sphere of civilisation is very much a culture of letters. Written works (published and unpublished) were of great importance to common folk long before the general spread of literacy, even though an unlettered culture always existed alongside it.[4] When the clergyman[5] preached to his illiterate congregation, it was the text he expounded, just as the master dictated the catechism and the burgher read aloud to his servants from chronicles of folk tales.[6] Books, on the other hand, have sometimes been used simply as trophies or objects of beauty, even by owners who should have been able to read them.[7]

The ability to read would not seem to have been either a necessary or a sufficient prerequisite for knowledge of the contents and messages of books. Nevertheless, the general spread of literacy has strongly influenced people's relationship to the written word. Some would even say that the process has been decisive to the development of civilisation. The American culture researcher Walter J. Ong is one of those to have emphatically emphasised the significance, in terms of civilisation, of the transition from oral to written culture.[8] This, then, is an important piece in the puzzle to which I shall return towards the end of this chapter.

Numerous attempts have been made to map out the spread of literacy in Europe since the development of printing, and many have associated the process with the ambitions of the burgeoning national state to cultivate the beliefs and customs of the people. Peter Burke has summarised the research results and claims that:

> ... historians have concluded that a substantial minority of ordinary people in early modern Europe were in fact able to read; that more of them could read in 1800 than in 1500; that craftsmen were generally much more literate than peasants, men than women, Protestants than Catholics, and Western Europeans than Eastern Europeans.[9]

Unfortunately, research on literacy has often been based on studies of signatures, such as in series of fiscal documents – in other words, more on observations of the ability to write than on literacy itself.[10] As far as Sweden is concerned, however, the situation is much better, because material consisted of records of parish catechetical meetings in which clergymen recorded not just whether, but also how well, their parishioners understood the written word. It was these catechetical meetings which Egil Johansson used when he established that approximately half of all Swedes could read by the mid eighteenth century and over 80 per cent by the end of the century, probably a very high proportion seen from a contemporary European perspective.[11]

But even if the findings of Swedish research on the spread of literacy rest on firmer foundations than much international research, most results still point in the same direction.[12] At the same time, the implications of literacy have scarcely been clarified by the ministers' notations in parish records. Their tests concerned writings, the contents of which were familiar from oral preaching, so it is difficult to say how the farmer or artisan would have fared with writings other than those included in the official selection.[13] In order to analyse this, material other than the records of the parish catechetical meetings is needed.

The production of books

The printed word expresses thought, which is not to say that, in so doing, it is also perceived by its contemporaries or is incorporated with its spiritual traditions. But in works of intellectual history, it used to be quite common to put an original or challenging message on record in a new book as a sign of a change of outlook in society as a whole, and not just as a manifestation of more-or-less unique thoughts on the part of the author of the book. Of course, there are also samples of older attempts to assess the dissemination of ideas as well. Yet, these were seldom based on solid foundations, more often on impressions gleaned from haphazard forays into the sources.[14]

The old method is now considered questionable, especially, perhaps, thanks to Robert Darnton's efforts to establish – partly quantitatively – the limits of the importance of the philosophy of Enlightenment to opinion-formation in Paris in the decades preceding the French Revolution.[15] Although modified, the tradition continues to this day, in Swedish intellectual history as elsewhere.[16] Besides, the new orientation has already been called into question by a number of cultural historians, who are of the view that literacy research must once again concern itself more with textual analysis than with superficial frequency measurements of the dissemination of books and other similar things. Chartier is perhaps the most outspoken of these critics; Ginzburg is also among them, even if neither entirely dismisses quantitative studies.[17]

There are no good reasons for allowing one method to displace another. Instead, they should be combined, something which may seem self-evident, but only as long as anti-quantitative arguments are not borne in mind. As soon as one argument is used to counter another, everything immediately becomes less self-evident. But I shall wait until the next chapter to complicate what seems simple and instead go on to some quantitative features of the development of book production in Sweden in the eighteenth century.

The prospects for following this expansion are good because the Svensk bibliografi (Swedish bibliography) database for the 1700–1829 period has at last been opened for searches.[18] At one fell swoop, it has become dramatically easier to make a great number of interesting measurements which previously required near Herculean efforts.[19] No longer are unreasonable amounts of work required in order, for example, to identify changes in the distribution of subjects, language or format. Quantitiative management of such half-obscured aspects of the production of books, has increased our chances of discerning a number of insidious cultural changes which people of the time did not really see, in spite of their being involved in them. But then, they did not have access to the new database either.

The bibliography, containing some 43,000 entries, is based primarily on the Royal Library's catalogued collection of Swedish publications and so does not cover all the publications of the period. However, dissertations and occasional papers (tillfällestryck) have been excluded, as have some period- icals and books published in the provinces if they were written in foreign languages. What were then called ettbladstryck (broadsheets) are included, but neither broadsheets (except in a few cases) nor yearbooks appear (årstryck – a series of annual publications, that has existed for centuries, containing new laws and regulations).[20] Nor are there any figures pertaining to circulation, as they tend to be very difficult to come by. Scattered details can be found in publishing contracts, in letters, among the claims of estate inventories and, on the odd occasion, in the literature. But compiled information does not exist, even if it is widely thought that a standard edition was about 500 copies.[21] If one wants to glean anything about the possession and reading of books, the bibliography is almost, but not entirely insufficient or irrelevant, as will be demonstrated shortly. One more thing: supply on the Swedish book market also consisted of imported literature, which needs tracing to other sources.[22] In spite of the limitations, a great deal of knowledge can nevertheless be extracted from the material, partly in combination with other sources. A little will be presented now.

The production of books increased greatly during this period. In 1700, a total of 183 titles appeared in print; 130 years later, 812. The difference reflects a general expansion, which, admittedly, suffered a good many ups and downs. This development can be seen, in rough terms, in Table 3.1.

Table 3.1 The production of books in Sweden 1700–1829. Ten-year periods, absolute num- bers. Source: SB17.

Period	Number of titles
1700–09	1019
1710–19	897
1720–29	938
1730–39	1164
1740–49	2132
1750–59	2117
1760–69	3778
1770–79	4447
1780–89	3229
1790–99	3890
1800–09	4848
1810–19	7171
1820–29	7306
1700–1829	42936

It is possible that the greatest variations can be traced back to political events, to which the people involved would seem to have reacted very emotionally. Perhaps the 1766 freedom of the press law – which abolished the public censor – can explain the sharp increase which now took place largely as a result of a flood of political pamphlets.[23] But following Gustavus III's coup in 1772, the creators of ideas withdrew from the public view, and the production of books fell as quickly as it had just risen. This cannot be seen from Table 3.1, but if each year is scrutinised individually, it is obvious enough: in 1772, 864 books left the printers, the following year only 378. The decline continued and culminated in 1777 (264 titles), at which point a recovery began. A similar peak can be observed at the time of the freedom of the press law of 1810, although the increase around 1740 cannot be related to a corresponding relaxation. This can be seen from Figure 3.1.[24]

Gustavus III wanted to be a patron of the arts. Instead he drove writers away from the scene he had usurped, but this did not prevent the expansion from gathering steam again soon. In time, there were fewer fluctuations, although the freedom of the press would be restricted and extended many times.[25] For example, Gustavus III was greatly affected by the events taking place in France.[26] In early 1790, he introduced a ban on the dissemination of printed news of the revolution, although he was powerless in the face of unpublished gossip.[27] The ban had discernible effects on the periodical press, and books also became fewer. But the newspapers did not by any means

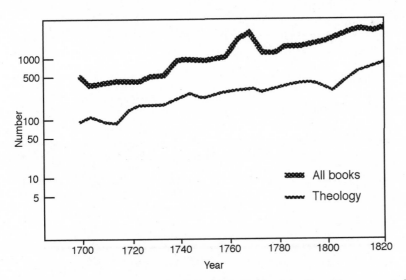

Figure 3.1 Book production in Sweden 1720–1829. Total and theology. Five-year periods, absolute figures, semi-logarithmic scale. Source: SB17.

observe the strict silence the king desired, and the decline in book production was so slight that it can hardly be linked to his interference.[28]

Measured in terms of subject classification, the eighteenth century entailed a slow but steady secularisation in the production of books. Theology – calculated by the number of titles – remained the largest area, by and large, throughout the entire period (1700–1829).[29] But books with religious subjects were becoming less important.[30] The question is, however, whether the authors, publishers and reading public were aware of what they were taking part in; they may have been actors in a process, the direction of which they could not see and the consequences of which they were even less able to forecast.[31] Indeed, it was scarcely possible for anyone in the midst of it to perceive the change, a change cannot be grasped in retrospect either, if one proceeds impressionistically. But it can be discerned statistically and depicted along the time axis as a falling wave. Figures 3.1 and 3.2 provide clear evidence of this. The production of theological books increased with the general expansion, but more slowly than literature in general.[32] The production of broadsheets underwent the same shift towards the secular.[33] On the whole, the development was not dramatic, even if it unfolded more rapidly in the capital than in the country as a whole.[34] Calculated in absolute figures, nothing sensational happened with theology, even if the subject area's share varied with the long-term receding trend. The production of spiritual books was not affected by political upheavals.[35]

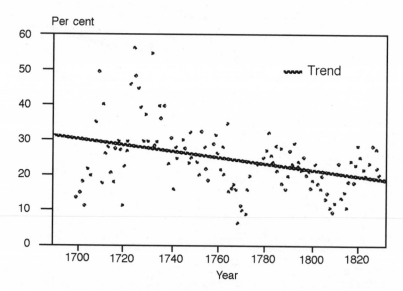

Figure 3.2 Theology's share of book production in Sweden 1720–1829. Source: SB17.

The movement towards secularisation would thus appear to have been slow. The direction it followed was, however, clear and also coincided with one of the objectives which many of the leading lights of Enlightenment had set themselves. But the secularisation process can scarcely be traced back to explicitly collective aspirations and was not based on any programme. Instead, it proceeded silently – as an insidious change in the cultural climate. And yet, if Enlightenment is considered more as a process and not as a programme, secularisation could, perhaps, be tied in with it, precisely because it was an unarticulated change of attitude towards the materialisation of the idea of Enlightenment.[36]

Judging from information about the quantitative variations in book production in the eighteenth century, then, it would seem to be possible to construe a great deal about the cultural renewal and renewal of mentalities which were under way during this period. But what is measured could, naturally, be explained in another way, and without reservations, any interpretation runs the risk of being an over-interpretation. The investigation which has been conducted is biased; if its results point in a certain direction, others can point in another. The fact that books were produced says nothing about their dissemination. A process is not irrevocable just because it is slow. Thus, for example, the figures indicate that religious literature regained something of its lost importance at the beginning of the nineteenth century (Figure 3.2), a result which is reminiscent of other enquiries.[37] Was it nevertheless that the Romantic period transformed what had been achieved by Enlightenment into a lamentable Pyrrhic victory?

The bibliography of eighteenth-century book production reflects a remarkable expansion of the printed word, an expansion which in itself must have facilitated the spread of written culture, because it is easier to read printed than hand-written texts.[38] But apart from that, the bibliography is ill-suited to studies of the dissemination of books; other sources are needed for that. A number of indirect measurements can, however, be made with the help of SB17. One has to take into account variations in the format of books. Roger Chartier argues that pocket format was of importance to the spread of written culture, not just because a small book was cheaper than a large one, but also because it could be carried about in the pocket. He is probably right.[39]

In general, small books were cheaper than large ones and the common people were, of course, poorer than the élite.[40] A growth in the importance of small volumes would thus say something about the dissemination of written culture to social strata beyond the circle of those already educated.

The folio was the preserve of the affluent collector, an octavo psalm book or a duodecimo almanac a relatively inexpensive everyday book for the poor.[41] But it was, perhaps, the octavo volume in particular that came,

more than any other, to be the book of the people, at least judging by the
distribution of the format of the titles. During the first ten years of the eighteenth century, 1,019 books were produced, all told. Of these, only 191 were
printed in octavo and 69 in duodecimo format, or 18.7 and 6.8 per cent
respectively. Slightly more than a century later, the situation was reversed.
The duodecimo format had, certainly, not advanced notably from its
modest position, but the octavo format now amounted to about 65 per cent
of the supply. Together, the years 1820–29 represented three-quarters of the
period's total book production, or 5,389 out of a total of 7,306 titles. This
dominance was a consequence of a steady growth in the importance of the
octavo volume, as can clearly be seen in Table 3.2 and Figure 3.3

But here it is also possible to discern clearly the fact that the 1760s represented a temporary interruption in the general expansion of small book
production. The quarto format regained something of its lost status, and by
the beginning of the 1760s comprised approximately 45 per cent of the
number of titles on offer. The peak was reached in 1766 with 81 per cent.
The increase in the small volume continued, however, and the relative
decline cannot be interpreted as a setback for the popularisation of culture.
The setback was presumably more related to the second half of the 1760s
having been a hectic time for pamphlets, because the politically militant publications were often in the larger format.[42]

*Table 3.2 Book production in Sweden 1700–1829 with reference to format. Ten-year period,
absolute numbers and percentage. Source: SB17.*

Period	Total	Octavo	Octavo %	Duodecimo	Duodec. %
1700–09	1019	191	18.7	69	6.8
1710–19	897	174	19.4	54	6.0
1720–29	938	259	27.6	91	9.7
1730–39	1164	397	34.1	79	6.8
1740–49	2132	813	38.1	115	5.4
1750–59	2117	861	40.7	92	4.4
1760–69	3890	1291	33.2	111	2.9
1770–79	4848	1704	35.2	161	3.3
1780–89	3229	1927	59.7	217	6.7
1790–99	3890	2434	62.6	242	6.2
1800–09	4848	2792	57.6	355	7.3
1810–19	7171	4299	60.0	456	6.6
1820–29	7306	4697	64.3	692	9.5

Note: The ten-year values are based on yearly values, while the ten-year values for the
formats are based on ten-year searches in SB17. This means that the series do not exactly
correspond. The differences are, however, negligible.

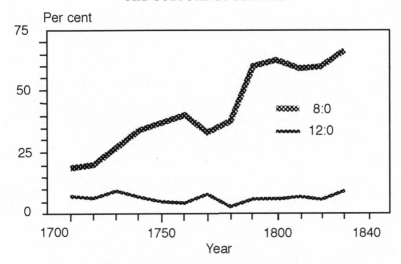

Figure 3.3 The proportion of octavo and duodecimo format of Swedish books printed between 1720 and 1790. Ten-year periods. Source: SB17.

As book production increased, books themselves became smaller, and a slowly diminishing proportion of them debated spiritual matters. Moreover, simple broadsheets were hawked as never before,[43] as pocket format almanacs were spread in hundreds of thousands all over the country.[44] The steady growth in all the myriad newspapers was also essential to the popularisation of written culture, even if many of them existed for only a short time, some for not more than a few months. The newspapers were read or read aloud in all manner of places: in the affluent tranquillity of homes as well as in noisy cafés. They could contain anything and everything: advertisements, short, droll anecdotes and philosophical essays. And, of course, news correspondents from all the corners of the earth, an invariable feature which dramatically extended the horizon of the public imagination, at times made those in power nervous – like Gustavus III in the face of all the horrifying reports of revolution from Paris.[45]

That this took place in the name of 'enlightenment' is, in fact, quite apt, especially as the population became literate at the same rate as the expansion, and the burgeoning literature shifted the cultural frames of reference towards the temporal. While still far from godless, the population – taken as a whole – debated theological or religious issues to a lesser degree. But note that this was an Enlightenment before the proud French Enlightenment movement: the process had begun several decades before it – long before its Encyclopaedia and long before Voltaire and the other philosophers became general topics of discussion in Sweden. One could, perhaps, even say that the spectacular enlightenment movement itself emanated from the gradual cultural changes, more an effect than a cause.

Similarly, a secularisation of the values of official society was also in progress, especially during the latter part of the eighteenth century. Here, however, it is quite clear that the campaigns of Enlightenment philosophers came into play, not least by ensuring that the Bible provided less and less guidance for the morality of society's criminal law. The death penalty, for example, became both more uncommon and less painful, and when it was imposed it was no longer done to avert the wrath of God, as it had been earlier.

The temptation thus exists to link all these simultaneous changes to perceive, for example, the secularisation of book production as a sign of the secularisation of the people, as an expression of a de-Christianisation that penetrated all of society. This is the case particularly as the same tendencies are also apparent when attention is focused on the production of octavo volumes in the vernacular which was in a particularly good position to achieve a broad dissemination.[46] Figure 3.4 illustrates this conclusion. Let me just add that the picture would be virtually the same were the canonical writings left aside and only the theological secondary literature recorded. I have, therefore, repeated the investigation, this time excluding all bibles, New Testaments, psalm books, catechisms, gospel books, psalters and funeral sermons. The result is almost the same as when they were included.

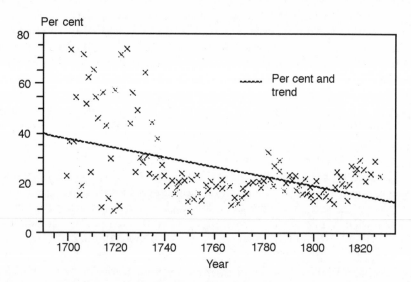

Figure 3.4 Book production in Sweden 1720–1829. The proportion of theological books out of all books in Swedish in octavo format. Source: SB17.

But here, the possibilities for interpretation have perhaps been stretched a bit far. A similar cursory survey of the very smallest format (duodecimo) in fact suggests the opposite interpretation, partly because the theological proportion of duodecimo printing does not appear to show any long-term decline, and partly because bibles and catechisms, psalm books and funeral services were as important as much as secondary literature, and have perhaps even increased in importance over time.[47] In other words, a canonical culture of letters in micro format perhaps attained a really wide dissemination just at the time that the educated élite turned increasingly away from eternal evangelical truths.

Whatever the case, the cultural frames of reference had been dislodged and the opportunities had increased for ordinary people to attain a little of the education from which they had previously been excluded. But what they did with those opportunities has not been established. What was on offer is one thing; what was bought and read another. The discussion, then, must continue on other aspects of the development of written culture, even if the results reported up to here, taken on their own, can be interpreted as an indication of an increasing spread of culture.

Some thoughts about the book trade

People meet at a market and exchange money for thoughts which have been transformed into writing. It goes without saying that this traffic is very interesting to anyone who wants to distinguish the flow of ideas which caught contemporary interest from those which attracted less attention or left the majority unmoved. By directing interest to the sphere of distribution, it is possible to gain access to what remains inaccessible with an analysis of production alone, even if the results, in this context too, are more indications than direct evidence. The literary sociologist Anita Ankarcrona gives a reasonable defence of the study of both auction catalogues and book auctions, which cannot provide direct information about people's reading. She says that these sources nevertheless 'tell about fulfilled and thwarted ambitions'. In short: one comes closer to an interest in reading. But that does not mean that the former can entirely replace the latter; each new piece only makes it a little bit easier to work out the rest of the puzzle.

Material evidence of such transactions are to be found in different places: in preserved bookshop catalogues, among the book advertisements in and subscribers lists of newspapers, in the records of transactions in the Stockholm book auction room, for example, and in the lists of books on offer there and so on. Catalogues from deceased book collectors could also be included here, but are usually (and, in my view, quite rightly) consigned to the category of 'book ownership'.[48]

Apart from a smaller survey of some book auction catalogues, I have not myself made any studies of the trade in books. But there is plenty of research in this area at present in Sweden and elsewhere. This is certainly in large part a result of Robert Darnton's inspiring study of the book market in France in the decades preceding the revolution.[49] Knowledge is steadily increasing, and a good many interesting results have already been presented. Anita Ankarcrona's study of business·in the Stockholm book auction room fits particularly well into the discussion that has taken place here.[50] I will content myself with touching briefly on what this has produced, but will also make some comment on its limitations.

Ankarcrona's study concerns a number of different aspects of the trade in books: mostly genres, language, format and prices, but also sellers and buyers. The enquiry only concerns the years between 1782 and 1801, a time frame which is justified by the limitations of the source material or, to be more specific, by the fact that what are known as 'inlagorna' are missing for other years. The 'inlagorna' are lists of books on offer and are therefore of central importance in a literary-sociological study such as this. In the auction records (which cover a much longer period), there are references to the lists of books on offer, but also details about the name and title of seller and buyer.[51]

The two sources can thus be used together, which is what Ankarcrona has done. A random selection of approximately 600 transactions and close to 850 titles comprises the basis of her enquiry, which has produced much new knowledge, but also guaranteed a good deal of natural suspicion.[52] I will comment on some of the results.

There was great variation among the titles. When consigned to categories, a pattern nevertheless emerges, with theology the single leading genre, in spite of bibles having been counted separately; counted together, these represented barely a fifth of the transactions (18 per cent). History and literature were also well represented genres, each with a little more than a tenth of the market (13 and 12 per cent respectively). The result corresponds to the subject classification in SB17 for the entire period between 1700 and 1829, if one disregards the fact that political literature had a much weaker position on the auction market than in the sphere of production (2 and 14 per cent respectively).[53] Books in Swedish took up almost half of the section, and among foreign languages, 'the more fashionable French' was stronger than the old classroom languages, Latin and German. The lesser and cheaper formats (octavo and duodecimo) accounted for three-quarters of the volumes auctioned off.[54] Even so, the price level was high enough to exclude most people from the auction room,[55] which was above all a place for the regulated exchange of books between members of the 'middle class' of the city, its officials and clergymen, merchants and doctors, as well as the odd artisan.[56] But whether it was the leading place of exchange is more difficult to say.

Johan Hjerpe, for example, seems neither to have bought nor sold a single book at the Stockholm book auction room during the first decades of the nineteenth century, and this in spite of his having acquired the greater part of his considerable book collection precisely during those years.[57] Perhaps he did this in his own neighbourhood, because there were several book stalls around the corner from his dwelling in the Old Town.[58]

In Ankarcrona's view, a number of expressions of general changes in mentality can also be discerned in the particular area she has chosen to study. Guided by the subject classification in the trade in second-hand books, she speaks, for example, of 'increasing secularisation and its vital interest in the subjective and the societal'.[59] Now, the author has neither followed the trade from year to year, nor conducted any comparative cross-section analyses. Instead, she attempts to trace the change in an indirect way, through comparisons between the genre patterns of the purchases and sales of the different groups. She sees the pattern which emerges from this muddle as an indication of 'generational change'[60] laden with significance. The clergymen, who are consigned to one group, sought in particular to dispose of books on religious subjects, thus returning home less burdened by religion. Theological literature comprised more than 40 per cent of their offerings, but scarcely 35 per cent of their purchases. Officials, merchants and booksellers also used the auctions to make their book collections less spiritual. But surely someone must have bid for the books which the educated 'world' wished to be rid of. The unnamed people under the heading 'Anonymous' shouldered the burden, and bought more religious books than they sold,[61] thus reducing the impression of the change of mentality Ankarcrona thought she saw.[62]

Interpreting books' 'generational change' as an indication of a more general change in mentality is a risky business, because, among other things, the generational change of books need not correspond to that of those who bought and sold them. But I will pass over these problems to deal with a more pressing complication. Ankarcrona's results deviate considerably from what, time and again, has emerged from studies of book ownership in the estate inventories of common folk, be they early eighteenth or mid nineteenth century. Among traces of learning in humble estates, spiritual literature reigns supreme like a king among books, not only as the largest, but as the completely predominant genre.[63] At times, Ankarcrona displays the belief that the two source groups are not entirely comparable.[64] The comparatively well-off members of the public at the book auctions in the capital presumably had a taste for more profane subjects than the majority of peasants, artisans and merchants whose meagre libraries have been recorded in estate inventories with other personal property of limited value. The results can not that simply be considered mutually contradictory.

Even with her own results before her, Ankarcrona wavers and ends up making the sort of comparison she earlier cautioned against. For example, she seeks to explain the wealth of religious literature in estate inventories from eighteenth-century Gothenburg with the hypothesis that the secular books in a deceased person's estate were presumably often disposed of before the inventory had been carried out, while the religious books were passed on, unsold, to the next generation.[65] The implications are clear: if this possibility is not taken into account, the result is a considerable overestimation of the importance of theology in estate inventories.

Ankarcrona does not consider the possibility that the deviations from her own results could also be the result of the different sources perhaps reflecting the genuinely different reading interests of different groups. Moreover, there is an inherent contradiction hidden here. In her debate about literary generational change, she imagines that books offered for sale were no longer wanted by their owners.[66] That the greater weight of theology in estate inventories was perhaps due to the survivors having grabbed the bibles and catechisms while allowing the secular books to be sold should therefore speak for, rather than against, the usefulness of the material.[67]

The shortcomings in Ankarcrona's sceptical debate about estate inventories also says something about the limited scope of her own results. They are not upset, but for the time being we do not know the extent to which the book auction room's socially distinct habitué represented anyone other than himself.

Books and estate inventories

A volume once purchased can soon disappear again, through the market or in a thousand other ways. Those books which survived their owner, and which remained in his estate, perhaps better reflect an enduring reading interest that was extinguished at the moment a life was snuffed out. But then, another sort of invariable has been assumed from the start, and such surviving traces resist attempts to gain an insight into what happened along the way. And so again, if one looks in one place, another is neglected. Whatever the case, if one wants to learn something about people's collected ownership of books, two types of source in particular can be consulted. One is the *printed auction catalogues* of individuals' book collections, the other, *estate inventories*.

Auction catalogues are easy to come by and to edit systematically, often with the format as the governing principle.[68] Unfortunately – and as expected – it seems as though, more than anything else, all they reflect is the 'frozen' reading interest of the book-collecting upper strata. This observation is confirmed by the massive inventory which Henrik Grönroos made of the book stock in preserved estate inventories from Finnish cities during the period.[69] I have therefore not delved more deeply into the material, but a modest survey of the 38 preserved book auction catalogues of 1825 produced the following result, among others: the average number of items is 862, i.e., notably more than Hjerpe's 329, in spite of his being an assiduous collector. The proportion of theological and religious books varies considerably, and it is thus pointless to try to report the average value.[70] For example, theology comprised a full third of the stock of Dean Olber (581 items), while one searches in vain for such spiritual nourishment in the catalogue of rural doctor Brusin's collection, which with 1,414 entries was very large for the time.[71] The collections, then, seem to have been varied and cannot be arranged according to a simple pattern, which is also interesting; it should be possible to test it through more extensive analyses than I have carried out.

What, then, can be extracted from estate inventories? The question has been posed countless times before and answered in different ways. My impression is that the scepticism Ankarcrona has suggested for this source has become quite widespread among the historically-inclined literary sociologists of today.[72] In my view, this doubt is connected to the Swedish historian Arne Carlsson's 1972 thesis on books in estate inventories from Bohus county for the period 1752–1808 (*Böcker i bohuslänska bouppteckningar 1752–1808*), or rather with the withering criticism which Gunnar Qvist aimed at it in a review.[73] Since then, it has been necessary to tread cautiously, as the spring flows in a place which is mined with Qvist's many doubts about the possibilities afforded by the material. This has not prevented the odd historian from resorting to estate inventories without referring to Qvist,[74] and researchers outside Sweden are as yet unfamiliar with his comments.[75] Quite rightly, many Swedish literary sociologists appear to have decided to abandon the source for other, less dangerous waters.

This is natural, as there are so many question marks pertaining to source criticism. Do the inventoried books actually say anything about reading interests? Were the books purchased by those who left them behind, or were they inherited from another estate? And if they were purchased, what, in that case, would they have been used for: reading or the bestowal of status and beauty? How long did it take after death before the inventory was completed, and did precision not fluctuate with the varying discretion of the stock-takers? Moreover, as, in time, the books fell in price, fewer titles were recorded. Forbidden books were perhaps hidden, or misappropriated in some other way, before the inventory. According to a law of 1734, estate inventories were to be made for every deceased adult.[76] But for many – perhaps most – this did not happen, and the question is whether the inventories that were taken are socially and economically representative of all the dead.[77] This can be put to the test, but such an analysis poses new difficulties, one reason being that the property details in estate inventories were in some respects a matter of form and because such information was evidence of the finances of the dead, and not of living people

Many problems relate to source-criticism, but they can be tested empirically, and are not too numerous to be investigated. Moreover, for a long
time, estate inventories have successfully, and with considerable awareness
of criticism of the source, been used for research on social and economic
history.[78] The problem should not deter anyone who wishes to try it. Personally, I have not shied away, but have conducted a modest study of the books
included in the estate inventories of 561 merchants, artisans and journeymen
who lived and died in Stockholm. The material is quite evenly distributed
between women and men, but unevenly over the three years which have
been selected – 1751, 1791 and 1821. The cross-section was chosen with reference to Johan Hjerpe: basically it covers his life and can throw into relief his
distinctive reading interest. A less detailed study has, however, also been
made of the estate inventories of 1711. An unusually large number of estate
inventories made in Stockholm that year have been preserved, including
some for quite ordinary people, such as tailors, coopers and fish buyers. The
reason is that the plague had claimed many lives in the city the year before.[79]
(The problems pertaining to source criticism are not dealt with individually,
but together with the reports of the various results.)

Judging by the number of estate inventories which remain, a total of 1,469
adult Stockholmers departed this life in 1751, 1791 and 1821. Of these, 561 – a
good 38 per cent – were merchants, master artisans and journeymen, or their
widows or wives.[80] Naturally, many more people, adults and children died in
this period who should have been the object of an inventory but who apparently were not.[81] The discrepancy is not so disturbing, however, if the representation of the groups surveyed in the material roughly corresponds to their
importance in the real world of learning. This can be tested in different ways.

From Table 3.3 it can be seen, first, that the incidence of estate inventories
in total and for the surveyed groups varies from year to year. But, fortunately, they *co-vary*. Of all the inventories, 25.5 per cent (375) are from 1751,
slightly more for the artisans and others (28.5 per cent or 160). Slightly more

*Table 3.3 Incidence of estate inventories in Stockholm in the years 1751, 1791 and 1821, (a)
for the city as a whole, (b) for merchants, artisans and journeymen. Absolute figures and percentages. Source: SSA, bou.*

Year	(a) abs	%	(b) abs	(c) %	(b) as % of (a)
1751	375	25.5	160	28.5	42.7
1791	611	41.6	233	41.5	38.1
1821	483	32.9	168	30.0	34.8
Total	1469	100	561	100	38.2

than 40 per cent are from 1791, both when it comes to the sample and to the population as a whole (233 and 611 respectively) and roughly 30 per cent, in a similar way, from the final year (168 and 483 respectively). The variations, then, correspond to each other, and also rather well with the fluctuations in mortality for the capital as a whole.[82] At the same time, it is clear that the sample's share of the total number of estate inventories fell between the three measurement points (from 42.7 to 34.8 per cent). A comparison between the taxed artisans of the capital and all tax-paying Stockholmers gives a similar result: a decline between 1750 and 1790 from 42.9 to 32.6 per cent for the artisan share.[83]

The material thus passes a first source-critical test. There are no good reasons for not using it yet, and we are free to continue. The first question concerns the incidence of books in general, the second which subjects were common.

In the estate inventories of 1751, one or more books are already recorded for the sample of Stockholmers which the study concerns. Forty years later they are even more common, while the study of the inventories of 1821 reveals an insignificant decline compared with 1791. Estimated according to the share of estate inventories with books, then, book ownership among the burghers and humble folk of Stockholm increased during the period, although the final year represents a slight decline. The results can be seen in Figure 3.5.[84]

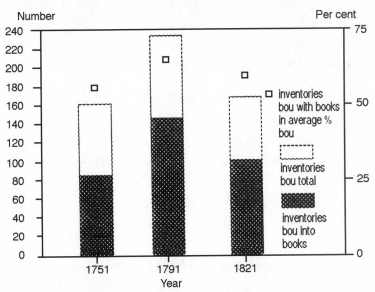

Figure 3.5 The incidence of books in estate inventories (bou) of merchants, artisans and journeymen in Stockholm in 1751, 1791 and 1821. Source: SSA, bou.

The decline, or rather the lack of a continued recorded expansion after 1791, could, perhaps, be explained by stock-takers having increasingly considered books to be trifles, and having thus become careless about recording them. In any case, the records of book ownership in 1821 were very poor in detail. Titles were mentioned only in exceptional cases, while older records had a wealth of detail.[85] Furthermore, measured per capita, book ownership increased throughout the period, and even if distribution increased at the same time, very few of the deceased seem to have left real book collections behind them.[86]

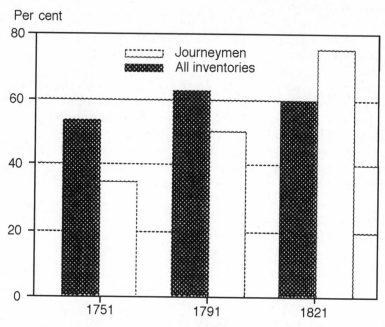

Figure 3.6 Percentage share of owners of books among journeymen and among the entire group of inventoried merchants, artisans and journeymen in Stockholm in 1751, 1791 and 1821. The percentages apply to each individual group. Source: SSA, bou.

I have already implied that the rapid growth of the smaller format during the course of the eighteenth century could have been a manifestation of the increased spread of written culture to common folk. The written word could, more than before, reach ordinary people directly, i.e., more frequently not the spoken word. The question is now whether it is also possible to discern traces of the popularisation of culture in estate inventories as well. In my view, there is much that speaks for this, apart from what has already emerged. In the first place, the occurrence of books increased more among the journeymen than in the group as a whole. As can be seen from Figure 3.6, the journeymen were initially among those with fewest books, but came instead to be over-represented among the owners of books by the end of the period under investigation. This could, of course, be associated with it having presumably become generally more difficult to establish oneself as an independent artisan entrepreneur towards the end of the eighteenth century.[87] But, secondly, the connection between economic position and book ownership seems to have grown increasingly weak over time, regardless of whether the gross or net values are compared with the number of books or with their recorded monetary value. This is easy to ascertain from Table 3.4: for example, the correlation which existed in 1751 between the value of the books and the net balance had disappeared entirely seventy years later.

Table 3.4 R_{xy} for gross balance (gb), net balance (nb), number of catalogued books (niu) and the noted value in money of the books (va) in estate inventories of merchants, artisans and journeymen in Stockholm in 1751, 1791 and 1821. Source: SSA, bou.

		gb	nb	niu
nb	1751	0.89		
	1791	0.98		
	1821	0.96		
na	1751	0.31	0.36	
	1791	0.05	0.02	
	1821	0.02	0.03	
va	1751	0.48	0.54	0.80
	1791	0.13	0.11	0.73
	1821	−0.02	0.00	0.67

The figures are precise and easy to interpret, but they can be credible only after having been put to the test of source criticism. The group of people which can be covered using estate inventories was naturally differently constituted in terms of age than the active population as a whole, and some of the details were, moreover, recorded as a matter of form rather than according to the real situation.[88] I have thus made a random selection of the estate inventories of 61 persons and compared the economic details contained in them with the income information about them in the register of taxpayers.[89] It is clear, admittedly, that taxation was also a matter of form, but it followed different forms than those of estate inventories, which therefore makes comparison meaningful. The statistical connection (r_{xy}) between the gross balance (in the estate inventories) and taxation was 0.46, but only 0.27 if the net income is used as the basis of comparison. Both connections are, however, significant, the former at the level of 1 per cent and the latter at the 5 per cent level.[90] In my view, the gross balance says more about the earlier living standard of the dead than the net balance does. The result should thus be satisfactory and the income information contained in the estate inventories usable.[91]

But the problems concerning source criticism are not solved by this. The weak connection between fortune and the possession of books – as it emerges in estate inventories – could be related to the very thing that Ankarcrona warned against: perhaps the libraries of the departed rich had already been auctioned off when the stock-takers came to make an inventory of their property. The poor had no book collections; the little they had was left behind in the home and could be recorded. I have also attempted to investigate this somewhat. From 1791 and 1821 I found 33 estate inventories which accounted for large fortunes but oddly few books, in some cases not a single one. Finds of preserved published catalogues from the auctions of their books in the large stock of the Royal Library should have confirmed Ankarcrona's suspicions. I have searched, but not found a single one. Now, it is naturally possible that unpublished book auction catalogues were put together for these well-to-do women and men at one time. This cannot, however, be investigated, as no unpublished catalogues remain from these years. But, assuming that some of them left book collections behind, it would be an unlikely coincidence were none of the libraries to have been registered in a published catalogue.

So, even after being put to the test of source criticism, the conclusion holds, albeit conditionally: during the course of the eighteenth century, the culture of print was spread increasingly far beyond the circle of the already educated. This leads naturally to the second question, about what sort of books were common.

Estate inventories usually put book ownership under a special heading. The registers of 1751 and 1791 contain a large number of entries specified in at least some way, 123 for the former year and 285 for the latter, to be more precise. In the estate inventories of 1821, it was the reverse: most is unspecified and the number of entries few (13). In spite of the multitude of titles, the thematic variation is rather slight (the question is, moreover, whether the latter increased when the former decreased). Certainly, one finds all manner of things recorded in estate inventories: among other things, Urban Hjärne's book on ore and types of rock, Defoe's *Robinson Crusoe*, an arithmetic book or Björnståhl's travel book. And although newspapers and broadsheets were, on the whole, much too simple and cheap to be noted, even among the remains of poor people, one can nevertheless conclude with confidence that many were reached by their increasingly worldly and at times sensual 'preaching'. Nevertheless, it is the canonical handbooks which form the predominant genre, here as in so many other estate inventories from the eighteenth and nineteenth centuries.[92] Again and again, bibles and catechisms, psalm books and sermon collections are recorded. For the time being, it is difficult to say anything well-founded on the basis of the 1821 estate inventories, as scarcely a fifth of the books can here be tied to a fixed theme. Things are different when it comes to the two other years, as can be seen from Table 3.5: it has been possible to sort the majority according to subject heading. If the unspecificed part is thus excluded, it emerges that theological literature was entirely dominant in 1791 as well as in 1751. But it is just as plain that theology, in spite of its lasting dominance, declined in importance between the two points of reference.

Table 3.5 Book possession among merchants, artisans and journeymen in Stockholm in 1751, 1791 and 1821. Total number of books, percentage share of unspecified books and theology in absolute figures and per cent. Source: SSA, bou.

Year	Total	Unspecified	Unspecified %	Theology	Theology % minus unspecified
1751	588	188	31.9	348	87
1791	1343	446	33.2	691	77
1821	1051	850	81	190	94.5
Total	2982	1484	49.7	1229	82

This is trivial and interesting at the same time. Trivial and hardly surprising, as the result is familiar from other studies of this sort;[93] interesting bearing in mind the earlier gist of this study. If one looks at the development of book production during the eighteenth century, an insidious secularisation of the cultural frames of reference was in progress.[94] Judging by the changes in book ownership among merchants, artisans and journeymen, a similar displacement was taking place in the conceptual frameworks of these people. The question is therefore, once again, whether it is correct to see this process as an indication of the 'people's' de-Christianisation as well. Was the declining importance of spiritual literature among city folk an expression of a corresponding change in intellect among the common folk, corresponding in relation to the scarcely discernible process of cultural change?

It is possible, but not certain. In the first place, the unspecified part of the recorded ownership of books is so large that the impression of change runs the risk of being weakened by every new entry that can be identified. In the second place, the total number of books is based on estimates and not on precise measurements. Third, an assessment of the importance of spiritual

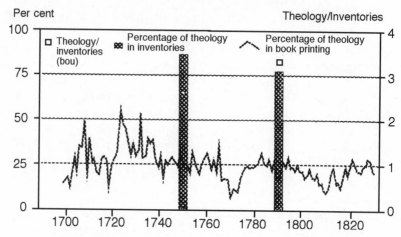

Figure 3.7 The importance of theology to Swedish book printing 1700–1829 and in estate inventories (bou) of artisans and merchants in Stockholm in 1751, 1791 and 1821. Per cent and per capita (i.e., per inventory or bou). Source: SB17; SSA, bou.

nourishment measured as theology per capita (i.e., per inventory) gives a somewhat different result, as can be seen from Figure 3.7: in 1791, the deceased in the sample left behind them an average of 3.3 volumes on religious subjects, but only 2.6 in 1751. Seen in this light, then, the Christian culture of print would seem to have achieved a broader dissemination towards the end of the eighteenth century than it had by the middle of that century. But the dead of 1821 were even more restrained, with an average of only 1.4.[95]

Yet, supported by these figure series, one could thus say, that the secularisation of culture was followed by a change in mentality – albeit with a certain displacement - in the same direction among common folk. But this would still be much too simple a conclusion, and I will shortly conclude with a discussion about what is problematic with such an interpretation. First, however, yet another sort of source-critical reliability test must be made. How is one to know that the books which are recorded in an inventory really are the evidence of the reading interests of the recently deceased owner? Could the books not just as easily have been bequeathed by long-dead relations? Are they thus not more a material and cultural legacy of the spiritual interests of bygone generations than of those who had just passed away? In short, who it was who acquired a book is not determined by its appearance in an estate inventory.

I have tried to solve the problem. The task has been to test whether the books in the estate inventories of 1791 were markedly more recent than the books of 1751. If it could be established that the book stock was renewed between two points of reference, this would speak for a younger generation having made independent book choices and not having mainly old treasures passed down. In concrete terms, the test entailed first identifying as many titles as possible, then finding corroboration in SB17 and, finally, identifying the year of publication of the original edition.[96] I have ignored theology, because canonical publications were undoubtedly read just as much, regardless of how old they were. And if the journeymen or his wife seldom, if ever, opened their old bible, they could nevertheless not help but be exposed to this spiritual material, however secularised the age had become.[97]

Of the entries whose subjects are more-or-less identified in the two stocks (123 and 285 respectively) I have succeeded in corroborating and dating the majority: 73 (59 per cent) in the estate inventories of 1751 and 183 (64 per cent) in those of 1791.[98] The series are mutually uncorrelated,[99] as the averages for the earliest conceivable years of publication deviate markedly between them. The books in the estate inventories of 1751 were, on average, printed in 1712, in the later stock in 1743. The source-critical test does not end here. As can be seen from Figure 3.8, the spread around these averages was very large (28.7 and 32 respectively). It is thus not possible to be entirely sure that the averages significantly deviate from each other, which a Mann-Whitney U-test has, however, shown that they do.[100]

The conclusion would seem to be clear: between 1751 and 1791, there was an unmistakable rejuvenation of the book stocks of middle- and lower-middle-class estates. Judging from Figure 3.9, moreover, the age distribution of the books in the estate inventories of 1791 would appear to correspond

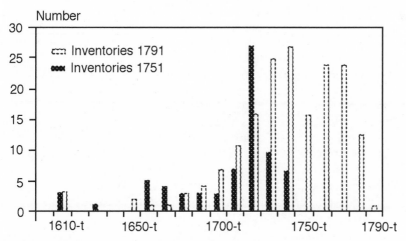

Figure 3.8 Earliest year of publication for identified titles in estate inventories (bou) of merchants, artisans and journeymen in Stockholm in 1751 and 1791.

rather closely with the quantitative variations of book production during the eighteenth century, at least from 1720. This provides support for the notion that book purchases followed book production, even if the buyers' choice of subject cannot be made to fit the pattern in the same way.

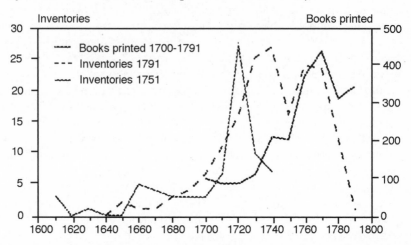

Figure 3.9 Earliest year of publication of identified titles in estate inventories (bou) of merchants, artisans and journeymen in Stockholm in 1751 and 1791 compared with book production in Sweden 1700–1791. Sources: SB17; SSA, bou 1751, 1791; Ankarcrona, s 188ff; Bring, s 180, 343; Carlsson, s 128ff; Holmberg, s 44, 596; Lext, s 282ff; Swedish men and women, del 4 s 492, del 5 s 619; Warmholtz, del 3 och 5

It might seem obvious that the test must turn out this way, as the older estate inventory stocks have an absolute time limit which the later stock can exceed by forty years. It is nevertheless possible to make the source-critical test more difficult by altering the preconditions so that the effect of the two stocks having come into being at different times is neutralised. I have done this in two ways, first by repeating the Mann-Whitney test under the simulated precondition that each book identified in the inventories of 1751 would have been published forty years after the actual years of publication. The measured difference is still significant, albeit to a somewhat lesser degree.[101] In the second modified test, all books printed after 1751 were removed from the later stock. The average publication year of the remaining books was 1722, compared with 1712 for the identified titles in the estate inventories of 1751. Once again, the concluson must be that, on this count, the material is serviceable as a source.[102]

Back to Enlightenment

I have studied some of the external features of the cultural change and at the same time have gradually worked inwards to the ideal meeting between the reader and the written work. The psychological drama which developed with the very act of reading is, however, the main topic of Chapter 6. It is thus time to pause for a moment and discuss what conclusions have been reached. The enquiry has exposed a number of different circumstances, but one is common throughout and especially interesting: the popularisation and secularisation of lettered culture in eighteenth-century Stockholm. What is now required is to bring Enlightenment and the acculturation process back into the assessment of the further and deeper meanings of the events.

To say that written culture became increasingly worldy is not the same as saying that people in general turned away from God. To be sure, the shift in the cultural frames of reference appears to have left an impression on burghers and common folk as well. But it was only now, towards the end of the century, that the Christian culture of letters achieved a really broad distribution in printed form, just when the educated élite, under the influence of Enlightenment, had already begun to gravitate away from the eternal evangelical truths. Note, however, that written culture spread more rapidly to common folk at the beginning of the eighteenth century than at the end. The road to Enlightenment was paved by a proto-enlightenment.

It has been claimed by several researchers that the bringing of literacy to the European rural and urban industrial classes by the authorities was a form of Christian acculturation. Once the farm-hand and journeyman had both learned to decipher written symbols, godlessness and other wayward notions would eventually disappear by themselves.[103] What has emerged from the studies conducted by myself and others would appear to conform to this. For, on the surface, it would seem that the acculturation process was successful, indeed perhaps particularly successful in Sweden: the vast majority learned to read well and eventually had at least some of the decreed works among their possessions.

Perhaps the authorities, or the powers-that-be, if you like, knew where they wanted to lead the people. But at the same time, the acculturation process had consequences which cannot have been intended, consequences which in one way came to confirm the fears of Voltaire and others of an overtly generous popular enlightenment.

I am convinced that the religious revival movements of the eighteenth and early nineteenth centuries can be seen as one of the unanticipated effects of the process. To put it in a somewhat speculatively generalising way, one could say that most of these revival movements distinguished themselves by having more of an orthodox than a heterodox tendency. It was in this very way that they came to irritate the high priests who laid claim to the right to interpret established doctrine. The revivalists did not generally dismiss the *Bible* as the ultimate source of truth. On the contrary, it was precisely the *letter* of the scripture they turned against those they believed were threatening the living faith: against the 'spiritually dead' clergy and against the educated élite who were charmed by science and strayed further and further away from a state of openness for spiritual experience which was considered the foundation of an enduring faith.[104] If one is looking for a typical example of this process, the literalist movement which took off in northern Sweden towards the end of the eighteenth century is a case in point.[105]

The question now is whether the strict adherence of this revival to the holy word can be associated with the contemporary spread of literacy to broad strata of the population. In time, the forward march of literacy came, admittedly, to alter fundamentally the relationship between the people and the printed word. When reading became a private matter and an act that took place in silence, a space was also created for an inner dialogue. Now, the interpretation of the holy canon could be more personal and the absolute truth of the word reduced to a relative one.[106] But in the beginning, the congregration related to the laboriously read text as it had a short while before to the spoken word; it was now, as then, a matter of imprinting these incontrovertible truths on the soul. The difference was, however, an important one: now, each and every person could compare the fruits of his reading with the preaching of the minister. And this was the very place the orthodox revival originated. To be sure, the acculturation process led to many people seeing the light, but in so doing, they also obtained a weapon which could be used against those very powers which were incorporating enlightenment notions into their world view. It is thus, perhaps, possible to say that the representatives of the popular revival rejected the notions of Enlightenment. And this regardless of some of the most prominent representatives of these notions being nevertheless afraid of spreading them to the common folk.

As already mentioned, these hypotheses are speculative and call for more research. Moreover, they require more detailed analyses of the very act of reading, i.e., of the meeting between the ordinary man or woman and the growing number of materialised ideas which gradually became increasingly available to both. In Chapter 5, I will attempt such an analysis. But first, it is necessary to make a case for what is significant in the clusters of figures strewn about this chapter.

Notes

1. A. Ankarcrona, *Bud på böcker: bokauktioner i Stockholm 1782–1801*, p. 77.
2. Ibid., pp. 62–72; R. Chartier, 'Les pratiques de l'écrit', pp. 126, 135–36, 141–59; F. Furet and J. Ozouf, 'Three centuries of cultural cross-fertilization: France', p. 219.
3. W. J. Ong, *Orality and literacy: the technologizing of the word*, p. 85.
4. See Burke, *The historical anthropology of early modern Italy*, Chapter 7; Furet and Ozouf, 'Three centuries of cultural cross-fertilization', p. 217.
5. As far as this concerns the pre-reformation era the word should be 'priest'; not 'clergy-man'.
6. Ankarcrona, *Bud på böcker*, pp. 70–71; Chartier, 'Les pratiques de l'écrit', pp.147–56; Davis, *Society and culture in early modern France*, p. 201.
7. Å. Åberg, *Västerås mellan Kellgren och Onkel Adam: studier i provinsens litterära villkor och system*, p. 92, bases his scepticism about estate inventories serving as a source for popular reading habits on that fact.
8. W. J. Ong, *Orality and literacy*. See especially Chapter 4.
9. Peter Burke, *Popular culture in early modern Europe*, p. 251.
10. For example, Chartier, 'Les pratiques de l'écrit', pp. 119–21; Davis, *Society and culture in early modern France*, pp. 209–10; Houston, *Literacy in early modern Europe*, pp. 120–29; E. Le Roy Ladurie, *The peasants of Languedoc*, pp. 150, 161–64; Muchembled, *Popular culture and elite culture . . .* , pp. 282–83; M. Spufford, 'First steps in literacy: the reading and writing experiences of the humblest seventeenth-century spiritual autobiographies', p. 126; M. Vovelle, 'Le tournant des mentalités en France 1750–1789: la "sensibilité" prérévolutionnaire', pp. 609–11; M. Vovelle, *La mentalité révolutionnaire: société et mentalité sous la Révolution française*, pp. 36–38. See, however, P. Burke, *The historical anthropology of early modern Italy*, pp. 111f and Houston, *Literacy in early modern Europe*, pp. 48–55, for an attempt to isolate literacy through information about how many attended school in late medieval Italy and in various parts of Europe between the sixteenth and nineteenth centuries.
11. Johansson, *The history of literacy in Sweden*, p. 64. Literacy in France at the end of the eighteenth century has been estimated as being 47 per cent. On this, see R. Chartier, *The cultural origins of the French revolution*, p. 69. That there is material of an unusually high standard available in Sweden has been acknowledged by researchers throughout the world. See Burke, *The historical anthropology of early modern Italy*, p. 111; Chartier, 'Les pratiques de l'écrit', p. 120; Houston, *Literacy in early modern Europe*, p. 129.
12. Mention can be made, for example, of France, where literacy, according to R. Chartier, *The cultural origins of the French revolution*, p. 69, rose between the end of the seventeenth and end of the eighteenth century from 14 to 27 per cent for women and from 29 to 47 per cent for men.
13. See for example Sahlin, *Författarrollens förändring . . .* , p. 45; Å. Åberg, *Västerås mellan Kellgren och Onkel Adam: studier i provinsens litterära villkor och system*, pp. 17–23.
14. Darnton, *The Great Cat Massacre*, p. 7. See also Houston, *Literacy in early modern Europe*, pp. 116–20 (but this concerns literacy research).
15. Darnton, *The literary underground . . .* , p. 12 and Chapter 6; Robert Darnton, *The forbidden best-sellers of pre-revolutionary France*, p. 210.
16. Two markedly topical examples from different areas are, in my view, J. Delumeau, *Sin and fear: the emergence of a Western guilt culture 13th–18th centuries* and K. Thomas, *Man and the natural world: changing attitudes in England 1500–1800*. Both have as their points of departure the doctrines in contemporary writings in the analysis of the development of morals in medieval France and the view of nature between *c*.1500 and 1800 in

England. A Swedish example is M. Nyman, *Press mot friheten: opinionsbildning i de svenska tidningarna och åsiktsbrytningar om minoriteter 1772–1786*, p. 126, who maintains that the view of Jews in the late eighteenth-century Swedish daily press reflects the mentality of its readership. The argument is that the newspapers wrote about what 'the readers had a need to be informed of'. It should, however, be said that Nyman is also influenced by Darnton and that he is conscious of the problem of representativity in this case (pp. 30, 59, 127).

17. See R. Chartier, 'Intellectual history or sociocultural history? The French trajectories', p. 43; R. Chartier, 'Text, symbols and Frenchness', p. 682; R. Chartier, *The culture of print: power and uses of print in early modern Europe*, p. 171; R. Darnton, 'The symbolic element in history', pp. 218–34; *The Great Cat Massacre*, pp. 10–11, 298–304; C. Ginzburg, *Ledtrådar: essäer om konst, förbjuden kunskap och dold historia*, pp. 24, 38–39. See also L. Hunt (ed.), *The new cultural history*, p. 7.

18. Gunilla Jonsson, head of reference at the Royal Library in Stockholm, has played a major role in the bibliography's coming into being. I am very grateful to her for the help she has given me in the use of the bibliography.

19. Partial measurements of certain aspects of the book production of the eighteenth century have been made before. See, for example, Heckscher, *Sveriges ekonomiska historia* ..., pp. 812–26.

20. SB17, *Användarhandbok* 1, pp. 2–3. The entries include everything from books in the real sense of the word to single-page publications. In SB17, all of these have been called books (*böcker*).

21. Conversations with the economic historian Lars Ekdahl and literary historian Gunnar Sahlin. Examples of scattered information on print-runs are E. Bollerup, 'Om franska inflytelser på svensk historieskrivning under frihetstiden', p. 245 n. 3; S. Lindroth, *Vetenskapsakademiens historia I:2*, p. 848. See also *Dialogues: English and Swedish*, p. 29. Five hundred is thought to have been the standard edition in the seventeenth century too. On this, see S. G. Lindberg, '500 år av svensk bokproduktion-och biblioteken', pp. 78–79.

22. L. Näslund, *Studier om importen av utländsk politisk litteratur under frihetstiden*, p. 6 singles out two types: book catalogues of different sorts (lists of books [*bokförteckningar*], for example catalogues of book auctions and estate inventories) and accounts of book purchases. Darnton, *The Literary Underground* ... has used book orders from Société typographique de Neuchâtel (found in Neuchâtel) as material for the analysis of the illegal import of books into France. See, for example, Chapters 3 and 5.

23. B. Åhlén, *Ord mot ordningen: farliga skrifter, bokbål och kättarprocesser i svensk censurhistoria*, p. 102. Research has long shown that the public debate took off at this time. See, for example, E. F. Heckscher, *Sveriges ekonomiska historia från Gustav Vasa II: 1*, pp. 817–19.

24. Ibid., pp. 87f, 211.

25. Ibid., pp. 114–66.

26. Lönnroth, *Den stora rollen*, pp. 252–61.

27. Åhlén, *Ord mot ordningen: farliga skrifter, bokbål och kättarprocesser i svensk censurhistoria*, p. 140.

28. Bergfeldt, 'Utländska nyheter från Paris', pp. 18–22. See Nyman, 'News from France in a Swedish provincial paper ...', pp. 35–41 for figures on the growth of the periodical press during the end of the eighteenth century. To avoid the authorities printed pamphlets were sometimes replaced by handwritten ones. On this, see Staf, *Polisväsendet i Stockholm*, p. 165.

29. But not every year. In 1800, for example, 142 volumes of fiction were produced but only 93 of religion and theology.

30. It is, naturally, debatable how the figures for book production are to be interpreted. The same conclusions have, however, been drawn in similar investigations pertaining to Paris. See Chartier, *The cultural origins of the French revolution*, pp. 70–71. Compared with other empirically-based secularisation theses, moreover, mine and Chartier's are based on more direct observations than is usually the case. See, for example, M. Vovelle, *La mentalité révolutionnaire: société et mentalité sous la Révolution française*, pp. 43–52, which is based on the decline in eighteenth-century Provençal wills including requests for reading masses for the dead. For a cautious critique of this interpretation, see R. Hagen, 'Historien om mentaliteterna', p. 10.

31. It is more difficult to establish which were the dominating tendencies in the academic environment. It is, however, quite clear that the 'material' subjects were growing in importance. On this see S. E. Liedman, *Den synliga handen: Anders Berch och ekonomiämnena vid 1700-talets svenska universitet*, pp. 62–80; Lindroth, *Svensk lärdomshistoria: frihetstiden*, p. 17. Academic theses have not been included in SB17 and, had they been, would presumably have nonetheless increased the amount of theology in Swedish book production. But it is not certain that the tendencies would in that way be displaced. Furthermore, the academic literature is less interesting as an indicator of changes in intellect among the burghers and ordinary folk.

32. R_{xy} for the connection between theology's share and the date is -0.39, $p = 0.01$.

33. M. Jersild, *Skillingtryck: studier i svensk folklig vissång före 1800*, pp. 1, 47, 69.

34. It is also clear that Stockholm's share of all Swedish letterpress printing was greatest when the difference was least between theology's share of letterpress printing in Stockholm and in the country as a whole.

35. This observation has also been made by G. Jonsson, 'N M Lindh i Örebro: 1798–1829 sedd genom Sveriges bibliografi 1700–1829', pp. 134–37. This concerns only one particular printer, however: N. M. Lindh's in Örebro.

36. See the preceding discussion. It seems, however, that the process was on the way even during the seventeenth century, although it is more unclear. See J. Svensson, *Kommunikationshistoria: om kommunikationsmiljön i Sverige under fem sekler*, p. 55.

37. Jonsson, 'N M Lindh i Örebro . . .', p. 135.

38. Ong, *Orality and literacy*, p. 122.

39. Chartier, *The culture of print*, p.162.

40. Ankarcrona, *Bud på böcker*, p. 135.

41. Somewhat approximately, it can be said that the concepts of folio, quarto, octavo and duodecimo indicate the format of the books, with the folio volumes being the largest and the duodecimo volumes the smallest. More precisely, the folio volume was a book with each sheet of paper folded once only and which consequently consisted of four pages, while the sheets of the quarto volume were folded twice and contained eight pages and so on. As the size of the sheet could vary, however, the size of the book was not entirely given by choice of 'format', even if this did not change much.

42. Conversation with Gunilla Jonsson, Royal Library.

43. Jersild, *Skillingtryck*, pp. 1, 47, 69.

44. Lindroth, *Svensk lärdomshistoria: frihetstiden*, pp. 325–26.

45. Nyman, *Press mot friheten*, pp. 35–49.

46. R_{xy} is -0.48, which suggests an even stronger negative connection between theology and year than when it comes to book production as a whole.

47. A survey of the theological duodecimo publications in Swedish including and excluding the canonical scripts (bibles, new testaments, catechisms, psalters books, gospels and sermons for the dead) has been made for every tenth year beginning in 1700.

48. For example, Åberg, *Västerås mellan Kellgren och Onkel Adam*, pp. 93ff.

49. Darnton, *The Literary Underground* ...; Ankarcrona, *Bud på böcker*; Nyman, *Press mot friheten*, pp. 78–81; R. Qvarsell, *Kulturmiljö och idéspridning: id'debatt, bokspridning och sällskapsliv kring 1800-talets mitt*, pp. 93–134; B. Petersson, 'Vad läste sundsvallsbon på 1840-talet?'; Sahlin, *Författarrollens förändring* ..., pp. 47–51; Åberg, *Västerås mellan Kellgren och Onkel Adam*, pp. 58–60, 76–80. Researchers in this area are acutely conscious of the complications. Qvarsell, for example (p. 104), has questioned the relevance of studies of book advertisements, and B. Petersson (p. 234, n. 1), has replied.

50. The source values of the book auctions have been previously emphasised, for example by Lindroth, *Svensk lärdomshistoria: gustavianska tiden*, p. 273, but it was not until Ankarcrona that they became the object of systematic and quantitative studies. On this see also Ankarcrona, *Bud på böcker*, pp. 73–78.

51. Ankarcrona, *Bud på böcker*, pp. 78–83. There are lists of books on offer again from 1831 onwards, which is obviously a period that did not interest Ankarcrona. Moreover, in order to identify the titles of books sold in years for which the lists of books on offer are missing, it is possible to combine the records with the auction catalogues over individual collections. These catalogues can be found in the Royal Library (but are unlisted). This is, however, time-consuming work. *SSA*, Stockholm book auction room, register of records and lists of books on offer.

52. To be more precise, 608 transactions and 847 titles. Ibid., pp. 97, 112. The difference between the number of lists of books on offer and titles is due to the possibility of the former containing more than one title. The results reported below all refer to the selection, not to the entire population.

53. Ibid., pp. 139–40 also compares her results with SB17, but has missed the difference on the matter of political literature. The difference is, however, partly deceptive, as a good 30 per cent of the political literature was produced in the years 1766–72, according to SB17.

54. Ibid., p. 135.

55. Ibid., p. 130.

56. Ibid., pp.147–49.

57. *SSA*, the Stockholm book auction room, protocol 1801–22. I would like to express my thanks to Solveig Hollari, who has made most of the excerpts.

58. *SSA*, records of the parish catechetical meetings 1819–21; M. Björkman, *Läsarnas nöje: kommersiella lånbibliotek i Stockholm 1783–1809*, p. 151.

59. Ankarcrona, *Bud på böcker*, p. 151.

60. Ibid., p. 143.

61. Ibid., pp. 284–88. In a similar way, a shift occurred from German and Latin to Swedish and French.

62. Ibid., p. 149. 43 of 303 buyers were anonymous, i.e., 14.19 per cent.

63. As far as Sweden is concerned, see A. Carlsson, *Böcker i bohuslänska bouppteckningar 1752–1808*, p. 34; G. Lext, *Bok och samhälle i Göteborg 1720–1809*, p. 221; Qvarsell, *Kulturmiljö och idéspridning*, p. 127. For the rest of Europe see for example P. Benedict, 'Bibliothèques protestantes et catholiques à Metz au xvie siècle' (on Metz in France in the seventeenth century), p. 349; Chartier, 'Les pratiques de l'écrit', p. 133.

64. Ankarcrona, *Bud på böcker*, p. 114.

65. Ibid, pp. 159–60. See also pp. 121–22 where in a similar way she compares her results with those of Lext on the matter of the distribution of languages among the books, albeit once again with the rider that the results are not actually comparable.

66. Ibid., p. 143.

67. If the state of affairs is as Ankarcrona says, it is naturally quite right that the studies of estate inventories give a distorted picture of book ownership. At the same time, ordin-

THE CULTURE OF LETTERS

ary people seldom offered their book collections for sale at auctions, as her own results confirm.

68. In most of them, the books are sorted so that the folio volumes come first and the duodecimo last. In other words, they are not sorted according to subject, which provides problems but also the freedom to sort according to one's own criteria. Printed book auction catalogues from the entire kingdom from the end of the seventeenth century up to the present can be found collected at the Royal Library. They are arranged according to year, but unfortunately are uncatalogued. Individual catalogues are to be found in parish and district libraries throughout Sweden.

69. Henrik Grönroos, *Boleen i Finland . . .*

70. *Bokauktionskataloger* from 1825; *Förteckning på Johan Hjerpes boksamling.*

71. *Bokauktionskatalog* after the Dean of Skara, Lev Olber and Uppsala for the ironworks doctor Anders Brusin.

72. See Åberg, *Västerås mellan Kellgren och Onkel Adam*, pp.92–93; Qvarsell, *Kulturmiljö och idéspridning*, pp. 124–26. This also emerges in conversations with sociologists of literature.

73. G. Qvist, 'Om bouppteckningar och deras bokbeståndsuppgifter som historiskt källmaterial'; Ankarcrona, *Bud på böcker*, p. 76; Åberg, *Västerås mellan Kellgren och Onkel Adam*, p. 92.

74. For example, C. Ahlberger, *Vävarfolket: hemindustrin i Mark 1790–1850*, pp. 150, 164. See H. Sanders, *Svensk forskning om den religöse väkkelse 1800–1850 problematiseret af dansk forskning om samme emne*, p. 20.

75. See, for example, P. Benedict, 'Bibliothèques protestantes et catholiques . . .', pp. 344–46; Chartier, 'Les pratiques de l'écrit', p. 129; Houston, *Literacy in early modern Europe*, pp. 187–97. There is a certain consciousness here of the complications with the studies of estate inventories, but the comments relating to the criticism of sources are much more limited than in Qvist.

76. Lext, *Bok och samhälle i Göteborg . . .*, p. 200.

77. Ibid., p. 205.

78. For example C.-J. Gadd, *Järn och potatis: jordbruk, teknik och social omvandling i Skaraborgs län 1750–1860*, pp. 53–73; J. Kuuse, *Från redskap till maskiner: mekaniseringsspridning och kommersialisering inom svenskt jordbruk 1860–1910*, pp. 21–30; G. Peterson, *Jordbrukets omvandling i västra Östergötland 1810–1890.*

79. He was born after the first year of the cross-section and died after the last. The justification for this displacement is, in part, that I would like to use the results of the starting year as a sort of cultural precondition for Hjerpe, and partly that the last year of the cross-section was also Hjerpe's last year in the capital. There is also much to suggest that by then he had written most of what has been preserved from his pen. More on this in Chapter 5.

80. *SSA*, estate inventories (subsequently abbreviated to Bou) 1751, 1791 and 1821.

81. According to the *Statistisk årsbok för Stockholms stad 1905*, p. 66, the absolute death figures for 1751, 1791 and 1821 were 2,735, 3,764 and 2,964 respectively. Variations in the general death figures can be found in U. Jonsson, *Mortality patterns in 18th century Stockholm in a European perspective*, p. 2.

82. *SSA*, Bou 1751, 1791, 1821; Jonsson, *Mortality patterns in 18th century Stockholm in a European perspective*, p. 2; *Statistisk årsbok . . .*, p. 66. The general mortality figures in Stockholm were, for the three years, 45.2, 53.9 and 39.1 per thousand respectively. Like the number of estate inventories, the mortality figures were 20 per cent lower in 1821 than in 1791.

83. Boëthius, *Magistraten och borgerskapet . . .*, p. 441; Söderlund, *Stockholms hantverkarklass,*

p. 316; Söderlund, *Hantverkarna 2*, p. 86. One additional test has been made, a random sample. The record of deaths for the Jakob and Johannes parishes in 1751 has been examined, and the proportion of deceased merchants, master artisans and journeymen has been calculated. Because they comprised scarcely 30 per cent of the record of deaths, they would appear to have been over-represented in the Bou material. See *SSA*, Jakob and Johannes parishes, record of deaths. I would like to thank Samuel Jarrick for having done the excerpt work.

84. Book ownership would seem to have been greater in Stockholm than in Paris, even if the direction of change was the same in both cities. See Chartier, *The cultural origins of the French revolution*, p. 69.

85. *SSA*, Bou for 1751, 1791 and 1821. In the Bou of 1821, only 11 different titles are mentioned (apart from some arithmetic and language handbooks). In the Bou of 1751, over 123 different entries were recorded, and for 1791 the corresponding figure is 285. These figures contain a few incompletely specified entries, however.

86. *SSA*, Bou of 1751, 1791 and 1821. When the Bou does not indicate the exact number of books, I have made estimations according to a scheme which systematically underestimates the number of books. The figures are thus on the low side. The following table shows the number of books per capita; the distribution is measured as standard deviation and maximum notation for the number of titles, respectively. Only a very few had enough books to lead one to suspect a collection. The peak of 1821 can be traced to a book printer and probably refers to a store rather than a collection.

Year	Books/capita	s (standard deviation)	maximum number
1751	3.5	5.9	34
1791	5.9	12.8	128
1821	7.0	23.6	255

87. Söderlund, *Stockholms hantverkarklass*, pp. 281–82.

88. Söderlund, *Stockholms hantverkarklass*, p. 150. Söderlund was critical of the estate inventories (Bou) as a source for the assessment of people's economic situation.

89. The intention was to select every tenth Bou. 61 people represent something more than 10 per cent of the entire sample.

90. That the connection is significant at a certain level means that the risk of these connections being coincidental is as slight or less than that which the level indicates. The larger the population, i.e., the greater the number of observations included, the greater is the probability that a random distribution will not yield any connection at all. That the connections which have been found could be entirely random in spite of connection and randomness being likely to be mutually exclusive has to do with the relative smallness of the investigated population (or, put differently, with the number of observations being few). If, for example, one throws a dice ten times and ends up with sixes nine times, it is usually possible (if the dice is not loaded) to assume that this skewed distribution (the connection) is due to chance. Because, if one continues to throw the dice, the skewed distribution will eventually cease. The connection I found could also be random, i.e., have to do with the distinctive qualities of the people I have happened to investigate, and thus not reflect a real distribution. But the significance measure says that this risk is small, one and five per cent respectively.

91. *SSA*, Bou 1751, 1791 and 1821; register of taxpayers. The income information in the register of taxpayers applies to the years 1735, 1750, 1765, 1775, 1785, 1786, 1787 and 1815. The amounts have been recounted in Swedish Riksdaler specie on the basis of Jörberg, p. 81. R_{xy} between the gross and net balance in the random sample was 0.73, which is very close to the situation for the sample as a whole. See Table 4.

92. Carlsson, *Böcker i bohuslänska bouppteckningar . . .* , p. 36a; Lext, *Bok och samhälle i Göteborg . . .* , p. 221; Qvarsell, *Kulturmiljö och idéspridning*, p. 127.
93. For example Lext, *Bok och samhälle i Göteborg . . .* , p. 221.
94. It had, perhaps, been on the way even during the seventeenth century. See Svensson, *Kommunikationshistoria*, p. 55.
95. *SSA*, Bou 1751, 1791 and 1821. Here I have risked making a comparison with the estate inventories of 1821, as I am convinced that the unspecified literature was more often non-religious than religious. Standard deviation for the three stocks was modest: 4, 5, 7, 3, and 2 respectively.
96. I have looked for the earliest conceivable year of publication regardless of when it is likely that the owner acquired the book. In this way, the age of the book will be over estimated, which makes it more difficult for the material to pass the source-critical test.
97. There is also an insurmountable documentation problem here, of course. The Bou often indicates simply 'bible' or 'an old bible', for example, which makes it impossible to date the particular copy. Established spiritual literature was continually published in new editions.
98. If one calculates instead on the basis of the number of books those identified represent and adds the canonical figures, the degree of coverage is still almost the same: 57 and 61 per cent respectively.
99. R_{xy} was -0.16, r_{xy} was -0.12. None of the connections were significant.
100. $p = 0.00$.
101. $p = 0.017$.
102. A number of additional tests of source criticism would need to be made, first of the relation between stock-takers and the occurrence of books in the Bou, second of the difference in the time between the time of death and the completed Bou, third of the relation between the income circumstances for the sample and the entire group of people practising a given profession in the different cross-section years and, fourth, of the age distribution of the heirs (testators). This remains to be done.
103. See Burke, *Popular culture . . .* , pp. 252–53; Johansson, *The history of literacy in Sweden*, pp. 18–22; Muchembled, *Popular culture and elite culture . . .* , pp. 262, 270, 282–83, 289, 294–95.
104. See, for example, Jarrick, *Den himmelske älskaren: hermhutisk väckelse, vantro och sekularisering i 1700-talets Sverige*, pp. 42 and 49; H. Sanders, *Den gudelige vækkelse på Langeland 1837–39*, pp. 53 and 62. There were, naturally, movements which emphasised the inner word more than the outer, including certain branches of pietism, not least so-called dippelianism. On this, see Jarrick, *Den himmelske älskaren*, pp. 27 and 34. These flourished, however, above all from the beginning of the seventeenth century and up until the beginning of the eighteenth century, i.e., before the general spread of literacy.
105. J. Holmgren, *Norrlandsläseriet . . .*
106. See Chartier, 'Les pratiques de l'écrit', pp. 126–28; Furet and Ozouf, 'Three centuries of cultural cross-fertilization', p. 219.

Chapter 4
New cultural history
and old history of mentalities

In the preceding chapter, I tried to build up a picture of a certain change in mentality among merchants and artisans in eighteenth-century Stockholm. The picture that emerged demonstrated that a shift was taking place in the cultural frames of reference. But because the change was very slow, it must have been difficult for those involved to notice it, however much they themselves contributed to it. In time, however, its effects became evident to all, and it is conceivable that, in retrospect, the change can be registered with the help of statistics, for instance.

But can it? What do quantitative series say about the way in which human thought changes with the passage of time? Nothing, some would say – for example, the French historian Roger Chartier and several of the other advocates of *a new cultural history*. They would be doing so in the face of the tradition from which they themselves have come, the French *Annales* school, which has always lauded *histoire sérielle* as the easy road to discerning gradual changes which have an enduring, long-term effect on society.

Those who resist the a priori assumption that the old is already *passé* would be wise to listen to what these opponents have to say. Because if renewal really is necessary, the structure which was erected in the preceding chapter will topple; if not, it may topple anyway, but for other reasons.

What is new about new cultural history

In the spring of 1987, a group of historians from the old and new world gathered at a conference in California on the subject of a new cultural history. According to the programmatic contributions to the conference report which was subsequently published, this 'new' is not simply an alternative to old cultural history, but also research into the mentalities, which is considered obsolete.[1]

For Swedish historians it is, perhaps, surprising that research on mentalities is already considered *passé*, as it has only just reached here.[2] But in other countries, the critical discussion has been under way for quite a while, and the conference on new cultural history may indeed be seen as a natural first culmination in this exchange of views.[3]

From one perspective, what has been hailed as new cultural history is simply a renewed interest in something old within historical research: human thought. Also, the word culture comes up increasingly often in historians' studies of the past, either as an addition to or substitution for the concepts social and intellectual. The new-old word has inspired empirical research on areas of life which have long been neglected.[4]

What is new, though, is not mainly long-forgotten themes being born again, but current cultural historical research being in some way fundamentally different from the old. According to its advocates, cultural history research is no longer about materialised thought in itself, art and literature. Nor is interest chiefly focused on recurrent features of the manner in which people pick up the intellectual content of cultural artefacts. Often – but not always – it is even denied that quantifiable patterns can be discerned at all. The object instead is to study the personally unique way in which particular individuals have actively appropriated texts, pictures and other messages. Roger Chartier is perhaps the leading advocate of this sort of individualising cultural research, and it is thus only natural that the contributions in a recent anthology on cultural history mostly deal with particulars: one work, one author, one reader, and so on.[5]

One can ask why the new current continues to drag with it the old word when it would seem to have let go of most of its established contents. The answer is that a connection can be discerned between the new and the old, particularly in the most far-reaching renewal à la Chartier. The connection is barely stated, but it can be reconstructed. The constant thread is the notion that man is a cultural creature, as he not only labours away but is also incessantly preoccupied with reflection on his own predicament. Traditional cultural history has studied the more brilliant symbolic expressions of self-reflection, above all the unique work or the great scientific notion. New cultural historians have finally discovered that this intellectual activity is to be found wherever people are active. But they go further than this. In an anthropological spirit, they claim that every context of life can be treated as a text in which a sub-text is to be sought.[6]

Cultural artefacts and great thinkers or artists lose their unique position with the new current, and each person – from philosopher to artisan – becomes worthy of study. But this is not just a consequence of an extended definition of culture; it is also related to the idiographic notion that each individual assimilates materialised thought in his own way. By focusing on the symbolic aspects of human life and by emphasising the unique, an old tradition of cultural history research is carried on, a tradition which is also surpassed, in that the unique is no longer located in the work, but rather in the person who makes use of it.

But because new cultural historians refrain from any attempted post-modern dismantling of the individual identity, they are nevertheless rather reminiscent of traditional hermeneutists. Faithful to a sort of individualistic holism, the hermeneutists - like the new cultural historians – come to a halt in front of the unique person, and on that basis they also dismiss every attempt to measure the expansion of certain mentalities.

The Swedish scholar of religion, Hans Åkerberg, is an advocate of this sort of fundamental hermeneutics.[7] His view is that particular individuals can only be understood as unique, and the human researcher must therefore work with qualitative material when he goes around in the hermeneutic circle or spiral. According to Åkerberg, qualitative information is the sort which has come into being without the involvement of a researcher, while quantitative material has come into being at the initiative of the researcher following some sort of specified pattern. The implications are obvious: insights guided by the researcher can be broken down into measurable quantities more easily than others. But such operations would be a violation of the notion of the distinctive nature of each individual, a deviation from classical hermeneutics. It is not possible to interpret and count simultaneously, for that would be both to believe and not believe that man is bound by incorruptible laws, according to Åkerberg.[8]

Cultural historians of the new persuasion naturally do not behave like a unified body, but quarrel amongst themselves just as energetically as other scholars. The conflicts have been above all about two issues. One of these has to do with with the unique itself or, vice versa, the extent to which it is possible to talk about collective symbolic structures. In his cultural history studies of France in the age of Enlightenment, Robert Darnton has tried to identify such structures. Thus, for example, Darnton relates the juicy story about a group of Parisian artisan journeymen who executed all the cats in the neighbourhood, including their mistress's little pet. This bizarre event is attributed several symbolic meanings, common to the entire group, among other things, a ritual sexual violation of both the master and his wife.[9] Like a number of other researchers,[10] Roger Chartier has subjected Darnton to a rather caustic critique and, as expected, objected to the implicit generalising features of his interpretation. According to Chartier, it is not possible to know whether all the journeymen saw the cat massacre and their own participation in it in the same way. The criticism has triggered an exchange of words between the two historians, with Darnton seeking support from anthropologists and Chartier referring back to classical sociology and to modern, or rather post-modern, literary theory.[11]

The other contested issue concerns folk culture, a favourite theme of social history research, but also a concept which has been increasingly questioned. Here, too, Chartier has played the role of leading critic. At the same time, it seems clear that he has himself been inspired by research on folk culture. Chartier's interest in the anonymous individual can without doubt be seen as emanating from the popular focus of social history research. I will soon comment on the critique, but first take a look at the research with which he and his supporters have found fault. This research has already been mentioned several times, most recently in Chapter 3, and it will be discussed again later, in Chapter 6. No lengthy expositions are required at this point, then.

As already mentioned, a number of scholars have, in recent years, claimed that a distinctive and independent folk culture existed in early modern Europe. They have also sought to demonstrate how the lay and clerical élite attempted to reform, discipline or repress folk culture with the help of the power of the absolute monarch. An important aspect of this acculturation process was the attempt to distinguish the profane aspects of life from the religious or ecclesiastical. The reformers also sought to force the superstitious and other pre-Christian elements out of popular belief, and this attempt was noticeable not only in the countries of the Lutheran reformation but also in those countries in which the counter-reformation came out on top.[12]

That the intellectual élite was gravitating towards the temporal at that time did not stop it from finding it difficult to put up with the 'primitive' heterodox variety which prevailed among peasants and artisans. But in spite of disciplining efforts, official culture was not easily spread to common folk. The congregations in the Europe of the new epoch attempted, for a long time, to withstand the spiritual influences from the authorities, who pressed them hard with the true faith, but at the same time withdrew from ritual occasions – carnivals, for example – which had previously been a common social sphere for all social classes.[13] In several cultural history studies or studies of the history of mentalities it has emerged that people remoulded the élite culture which reached them: it was filtered through a folk culture which was, in certain respects, independent, something into which I will go in more detail in the next chapter. Nevertheless, it would seem clear that ultimately they gave in to outside pressure. The struggle culminated in the eruption of witch trials throughout Europe, with confrontations which ultimately sealed the fate of folk culture.[14]

But as I tried to show in the last chapter, the outcome of the Christian acculturation process was not the society of disciplined or impulse-controlled people which some of the upper classes desired. Its spiritual result was division rather than unity: continued half-Christian irreverence combined with newly aroused fundamentalism, but eventually more of secularised disbelief than ordered belief.

The process of secularisation has been observed by many, but the *Annales* historian Michel Vovelle has, perhaps, distinguished himself in the area with his comprehensive attempt to capture the process with quantitative methods. He deserves to be mentioned in this context, as he is a typical example of the research into the intellect from which the advocates of new cultural history have sought to distance themselves.[15]

There is, of course, much more to be said about the results of research into popular cultural history, and the savagely concentrated summary which I have just given cannot do justice to the nuances and differences of opinion which characterise this, as other, areas of research.[16] One of many contentious issues has been the concept of mentality. It has been rejected by several researchers who have chosen to use the concept of folk culture in its stead. One of the reasons for this, as I have already suggested, is that the concept of mentality is considered to be a consensus term, i.e., a term which designates that which is common and enduring in a culture. It would thus not be of use in the historical analysis of all the vertical group and class conflicts which marked the spiritually varied acculturation process.[17]

The new cultural history's critique of the old

Chartier and the other opponents attach little importance to the dissension within research on folk culture. When they attack research into mentalities, it is for failings of a different sort.

What is special about society is that the interaction between people is symbolic to such a great degree. The claim is an old one, has been repeated by many and by now lacks all freshness. But it can nevertheless be true, and has again become topical after Marxism's *Sturm und Drang* period. It has been used, among other things, as a formula for dissolving the dichotomy between base and superstructure, and is once again (or still) a guide to many influential researchers. Anthony Giddens and Jürgen Habermas, for example, maintain from such a point of departure that the human sciences must be *doubly hermeneutical* because, compared to the natural sciences, they are occupied with the interpretation of a world which has already been interpreted.[18]

A number of the advocates of the new cultural history have pushed this thesis further in an 'idealistic' direction. Among these, Roger Chartier and Lynn Hunt have perhaps been particularly prominent. If the human world is symbolic, it is not possible to distinguish separate levels in social life. Economy as politics, culture as mentality, both base and superstructure are themselves intellectually constituted, and therefore cannot have any independent 'material' existence. The criticism has been raised in particular against *Annales* historians who localise mentalities on a 'third level', but at the same time stand generally against all aspirations to detach the material from the symbolic.[19] In retrospective analyses it is increasingly frequently said that research into mentalities represents both the third generation of the *Annales* school and *histoire sérielle* (roughly quantitative history) and the third level (*troisième niveau*).[20] In other words, research into mentalities is thought to be the third stage in a three-stage project, i.e., in a way just the top of what is actually an economic history research programme. The characterisation is based on the historical notion that the research of the *Annales* school has been driven by a programme modelled on Fernand Braudel's trisection of society, with politics and rapid developments uppermost. Stationary structures were to be studied first, followed by long-term cyclical changes and, finally, politics.[21] It is possible to get the feeling that there is a programmatic subtext in this critique, a more or less veiled *plaidoyer* for culture or the symbolic world as the ultimate determinant.

Now, the symbolic world – as mentioned – need not be a collectively shared world, as the quantifying historians on intellect conceive of it *according to their critics*. The emphasis on quantitative studies in itself is thought to be an indication of such a position. Moreover, these working methods are thought to follow logically from the assumptions of research on mentalities. If people's attitudes can be placed at a particular level and, in turn, *can be traced back* to another 'social' or 'material' level, the climate for example, it is probable that these attitudes are common or collective to the same extent that primary experiences are. The task is thus to reconstruct such thoughts and customs which are to be found among the masses and which can be brought together in all-embracing categories. The consequence of this is that the individual has a voice only as a number in a statistical presentation. He is reduced in that way to a case, to an impersonal part of overlapping social processes of change such as secularisation, increased tolerance, disciplining and so on.

The advocates of new cultural history raise objections of a historical-philosophical rather than sentimental nature to quantitative mentality research, even if they do not entirely dismiss the value of statistics as an analytical sorting instrument. A central notion is that symbolic structures have short ranges both socially and over time. In my account of the exchange of views between Chartier and Darnton, I have already mentioned the spatial or inter-human limitations of symbols and will not develop the theme further. But apart from that, it is claimed that historical development cannot be described in macro terms related to culture or mentality (such as secularisation, for example), as these are continually recoded. It is not possible to say, for example, that the people of today are saner than those of yesteryear, as the meaning of the concept is as fluid as time. This idea is familiar from Michel Foucault and modern or post-modern literary theory, but the influences from these quarters are also open and acknowledged by the advocates of the new movement.[22]

The new cultural history critique can seem theoretically untraceable. But this perspective has also served as the basis for empirical complaints about some of the results of research on the history of folk culture. The discussion concerned the cultural effects of the continual spread of the printed word in early modern Europe.

After Gutenberg, wider circles of people were afforded the opportunity of personal encounters with distinctive texts, and the spoken word slowly became relatively less important. The world of spiritual experience was changed in a very decisive way, 'since what movable type and the printing press produced was not reserved (. . .) for the administrative use of the ruler but penetrated the entire web of social relations, bore thoughts and brought pleasures and lodged in people's deepest self as well as claiming its place in the public scene'.[23]

Researchers of the new movement have shown a special interest in the act of reading. The acculturation process entailed the masses becoming literate, among other things.[24] Their view of what happened when the established culture of letters reached further and further beyond the circle of those already educated corresponds, in part, with the results which Carlo Ginzburg and other folk culture historians have reached. Both dismiss the traditional view that the spread of culture was a simple top-down transmission of enhanced knowledge. They describe, instead, the reception of the printed word as an active, selective and creative appropriation, and also emphasise that influence has been exerted in both directions: from the top down and from the bottom up. But after that, views diverge.

Unlike Peter Burke, Carlo Ginzberg, Robert Muchembled and others, historians of the new movement are not particularly convinced that a delimited or independent folk culture emerged in late medieval or early modern Europe. It is impossible to identify class-specific cultures or collective mentalities, they argue. The task is, instead, to try and identify the individual variety in use in a common culture. Furthermore, they dismiss the notion that there could be a simple connection between the distribution of material and cultural resources, a notion which is implicit in many studies of folk culture.

Although new cultural history recognises the study of the unique or the particular, the discussion is more often conducted in principle than in empirical terms. For example, it is never really made clear what is meant by people making different use of a common culture, and as yet, no one has demonstrated empirically that material resources were distributed differently from cultural ones. The discussion produces a number of concrete associations, however; it is possible to get some idea of what the innovators are looking for. Let me give an example.

There is much to suggest that people – of both higher and lower status – long believed that what they dreamed at night really did happen, although in a spiritual and not in a physical sense. The sleeper did not just lie there in his bed and dream: it was thought that the soul really was able to go off on adventures of its own when the house was swathed in sleep. This was still how people imagined it to be in the seventeenth century, or in the Baroque era, to use the traditional cultural historical designation. But does this not reek of the mentality? No, because even if these notions represented a collective cultural legacy, the point is that people made use of this legacy in very different ways. Compare, for example, the Mexican nun Sor Juana with the witch from Spanish Navarra: while Sor Juana's soul rose to heaven each night, the spirit of the witch left through a hole in the wall for a carnal meeting with the devil. In the one case, it concerned liberation from bodily demands, in the other with their satisfaction. But these dream conceptions can also be linked to a symbolic structure which was common to both.[25]

This is my image of new cultural history. But if its advocates are right about each individual having his own legitimate manner of reading, it is not possible to determine whether I have understood or misunderstood them. A text constantly comes into existence in the meeting between new and old readers. When I now move on to defending quantitative mentality research against the critical view just presented, I do so on the basis of my (by definition) special way of grasping it. Nevertheless, one need not doubt that the measurements made in the preceding chapter can serve as an example of the sort of research which new cultural history dislikes.

Criticism of the critique

The new orientation has furnished research on the history of culture and mentalities with a number of interesting questions, and suggested answers which it can be productive to test. This applies in particular to the hypothesis of the significance of the silent act of reading to the import of cultural change. But this is precisely it: the orientation is new and the hypotheses thus still largely untested. Not everything is equally productive.

To start with, Chartier and Hunt give far too simple a description of what distinguishes mentality research, and they also give a distorted picture of the history of the *Annales* school. It is not as unambiguously materialistic and quantitatively oriented as these two, mostly in a logical way, infer that it 'should' be. Certainly, a number of leading figures within the *Annales* school – among them Fernand Braudel – have considered mental structures to be derived from or 'enmeshed in' material structures. The *Annales* school, under Braudel's aegis, was indeed relatively uninterested in the mentality, but this does not apply to all, and is hardly a clearly dominating view among the *Annales* historians. Perhaps it could even be said that the newly aroused intellectual interest of the 1960s represented more a departure from Braudelian materialism than an application of it. There are many internationally acknowledged researchers into mentalities who have refrained entirely from his reductionism. Philippe Ariès, among many others, with his studies of childhood and death[26] must be included here. Mentality researchers are not a body of quantifying societal researchers, even if a number of *Annales* historians have also, during certain periods, advocated a *histoire sérielle* in the study of the history of human thought.[27] If one looks at the research into mentalities which has actually been conducted, however, the calculator Michel Vovelle can be counted as an eccentric among the impressionists.

The mentality cannot be seen as a counterpart to Braudel's *troisième niveau*, in any case not like those framed, so to speak, by the *Annales* historians. On the contrary, it would be more suitable to consider the mentality as the 'spiritual' or psychological equivalent of the first level, of the immobile structures. As such, the mentality changes only very slowly. It would be more natural instead – from a Braudelian point of departure – to link political ideologies or doctrines with the rapid course of events.

Moreover, the materialism of the old *Annales* school was not Marxist, contrary to what is often implied, even if significant impetus from Marx is evident in that materialism. For Braudel, the restrictions imposed on man by nature play a virtually decisive role in the historical process. Stagnation is his leitmotif and nature its cause. It is because of this that society remains the same and people's habits repeat themselves.[28] In Marxism's historical scenario it is movement – social change – which dominates. Nature was thus discarded in Marx's causal reasoning. Like Braudel, he found it difficult to detect anything much happening in nature.[29] But while Braudel and Marx had different views of the importance of social change, they appear to have been in agreement about the independence of thought on the material. To that extent, one must acknowledge that the fourth generation's critics of its advocates are right. The error is only that Braudel was not a particularly distinctive representative of research into mentalities. At best he devoted a few chivalrous phrases to it.[30] Those *Annales* historians who paid more comprehensive professional attention to mentalities have been, as said, less reductionist. This applies not least to Michel Vovelle who, in his study *La mentalité révolutionnaire*, adopts a very open attitude to causal connections.[31]

In their critical historiography of mentality research, the advocates of the new cultural history occasionally overlook the fact that research into mentalities was present from the very first days of the *Annales* school, and long before Braudel introduced his hypothesis about distinct parts of historical development. For Lucien Febvre, historical psychology was, moreover, the main thing, even if he tried to anchor what he called '*outillage mentaux*' in social contexts.[32] The concept of mentality itself is borrowed, from Lévy-Brühl, for example, and his evolutionist-anthropological reflections on 'primitive mentality'.[33] The fourth generation of *Annales* historians is very familiar with these historiographic circumstances, and often point to them[34] – just as often as they overlook them.

I am more than ready to agree that the naïve talk of hierarchical societal levels should be abandoned. Interaction between people is symbolic to a great degree, and society's different spheres of activity intellectually constituted. But an analytical distinction between symbolic and non-symbolic phenomena, and between different spheres of activity, could nevertheless be significant.

There are different reasons for this. First, in the earliest phases of life, human beings have a pre-symbolic relationship to the world. Second, people not only interact with each other, but also respond to signals from both the surrounding physical and inner biological worlds. A third reason has to do more specifically with the conditions of historical science. A number of conditions become apparent only in retrospect; they have never been interpreted as such until the historian tackles them on the basis of information which was not accessible to those who were directly involved. This is the case, for example, with historical demography.[35] But apart from this, it is possible to trace human activity to finds which in themselves by no means contain any interpretative messages. Piles of ashes are an example.

These comments are not intended to discriminate against 'the material', which subsequently, in a Marxist way, would be considered extremes both in cognitive theoretical terms and when it comes to the causes of historical change. Material processes take place at one and the same time in the so-called 'world' and in the man's mind, even if the actual content of his ideas must be considered immaterial. It is thus not possible to determine what should be primary in a causal sense, and neither is this what I want to discuss.

On the other hand, the argument is relevant as a defence of a partially quantifying research into mentalities, i.e., in the attempt to identify thoughts which are not stated as ideas and which can be found in many people at the same time. A person wants one thing and does another, or does what he wants but for another reason, and not because he wants to, or he does something he both wants and does not want to. How is one to know which? If it is not possible, is it not possible, either, to assume that people who act alike do so for the same reasons? What, then, becomes of research into mentalities?

Let me try again. If a thousand people, one after the other, change their habits in the same way, most of them presumably share at least some motive with the rest, even if they each give their own explanation as to why they exchanged an old way of life for a new one. It could be the case that individual motives were as effective in bringing about the change as shared ones. On the other hand, it would be strange if no common notion whatsoever occurred to all those people who suddenly began to behave in a similar way.

The occurrence of general patterns in changes of human habits thus probably betrays at least *some* meaning in change which is common. Without denying the variety of motives, it is precisely this which quantifying research into mentalities seeks, and this was what I was doing in the preceding chapter. But need such research not also seek laws for human behaviour? I think not. There is nothing necessarily deterministic in making long-dead people comparable with each other. To trace recurrent psychological patterns is not to say that those patterns are necessarily regulated by laws (although neither is it to deny that they could be). On the other hand, by using such a method, one has naturally dismantled the 'whole' which the particular individual is said to be, and that is not always right (as I shall discuss in Chapter 6). But it is right sometimes, as wholes are only to be found as the conditional patterns we ourselves impose on phenomena. In my view, there is a contradiction in claiming a holistic view while at the same time denying all entities which exceed and contain the individual. The anti-essentialism of new cultural history contains yet another curious self-contradiction. Having said that level designations are cultural creations, the implication is that it is the concept which determines the content of the concept to which it applies. If one says that individuals assign different meanings to concepts and signs, one has, however, said the opposite: that it is the different positions or the like of individuals which determine the concept. In the one case it is claimed that it is the concepts which 'inscribe' meanings in the phenomenal world, in the other that it is different experiences in the phenomenal world which inscribe a mosaic of different meanings in the concepts.

*

The advocates of the new cultural history do not entirely reject measurements of intellectual processes, although it would be consistent of them to do so. It is also possible to find in their studies numerous examples of a sort of sweeping crypto-quantification under the idiographic surface. For example, reference is often made to a 'dominant paradigm', to 'majorities' or to how 'groups' of people make use of certain cultural forms.[36] And according to their interpretation, few people seem to have escaped the relativistic consequences of the growing dissemination of the printed word in the new epoch's increasingly modernised Europe. So even if cultural historians are wary of using concepts such as 'collective symbolic structures', they would seem to have nothing against pointing out a definite direction in the course of cultural change.

Anything else would be strange for historians with scholarly ambitions.

Notes

1. L. Hunt (ed.), *The new cultural history*, 'Introduction', especially pp. 7ff.
2. A. Jarrick, 'Mentalitetshistoria-parismode eller seriös forskning?', pp. 91–95.
3. For a relatively early contribution in line with the approach of the conference, see Chartier, 'Intellectual history or sociocultural history? The French trajectories'. See also L. Hunt, 'French history in the last twenty years: the rise and fall of the *Annales*

paradigm', pp. 212–22. See also H. Coutau-Bégarie, *Le phenomène 'Nouvelle histoire'*, a caustic reply to the *Annales* school which has been partially hushed up in France. See also U. Jonsson, 'Annales-traditionen: ett paradigm i upplösning eller förnyelse?' for a summary of the criticism.

4. Leading international examples include Burke, *Popular culture* . . . ; Burke, *The historical anthropology in early modern Italy*; Chartier, 'Intellectual history or sociocultural history?'; Chartier, *Cultural history: between practices and representations*; Davis, *Society and culture in early modern France*; Darnton, *The Literary Underground* . . . ; Darnton, *The Great Cat Massacre*; C. Ginzburg, *The cheese and the worms*; Ginzburg, *Ledtrådar: essäer om konst, förbjuden kunskap och dold historia*; Muchembled, *Popular culture and elite culture* . . . ; M. Sahlins, *Kapten Cooks död*; J.-C. Schmitt, *The holy greyhound: Guinefort, healer of children since the thirteenth century*. Among Swedish historians, L. Magnusson, *Den bråkiga kulturen*; R. Ambjörnsson, *Den skötsamme arbetaren: idéer och ideal i ett norrländskt sågverkssamhälle 1880–1930* have been noted. Cultural analysis is not new to ethnologists.

5. See R. Chartier, *The culture of print: power and the uses of print in early modern Europe*. In the introductory chapter, Chartier very clearly formulates his cultural history programme.

6. About the influence of Geertz on historical-anthropological research, see A. Biersack, 'Local knowledge, local history: Geertz and beyond', pp. 72–84; N. Davis, 'Anthropology and history in the 1980s', pp. 267–75; Magnusson, *Den bråkiga kulturen*, pp. 62–63.

7. H. Åkerberg, *Hermeneutik och pedagogisk psykologi: premisser för tolkning och förståelse inom beteendevetenskap*.

8. Ibid., pp. 21, 168–69, 175–84.

9. Darnton, *The Great Cat Massacre*, pp. 36–40.

10. Dominick LaCapra, 'Chartier, Darnton, and the great symbol massacre', pp. 95–107; James Fernandez, 'Historians tell tales: of Cartesian cats and gallic cockfights', pp. 113–27.

11. Chartier, 'Text, symbols and Frenchness'; Darnton, 'The symbolic element in history'; Chartier, *Cultural history: between practices and representations*, pp. 4ff, 63; Chartier, 'Intellectual history or sociocultural history?', pp. 26ff. See also L. Hunt, 'Introduction: history, culture, and text' in *The new cultural history*, pp. 15–16.

12. This is prominent in both Burke, *Popular Culture* . . . and Muchembled, *Popular culture and elite culture* . . .

13. Prominent are Bachtin, *Rabelais and His World*, pp. 33–34, 82, 101–02; Darnton, *The Literary Underground* . . . , Chapters 1 and 6; Davis, *The Return of Martin Guerre*; Davis, *Society and culture in early modern France*, for example p. 225; Ginzburg, *The cheese and the worms*, pp. xiv–xvii, xix, xx–xxii; Schmitt, *The holy greyhound*, pp. 7–8, 15–24. See also Chartier, 'Intellectual history or sociocultural history?', p. 30; P.-O. Christiansen, 'Construction of the past: from Montaillou to "The name of the role" '.

14. Burke, *Popular Culture* . . . , especially pp. 207–43; Burke, *The historical anthropology of early modern Italy*, pp. 187–90; Muchembled, *Popular culture and elite culture* . . . , part 2, especially Chapter 5. For a concrete description of a witch trial, see G. Henningsen, *The witches' advocate*, and for his discussion of folk culture pp. 340–42 in particular. For a Swedish contribution with a similar view, see P.-J. Ödman, *Konformismens triumf: utvecklingslinjer i svensk 1600-talspedagogik*, a study which is, however, limited to Sweden in the seventeenth century.

15. Conversation with Chartier, who pointed to Vovelle as a typical example.

16. For a survey, see, for example, Burke's discussion of Muchembled and himself in P. Burke, 'Popular culture between history and ethnology'; Christiansen, 'Construction of the past . . .'; W. Beik, 'Popular culture and elite repression in early modern Europe'; Ginzburg, *The cheese and the worms*, Preface to the Italian edition.

17. Darnton, *The Great Cat Massacre*, p. 7; Ginzburg, *The cheese and the worms*, Preface to the
     Italian edition; E. Le Roy Ladurie in an interview with Ami Lönnroth, *Svenska Dagbla-
     det*, 19 December 1989, p. 19. For an example of the critique in Sweden, see O. Löfgren,
     'På jakt efter den borgerliga kulturen'. See also M. Vovelle, 'Ideologies and mentali-
     tites'; J. Le Goff, 'Mentalities: a history of ambiguities'.
18. Giddens, cited in Habermas, *The theory of communicative action 1*, p. 110.
19. Chartier, 'Intellectual history or sociocultural history?', p. 30; Hunt, 'Introduction . . .'
     p. 7; Hunt, 'French history in the last twenty years: the rise and fall of the Annales para-
     digm', p. 217.
20. See, for example, Hunt, 'French history in the last twenty years: the rise and fall of the
     annales paradigm'.
21. Braudel, 'History and the social sciences'.
22. Chartier, 'Intellectual history or sociocultural history', p. 30; Chartier, 'Texts, printing,
     reading', pp. 154ff; P. O'Brien, 'Michel Foucault's history of culture'.
23. Chartier, *The culture of print*, p. 1.
24. Chartier, 'Les pratiques de l'écrit', pp. 126–28; Furet and Ozouf, 'Three centuries of
     cultural cross-fertilization, p. 219.
25. The example is based on my reading of O. Paz, *Sor Juana or the traps of faith* and Henning-
     sen, *The witches' advocate*.
26. No really comprehensive studies have been made of the *Annales* school with regard to
     these questions.
27. Cf. Christiansen, 'Construction of the past'.
28. Fernand Braudel 1976, p. 1239.
29. See, for example, Marx and Engels 1968, pp. 58–59.
30. See, for example, Braudel, 'History and the social sciences'.
31. Vovelle 1988.
32. See, for example, Febvre 1942.
33. Lévy-Brühl 1923.
34. See Chartier, 'Intellectual history or sociocultural history'.
35. Cf. J. Söderberg, 'Makrohistoria och lokalhistoria', p. 62.
36. Chartier, 'Texts . . .', pp. 165, 166, 171.

Johan Hjerpe's reading
and the individual in history

Chapter 5
Johan Hjerpe and the culture of Enlightenment

Within the relativistic framework of Enlightenment philosopy, a number of coherent thematic groupings stand out more than others: a secularised deism or atheism, an expanded awareness of the value of foreign cultures, and the transformative idea that history will never return to its starting point – a notion that for some like Fontenelle, Turgot or Condorcet was elevated to a belief in progress.

What concerns me in this chapter is how these attitudes were remoulded when they reached the man in the street. Indeed, the discussion is even more narrowly focused, as it largely concerns a single person who has already made his appearance, and therefore needs no further introduction. The person to whom I refer is, of course, the tailor's son and silk manufacturer Johan Hjerpe.[1] But for the sake of comparison, he has a companion – the Parisian master glass worker Jacques-Louis Ménétra.

Both men lived during the Enlightenment, but they were far from being part of the cultural élite that gave the epoch its name. They were unknown to the public of their time, although they have now achieved a certain renown thanks to the current enthusiasm among historians for typical but non-élite case histories from the past. In recent years, Ménétra has been as much in the limelight as Menocchio, Martin Guerre or Pierre Maury, those most famous and favoured objects of attention within the field of recent socio-historical research into popular culture and mentality.[2] Hjerpe, too, has occasionally been consulted as a witness from the masses, although in recent years I am the only historian to have paid him any real attention, and he still awaits his breakthrough.

It is obvious why these men of the people have caught the interest of social historians: Ménétra and Hjerpe were both copious writers; indeed, words positively flowed from their pens.[3] They were contemporaries; they were social equals, and to some extent were influenced by the same events, in particular Enlightenment and the French Revolution. But they reacted to these at least partially pan-European upheavals from separate cultural and geographical spheres. Furthermore, they were very different as people, and would hardly have found much pleasure in each other's company. Nonetheless, in certain fundamental respects they seem to have had the same outlook on the world and on life, a common mentality which is recognisable under the layers of cultural and individual peculiarities. It is this very combination of similarities and differences which makes the Parisian master glass worker deserve an important, albeit minor, role in the discussion that follows.

Hjerpe will be compared with Ménétra, and with the central themes of Enlightenment, and he will also be discussed from the point of view of the self-reflective relativism found under the surface of these burning questions. It is, for example, not at all certain, or even a priori probable, that Ménétra shared the basic relativistic outlook of Enlightenment simply because he shared its negative views of priests and Christian dogma. Similarly, it is not certain that Hjerpe considered the distinctive nature of Western culture as a factor of time and place, merely because he expressed regret over England's penetration into India, or spoke well of Mohammed. None of these has an answer: they are empirical questions.

It is, of course, possible to make well-founded objections to concentrating on only one or two individuals, and this happens fairly often. The old question about the value of biographical studies has been raised again, and since current debaters have also added a number of new viewpoints to the discussion, it must be touched upon. I shall do this in the next chapter. Until then, I shall act as if my task is free from complications, and let the discussion carry itself. However, those readers who do not wish to acquiesce to such irresponsibility are naturally welcome to skip to Chapter 6. The rest are hereby invited to a short presentation of Hjerpe and Ménétra, and then to a continued analysis of the reflections about Enlightenment in the minds of the two men.

Two members of Europe's petit bourgeoisie

Hjerpe
A biography of Johan Hjerpe would be a commonplace and uninteresting story, a portrait lacking contours. His tranquil life apparently lacked dramatic highlights, so there is no special reason to spend much time on it, especially as I have already mentioned the most important biographical points. However, for the sake of comparison, I shall touch upon some of these features later on.

The most interesting aspect of his life is the intellectual work which occupied his solitary life: his life-long association with books and periodical papers, as well as his own inexhaustible diligence with the pen. He surrounded himself with books, pamphlets and newspapers, and on his death he left over three hundred titles as well as his own manuscripts.[4] The majority were auctioned and met an unknown fate.[5] However, despite his admirable collection, Hjerpe was not a collector in the restricted sense of the term; he did not own books because they were beautiful or furnished his home. He did so to satisfy a hunger for reading and to nourish his writing, pastimes for which it is not possible to uncover a deeper motivation. I do not know whether he sought wisdom or learning or both, or merely sought answers to major philosophical questions, or whether he just sought diversion, company and comfort in his solitary existence.[6] I shall not waste time in speculation.

Other things can be said with greater certainty. First, his books and pen were very precious things to which he gave priority and used to salve his conscience. For example, one Sunday in July 1790, he stayed home from morning service because it was raining 'so heavily'. What he did instead is made clear in his diary:

> The 19th intercession day I was home and wrote during morning service since it was raining so heavily and had been doing so all the time. In the afternoon I went up to the cathedral and listened to a bad Minister preach the Evensong.[7]

Second, it is very clear that Hjerpe sought out, or in any case allowed himself to be exposed to, Enlightenment literature. For example, he regardly read *Stockholms Posten* – the leading proponent of Enlightenment – as is made clear both by his diary and in his calendar of world history, in which there are many references to and excerpts from it; and he had the relevant books, as is evident from the catalogue of his collection.[8]

Third, Hjerpe was a very independent, not to say wilful reader.[9] In many places in his own handwritten collected texts – especially in the historical calendars – traces of the literary originals are certainly clear enough. Sometimes, he also copied out exact transcripts. He was not particularly original in terms of his choice of subjects in these texts: it is strikingly similar to that in the contemporary press.[10] But in issues closest to his heart, he used these sources at his own discretion, most often just as a starting point for his own reflections. Indeed, it would almost appear that his deviations from his sources corresponded to the strength of his commitment to the particular subject at issue.

If that was the case, Hjerpe was not much affected by the tales of curious phenomena which contemporary writers of popular literature liked to relate, and which seem to have had a magnetic effect on the reading public.[11] For example, it was noted in an 1818 issue of *Allmänna Journalen* that in 1314 the parliament in Paris had condemned a bull to death for having 'gored a man to death'. The note concluded with the reflection that 'this action belongs to the Characteristics of the way of thinking at this time'. In Hjerpe's calendar of world history one finds the note repeated almost verbatim, and so it is not possible to determine whether he had made an original observation.[12]

News about the fates of kings, Enlightenment philosophers and revolutions must have upset him, especially if it concerned Gustavus III or the French Revolution, because Hjerpe seldom used any more information from his source than the formal details of name and date. The rest, he placed with angry free-hand descriptions.

As far as their form was concerned, and measured by contemporary cultural yardsticks, Hjerpe's writings were conventional, perhaps even old-fashioned. This was especially true of his historiographical efforts, which were modelled on almanacs. In neither the almanacs nor in Hjerpe's works is history presented in a chronological or thematic way, but rather according to the calendar. Events are brought together because they occurred on a particular day of the year: the move of the Stockholm borough administrators to the square of the House of the Nobility in 1732 is placed together with Leo I's appointment as 'Emperor of Austria' in 475, and with the judgment against the unfortunate Parisian bull in 1314, and so on. They are associated with each other on an old-fashioned but still vigorous astrological basis which provided a form, even if that form no longer controlled people's thoughts as much as it once had. But it was well suited to Hjerpe's view of history as a chain of eternally repetitive events. In addition, this was an organising principle which could be used while waiting for the standardised history of civilisation which the Western world still lacked. Even if historians already had a cumulative view of the past, this era witnessed the flowering of a wild assortment of divisions into epochs.[13]

Ménétra and Hjerpe

The fact that 27 years separated Jacques-Louis Ménétra and Johan Hjerpe did not stop them from being contemporary with the most important events of their century. Ménétra was the elder – born in Paris in 1738 – and was presumably also the first to depart this life, even if we are not completely sure when he died.[14]

Ménétra was the son of a master glass worker, and in time he had a son who would also follow the same profession. But while he passed on the family's professional tradition, he hardly bowed in respect to his own father. Rather, his words are irreverent and condemning: his father was temperamental and brutal, a man to be avoided by young Jacques-Louis. Instead, he turned to his kindly grandmother, who took care of him as he grew up.[15] Nonetheless, in time he grew taller than his father, and, strengthened by years of liberating travels as a journeyman, he could face his father without fear, indeed almost patronisingly, as a piteous old man.[16]

Things were different with Johan Hjerpe, who, unmarried and childless, held his own father in life-long respect. Unlike Ménétra he never said a disparaging word, even though he had considerable contempt for people who did not measure up to his standards.[17]

The contrasts between these two men thus have been as great as could exist between any two people. Still, both were the children of craftsmen, became journeymen, and then came to function as petit bourgeois professionals, each in his own city. It is true that Hjerpe would come to raise himself slightly above his social origins, but only a little, and, what is more, like the master glass worker, considerably more in terms of education than social status. As has already been mentioned, both wrote a great deal, even if it is uncertain how much Ménétra read over and above a number of books by Jean-Jacques Rousseau and a few others, and even if he, unlike Hjerpe, wrote in a free, childish manner, in short sentences without punctuation.[18]

Despite the fact that Hjerpe was a member of the Moravian Brethren, he appears to have been a fairly conventional Christian. In contrast, Ménétra hated everything that the clergy represented. But, although he was hardly a spiritual person, he expressed a confidence in Providence in times of change rather like Hjerpe. In May 1789, Hjerpe, then only 24 years old but expressing himself as if he already had his whole life behind him, wrote a reflective diary about God's benevolent guidance towards him. It can be put side-by-side with a similar excerpt from Ménétra's autobiography:[19]

Hjerpe

When I look back, I see how God has guided me. He made more of me because my father was poor, as did Bratt. Then I used my fists in School. Now they are both Gardies' men – who would have thought it, then their fathers were rich.

Ménétra

Aussi si j'ai été que je suis c'est l'Eternel qui m'a protégé car j'ai été induit en bien de mauvaises connaissances que je faisais par l'imprudence de mon père mais le peu de bon sens que je pus avoir m'a bien empêché de tomber dans des forfaits que mes camarades et voisins et autres de ma connaissance malgré que je les fréquentais sont tombés et qui ont été punis

Through the providence of God or the Everlasting, they had both been saved from the sinful and poor life to which their social lot seemed to have destined them. Here, too, amongst their differences, one finds similarities between the two men. But perhaps these passages can be used, not only to associate Hjerpe and Ménétra with each other, but also to place them socially. Perhaps their common notion of divine providence and earthly fate was also a socially distinctive mentality: a poor man could not save himself, therefore he did not need to engage in self-reproach for his sinfulness, but could at the same time be proud of the fact that God or the Everlasting had chosen him in particular. Or it could be only a matter of chance that the two men arrived at the same point of view. Or nearly the same, because even in the quotation above, one can see that Ménétra ascribed to himself a sort of inborn common sense (or 'le

peu de bon sens que je pus avoir), which is not found in Hjerpe's self-descrip-
tion. He was almost embarrassed by God's goodness to him, or 'ashamed' as
he expressed it at one point in his diary.[20] And as regards other moral issues,
their attitudes diverged even further.

Using the terminology of Lawrence Kohlberg (further developed by
Jürgen Habermas), one can say that Hjerpe was a conventional moralist: his
normative mentality was founded on support for a given social order and not
on independent ethical values or principles. Like Enlightenment, he lacked a
reflective foundation for his moral standpoints.[21] He seldom expressed com-
passion for all the unhappy people who had been conquered, tortured, and
even executed by history's righteous victors, despite the fact that he based his
arguments on sources which had a different tone.[22]

Early on, Hjerpe tried to get away from the popular ethics which were
natural for one born into his class, and so was not completely conventional.[23]
(If one is to follow Kohlberg, a conventional moralist takes as his moral starting point the social group to which he belongs.) He was afraid of the
tumultuous crowd, and was at once both admiring and condescending
towards it – in time, increasingly condescending. His admiration was for its
royalist and anti-aristocratic courage; his condescension was for its lack of
seriousness and lack of respect for social hierarchies based on tradition. The
following passage comes from a diary entry dated Christmas Eve 1790:[24]

> Titles are not properly used. The humblest servants fly about the ears when
> one sees someone. Everyone is called Sir from the simplest man by his
> equals. My sweet Maiden to the Maids & [. . .] there simply have to be
> Balls and masquerades to pass the time. Light-hearted people win when
> serious people must be silent. What will posterity say about this age? Yes,
> it has been great [. . .] A few years ago sex was generally the object, now,
> during and after the war, Bacchus has started to reign.

This was not just a passing phase, a youthful cursing of a cultural decline, for
he expressed himself similarly later in life.[25]

Hjerpe's embittered words applied to his own cultural circle but could just
as easily have applied to Ménétra, who was the type of person not to let himself
be put out by dreary considerations or serious admonition. He unashamedly
amused himself with a continuously changing throng of people. He let
himself be formed by his artisan childhood, by his extensive travels, limited
to France, as a journeyman, and by the profession which he practised. He was
neither a moralist nor consistent, and is generally difficult to place morally.
But it would still seem as if he held some values in high regard, ones that
were alternately moral and amoral. As I understand Ménétra, it was always
right and necessary to help a person in need, whatever the law said (for
example, that it was forbidden to help a drowning person from the water),

and that it was forbidden to keep something that one did not own – if it was valuable. Otherwise, a person was free to fulfil his desires. It would seem that no feelings of guilt, only shame, could keep him from practising the pleasure principle. Yes, he could blush at being caught out with his friend's wife, but he showed no signs of emphatic contrition, remorse or anguish.[26]

If Ménétra was a confident fatalist in a cosmic sense, he believed at the same time in the strength of his daily, happily self-absorbed, sometimes abrupt interventions into social micro-life. This would appear to be contradictory, but for him it fitted: he was protected by *l'Eternel*, and could do as he wished.

Still, Ménétra was not free to form whatever views he wished to. Despite the fact that he appears to have had a strongly personal moral temperament, both he and Hjerpe were bound by culturally transmitted ways of thinking, modified during the eighteenth century by Enlightenment influences. And it is from the viewpoint of the central themes of Enlightenment that they will now be compared. I will begin with religion, which will be discussed in more depth than their views about the outside world and progress.

The first theme: religion

Enlightenment and religion

It is common knowledge that Enlightenment philosophers each had an individual relationship to religion. There were atheists such as Holbach and La Mettrie, and those, such as Condorcet and Voltaire, who believed in God.[27] I am convinced, however, that it is still possible to distinguish characteristics which were shared to a fairly high degree. They include a contempt for Christian teaching, and in the case of Voltaire for Jewish teaching too, for the Bible, for the medieval church and that of the Counter-Reformation, and for old superstitions such as a belief in witches which adhered to no creed. God was good and Hell was an invention that was both unreasonable and ineffectual.[28] But in their strong attraction to deism and to a kind of timeless inner faith, most Enlightenment thinkers themselves adhered to no creed, which was regarded as being 'invariable', in contrast to the major belief systems:[29] 'le judaisme, le christianisme, le paganisme & le mahométisme'.[30] It is perhaps a little surprising that paganism was regarded as being one of the world's religions, but this may be regarded as being included in the concept of tolerance, which was one of the most definitive features of Enlightenment. In Swedish Enlightenment debate, the issue of tolerance (that is, of freedom of thought and the press) was very much to the fore, and references were repeatedly made to Voltaire. The debate about tolerance was very much interwoven with views of religion, and here, too, Voltaire's standpoint was vigorously discussed.[31]

It is harder to say whether secularisation was also definitive of Enlightenment, which certainly contributed to a declining interest in things divine. At the same time, this decline was part of a course of events which had begun much earlier, and which – despite nineteenth-century religious revivals – continued, and still continues.[32] It is true that the de-Christianising campaigns of the French Revolution, for example, must be associated with Enlightenment, and some of the Revolution's better orchestrated festivals can also be traced back to this project.[33] But the most hectic phase of the Revolution also saw carnival celebrations featuring inversion rituals – events which Enlightenment philosophers regarded as base and backward.[34] In addition, the fact that the course of secularisation presumably continued throughout the eighteenth century did not stop heterodox, perhaps pre-Christian, ideas from continuing to survive unrestrained, even among the clergy.[35] It may even have been that these kinds of unchanged pre-Christian ideas were added to modern post-Christian ideas in the continuing secularisation process.

In any case, the immediate successor of Enlightenment, the Romantic period, gave the question of guilt an easy answer, at least if one believes Lorenzo Hammarsköld. To him, Enlightenment was atheistic, materialistic, and a sworn enemy of religion:[36]

> ... individual well-being [is] the exclusive goal of everyone's efforts. Eighteenth-century educational theory depicted this goal as its highest principle, and Religion itself, transformed into a popular doctrine of bliss, became, depicted in this way by its public Preachers, as if it sought to regard duty and morality only as a form of capital which one loaned out, in order to win success in this life and salvation in the next. In the end, even this weak ignominy of Religion was declared to be not only an unnecessary, but also actually a dangerous superstition, since France's Encyclopaedists lit their so-called Enlightenment, according to which man is declared to be a machine, constructed by chance out of material parts, without connection to any predecessor or successor, because self-love is held up as the only right foundation for all his actions, and the good sense to satisfy this, as the single highest wisdom.

Hammarsköld's description of Enlightenment is plain and simple, but still focuses on real events, whoever was responsible for them.[37] In Sweden, the cultural framework had indeed been moved in a secularised direction. The religious freedom reforms of the Gustavian period also bear witness to the fact that the authorities no longer had the same interest in defending true evangelical teachings.[38] It is true that in the clergy's deliberations in the 1789 Riksdag, several members continued to stress that guarding the true faith was as important as it had always been. Yet, in contrast with earlier times, there was obvious support for Gustavus III's plans to increase freedom of religion, and increase it so that it also embraced Jews and Catholics to a limited extent. And as the threat against the faith was seen to have lessened, some members could even voice a principled defence of freedom of thought. Anders Chydenius, one of the leading members of the clergy at the time, is an example. He expressed himself as follows in one of his journals: 'The prejudices are, thank God, long since scattered, to seek to exterminate other points of view by moral constraint and persecution.'[39] It is also very probable that quite ordinary people were reached in one way or another by the Enlightenment message. But it is far from clear how the material was distorted, or the way in which it was incorporated into people's ideas, or whether it was simply rejected. Nevertheless, in the spiritual microcosms of both Johan Hjerpe and Jacques-Louis Ménétra, it is possible to detect traces of the tendencies of the age.

Hjerpe and religion

Hjerpe was a second-generation member of the Moravian Brethren,[40] but one searches in vain for the Brethren's somewhat stifling sincerity in the writings he left behind.[41] He mentioned very little at all about his religious experiences: a few descriptions of the sort of things he did with the evangelical brothers and sisters – eating, riding, dancing, going to a funeral, meeting and parting – but hardly a word about religious reflection.[42]

On the other hand, he could be very articulate, and even acute, in spiritual questions of an ideological nature. In these cases, he also happily referred to Enlightenment, as he did in a note about Voltaire's birth on 20 February 1694 in his calendar of world history.[43] He associated the French Revolution with the Enlightenment movement, and the Enlightenment movement with a threat to Christendom, and it would seem that he hated both these movements with equal intensity. But here there is more about the author of the note, because, compared with his source, he also appears to be an arbitrary reader. This note, like nearly every one of the over two thousand others, is conscientiously rounded off with references to its source. For the information about Voltaire, Hjerpe referred to Jacob Johan Björnståhls travels, part 2, page 70. That he dared! The reference is good and the exact location is easily found, so Hjerpe's note can be compared with suitable excerpts from the source:[44]

Hjerpe	Björnståhl
February 20 [. . .], 1694 France's great poet Voltaire was born in Paris, the great evil this man has carried out on earth, his hatred of the Christian Faith, and his inexhaus-	I said to him [Voltaire, AJ], that he could not die, that his Spirit was immortal [. . .] He spoke later with much joy about the great change, which had taken place in

tible zeal, to disguise all truth by means of his writings, and to overthrow all order, has been a mainspring of the bloody Revolution which overthrew his own Fatherland, and has spread out streams of blood over the whole Earth.

Jac: Joh: Biörnståls Resa 2ndra Del. p. 70.

Sweden during our absence; he said with great emphasis and raised voice: le Roi GUSTAVE est adoré En Europe. ce grand Roi de Svede [...] to a Compliment I made him about the verses he had written about the Revolution in Sweden I answered him, that His Majesty will rejoice at this; [...] Mr Voltaire was born in Paris the 20th of February, 1694, and it is an honour for Paris; because it has been observ'd, that such a great man has never before been born there [...]

As can be seen, very little is recognisable from the source, so why did Hjerpe use Björnståhl at all, and where did he get all the rest from? The choice of Björnståhl was natural because he found a date there, which was just what he needed in the compilation of his calendar. He picked up dates where he found them. The rest, he made up as the melted-down result of everything he had acquired in life, and he could then calmly disregard what was written in black and white in *Björnståhls resa*: that Gustavus III – his own beloved hero-king – had himself entertained a kind of enlightened admiration for the odious Voltaire.[45]

If one is to believe J. C. Bauer, a contemporary intellectual, Hjerpe's selective silence was not particularly strange. In his chronicle of the eighteenth century's most remarkable events, a chronicle which was typical of his times, Bauer argued that ordinary people tended to misunderstand Voltaire as an enemy of religion.[46] For those who simultaneously cherished the memory of Gustavus III, it was therefore necessary to disregard the praises which had once been exchanged between the king and the philosopher. Hjerpe did not allow himself to be led by Bauer, despite the fact that his calendar of world history is full of references to Bauer's chronicle.[47]

If one is to follow Bauer, it would seem that Hjerpe sifted ideas in the same way as others in his social surroundings did, but the similarity with the conception among the Romantic intellectuals is also fairly striking. So Hjerpe's cultural filter was certainly neither a purely personal one nor a social one in the narrow sense of the word.

There is still more to consider. If Hjerpe was unequivocally hostile to Enlightenment, he was far less clear in his views on religious fanaticism, on those of foreign faiths, or on those who were merely indifferent to God.

Unlike Ménétra he was not a completely intolerant person, but neither was he tolerant as a matter of principle. In general, his sympathy grew the more he dissociated himself from the form of piety he was discussing. Foreign forms were remote and therefore not dangerous; they were still shrouded in an exotically appealing mystery. Least valued were evangelical deviants close to home, despite the fact that he himself had been born into a visionary revivalist movement which had recently been severely persecuted and against which the clergy constantly warned.[48]

Closest of all was the pietistic Collin sect or the new sect, as it was also called. Within the space of a few years, this almost Dippelian sect both won and lost a large number of followers, approximately four thousand souls[49] – according to the Swedish literary historian Martin Lamm. The movement mostly kept itself within the poor Stockholm neighbourhood of Södermalm, but was also found in the Nicolai parish in the Old Town where Hjerpe lived during the 1780s.[50] He commented on the sect in his calendar of Stockholm history. Perhaps he had experienced what he described, because he did not give any references, although he hardly ever did in this particular work. He wrote as follows:[51]

1780
The Same Year an uproar occurred in the Town and its Districts, by the so-called new sect, in particular on Götgatan on Södermalm, where they held most of their meetings, but thanks to action by the Royal Police, everything was calmed down. These people preached and practised their strange faith, and seduced the very foolish people they preached to, they set themselves up against the Clergy, and once, at a hearing in St Nicolai Church they caused tumult when they wanted to confuse the Minister who was holding the hearing.

Here, too, Hjerpe was out of line with his more enlightened contemporaries. It is true that Uno von Troil – *praeses* (president) in the Stockholm consistory and later archbishop that same year – had requested permission from the king to intervene against the sect. Governor Carl Sparre also allowed the police to take measures against Anders Collin, the sect's leader. But von Troil's application is written in full awareness of the tolerance for differing religious opinions which was imposed at the beginning of the 1780s. The king did not like Sparre's intervention against Collin, something of which, however, Hjerpe was presumably blissfully unaware.[52]

However, he cannot have helped notice that the *new sect* was used as an example in the continuing debate about tolerance.[53] It was a debate in which many tried but almost no-one succeeded in maintaining a tolerant standpoint on principle. The debators continually slid away from principles and towards wanting to allow what they liked and forbid what they did not like. This attraction towards a *substantive* instead of a *formal* tolerance appears throughout the debate, in which everyone – due to fear of lingering intolerance on the part of those in power – participated under more or less imaginative pseudonyms.[54] I have not come across a strictly formal standpoint or one purely based on principle anywhere, although I have come across one contribution in which the author at least distinguishes in principle between truth value and usefulness. In *Remarks about the old folk-saying: 'It is better to have too much faith than too little faith' devoted to the friends of Enlightenment*, the anonymous author asserts that the question 'whether something is true has nothing in common, upon rational investigation, with the question of whether it is beneficial or harmful to believe in it'.[55]

With Hjerpe, things were both the same and yet different, because when he wanted to intervene with a ban on the dissemination of certain opinions, he was not, like other debaters, sliding away from any principles of tolerance. He had no such principles. If the clergy was strict while Gustavus was generous, neither party made much effort to distinguish between the different sects.[56] But Hjerpe did. The new sect denied one of the most crucial elements of the Moravian Brethren's preaching: the atonement for mankind's sins as the symbolic meaning of the crucifixion.[57] It was therefore good that the governor intervened against the sect but left the evangelical brethren in peace.

Tolerance for self-righteous pietists was also important within the justice system. At least, this would seem to have been the case, judging by a case of assault which was debated in the court of the southern suburbs (Södra förstadens kämnärsrätt) in 1780, the same year that the sect reached its peak. Shopkeeper Simon Kihl was accused of assaulting his five-year-old son so badly that the child died from his injuries. After much negotiation and investigation, the case ended with the father being absolved of responsibility for the boy's death. One important basis for the court's ruling was the man's attraction to pietism, a self-righteous form of piety which was regarded as being particularly irreconcilable with 'insensitivity to his own Child'.[58]

Hjerpe was if anything neutral or naïvely interested, when it came to Jews and Muslims, and his attitude was more in harmony with the continuing change of attitude within the country's political leadership. However, it was still not in line with the critical attitude of the Enlightenment philosophers towards Jews and Judaism, nor with the anti-Semitic gossip which dominated the notes about the Jews published in the periodical press.[59]

In the years around 1780, limited freedom of religion for Jews and Catholics was introduced in Sweden. The result was a certain immigration of Jews, which the young Hjerpe, with an innocent commentary, associated with the new regulation about the Jews.[60] He wrote that they came 'Because they had received permission to do so and besides the Estates of the Realm have permitted a free practice of Religion for all the Christian Religions'.[61] The comment is neutral in tone and makes a surprisingly unconscious impression. Didn't he know any better, or was he merely fishing with his pen when he made Judaism into a form of Christianity? Certainly the Moravian revival sought good relations with the Jews, but it made a distinction between creeds, and the aim was still to convert the Jews.[62] And even if the Jews tended to be praised for their alleged complicity in Jesus's sacrifice of atonement – in that they thereby helped to save mankind from eternal damnation and to found the new religion – they were not considered equal to Christians for that very reason.[63]

However it was with Hjerpe's youthful confusion, he subsequently wrote more unerringly when he made notes about the fate of the Jews. Nowhere in his world of ideas can any anti-Semitic impressions be found. For example, a late note about Spinoza says that he was a 'real Philosopher, temperate and unselfish', despite the fact that he abandoned Judaism 'without embracing Christianity' and based his system of thought on 'Atheistic principles'.[64] In another note, the mob in London in the deep Middle Ages was criticised for its persecution of the Jews:[65]

> 1189. The Jews were murdered in London. At the coronation of King Richard the Lionhearted the Mob availed itself of the lack of discipline allowed it owing to this solemn occasion. They murdered everyone of this Nation that they could come across, and plundered their Property, with the excuse of punishing them for their Usury.

Note that Hjerpe used the concept of *nation*, rather than *race* or *religion* in referring to the Jews. This was the convention of the day, and was not in itself disparaging, even if it later became part of the rhetoric of the anti-Semitic press.[66] It has been suggested that the disparaging comments about Jews in the periodical press must have reflected public expectations. The readership was presumably as hostile as the periodicals, otherwise the comments would not have been included.[67] Popular anti-Semitism also had a long tradition in Europe.[68]

But how sure can one be of this theory? A reading of Hjerpe casts a slight shadow of doubt over the suggestion, because the disparaging gossip made no impression on him, despite the fact that he was evidently a faithful reader of the periodicals. On the other hand, he did not abandon his reading habits because of the comments; they were often insignificant and short and could be ignored as irrelevant background noise. In his description of his travels in the summer of 1809, he also related with evident neutrality how, in the late Middle Ages, the Swedish king Sten Sture the younger allowed gypsies to settle in Sweden, and how they became naturalised in the small southern Swedish town of Gränna. He adds: 'It is believed that they originate from Egypt'.[69] It can also be mentioned in passing that on one occasion in 1784,

Stockholms Posten published a long and prominent article, in which the author critically compared other countries' rough treatment of the Jews with the tolerance they met with in Sweden.[70]

There are other examples of similar popular attitudes towards the Jews – for example those of the bookbinder P. J. Öberg[71] and Jacques-Louis Ménétra – and I suspect that, at this time, anti-Semitism was more widespread and far more articulated in the periodical press than it was among the petit bourgeoisie in general. Before it is possible to answer this question with any certainty, more investigation is needed, not least into how the Jews were usually portrayed in sermons, especially those preached during Easter. But even if unpleasant rumours had circulated about Jews for generations, the rumours had no concrete environment in which to exist as long as the Jewish settlement in Sweden remained insignificant, as was still the case at the end of the eighteenth century.[72] But not even after the Gustavian laws of tolerance had stimulated some immigration did the Jews meet with any anti-Semitism based on biological arguments. For a long time, they were widely spoken of as a nation,[73] and it was only during the nineteenth century that they gradually came to be identified as a separate race.[74]

Meanwhile, the Jews met with obstacles based on cultural and religious arguments, not genetic ones; in other words, conditional on the extent they refused to convert. Therefore, it was easy to put Jews on a par with Muslims or pagans, for, as the rhetorical question in *Stockholms Posten* phrased it: 'Do we not all have one Father? Has not one God created us?', and 'Should we therefore be completely unconcerned about our poor fellow men ... ?' Put differently, although they were led astray and as yet unenlightened by the evangelical faith, the Jews (and Muslims and pagans) were still the Christians' equals as human beings.

However, the Jewish presence in Stockholm and in a number of other places gradually became sufficiently obvious to give rise to popular anti-Semitism, in which the sardonically misspelled word 'natzion' became one element in an emerging racist rhetoric.[75] Stockholm, too, experienced its anti-Jewish mob riot.[76] In itself, however, the racism was not new; the renewal lay in a shift in the ideological centre of gravity. With progressive secularisation, religious distinctions lost some of their meaning, and hostile demarcations began to be drawn up according to new criteria. In this way, the biological argument gradually succeeded the cultural-religious one.[77] In addition, the new reasoning had its equivalent in contemporary science, where an evolutionism with Lamarckian overtones became increasingly dominant.[78]

So it is only to be expected that there are no traces of biologically-based racism in the literary legacy of young Johan Hjerpe. It is, however, stranger that he did not show any culturally or religiously motivated disparagement for foreigners of an exotic faith, either Jews or Muslims. Faithfully and ingenuously in the history of the world, Hjerpe reiterated what was written about Mohammed in Number 128 of *Allmänna Journalen* of 1818, for example that the prophet 'was a man of great character traits, wise, eloquent, brave and with a captivating exterior'.[79]

From a modern viewpoint, one can believe that in voicing these attitudes, Hjerpe shows himself to be a modern, broad-minded individual. Perhaps that was the case. But from the high-level perspective of contemporary Enlightenment, he would still have seemed to be old-fashioned. This was so, partly because he remained religiously intolerant close to home, despite his tolerance of foreigners, and partly because he remained faithful to attitudes that Enlightenment dismissed as the superstitious gossip of old women. I will give one example.

In his account of the history of Stockholm, Hjerpe briefly hinted at the witch-hunt that occurred in the city in 1676.[80] Within a year, witchcraft in the city peaked and faded away.[81] In a footnote he adds that many innocent people were hanged or burnt, a fact taken up in the trials that followed the turmoil. He also states that in these trials the prosecutors who could not completely prove 'their cases' were themselves sentenced to death.

The way Hjerpe expresses himself indicates that to him witchcraft was a reality, although not as comprehensive as was originally imagined. In my view, this conclusion about Hjerpe is validated when his remarks are contrasted with the source he referred to, *Swea rikes historia (The History of Sweden)* – the major work by the famous eighteenth-century historian Sven Lagerbring, one of the leading figures of early Swedish Enlightenment.

Clearly, Hjerpe's phrase that 'many were innocently destroyed' stems from the passage in Lagerbring's work, where it is stated that 'The worst thing was that many innocent were destroyed'. Although these phrases appear almost identical, they still represent divergent views on witchcraft. According to Hjerpe, many of the ill-fated were innocent, which means that *some were not*. What Lagerbring wanted to say was essentially different. Due to his enlightened conviction that witches had never existed, all the people who were killed were innocent, and these 'all' were many. It is also evident from other passages in his chapter on witchcraft, that this was Lagerbring's view. Afraid of being considered superstitious, he assures the reader that he has never believed in witchcraft and apologises for dwelling on such an out-dated theme.[82]

Hjerpe's conception of the witch-hunt in seventeenth-century Stockholm is another example of his incomplete absorption of Enlightenment. As stated, he was hardly a deliberately tolerant person. Rather, he displayed a *lack of intolerance* for those who professed foreign faiths which really hardly affected him, but at the same time he had difficulty tolerating zealots close at hand in his own neighbourhood. This was not the case with Jacques-Louis Ménétra.

Ménétra and religion

As we shall see, Ménétra, like Hjerpe, had no quarrel with the Jews, which is an interesting similarity between two men who otherwise adopted different stances on the question of faith. Whereas Hjerpe was decorously pious, Ménétra incessantly made fun of the clergy and of what he described as their narrow intolerance and superstition. He happily poked fun at the Christian God, at angels and nuns, and at people's fear of devils and ghosts. In time, he also took part in the de-Christianising campaign of the French Revolution. But for all that, Ménétra was not an anti-religious man, for he did have his own heavenly protection in the form of the Everlasting.[83]

For Hjerpe, tolerance must have been a foreign or inconvenient word – it is impossible to find the word anywhere in his surviving works. I have seen the closely-related word 'democracy' used in combination with rage and to characterise the unjust execution of Louis XVI, 'that innocent Victim'.[84] The word 'modern' also appears, although only as a description of a regrettable state of existence in early nineteenth-century Sweden.[85] It was different for Ménétra. In his conceptual 'toolbox', one of the most precious contents was 'tolerance'. It was a utilitarian word loaded with positive implications, a kind of weapon for separating friends from enemies.[86]

Everyone familiar with Enlightenment thought knows that Ménétra was in the company of thousands and thousands of his contemporaries when he ridiculed Christianity and argued for tolerance.[87] But to what extent Ménétra was directly influenced by 'les philosophes' is still quite unclear. Perhaps the philosophers and Ménétra were actually part of a greater course of events, in which both parties, largely independent of each other, reoriented themselves in the world, and to some extent reoriented in the same direction. For despite the fact that Ménétra could read and write – like most of the young men in Paris of the 1750s – one finds very few references to the fruits of his own reading in his autobiography: besides the Bible and one other spiritual work, only *Petit Albert* (a manual of white magic), two books by Rousseau and the popular paper *Le Journal des Dames* can be found.[88] It is very likely that he owned a few more books, at least if we are to go by what was normal for a contemporary Parisian artisan.[89] But we will never know, as an inventory of his estate has never been found.

Ménétra's relationship to culture was not the same as Hjerpe's – he did not acquire wisdom at home. Daniel Roche, the editor of Ménétra's autobiography, says the master glass worker seldom read and his book-learning was very superficial.[90] Instead, he learned mostly by observing the effects of his unremitting, self-absorbed and impatient dabbling in social microcosm. Of course, Ménétra *can* have been influenced by Enlightenment even if his reading was limited. Roche argues that this was the case, or at least that the successes of Enlightenment made room for his anti-clerical attitude. Enlightenment provided more space to choose, to express freely anti-authoritarian attitudes, regardless of how well it succeeded in disseminating its own distinctive body of thought.[91]

But let us now see whether any concrete relationship between Ménétra and his Enlightenment environment exists. Here, first, is an example of his flippant attitude towards the religious world, whose female representatives he gladly humiliated, or claimed that he humiliated, with frequent conquests. Ménétra worked for a short time in a Dominican convent in Paris, where one day he was alone with one of the nuns. Taking him at his word, he was hardly unfamiliar with such a situation, for in his diary he claimed that he 'yet again' made himself a successful rival to Jesus, the holy bridegroom of all nuns:[92]

Ménétra

Un jour j'étais seul avec Mère Sainte Ursule et étais dans sa cellule dont la vue donnait sur le jardin des Petit-Pères Elle me dit Monsieur le vitrier si j'eus été femme du monde je n'aurais jamais voulu avoir des relations avec ces hommes-là en me faisant apercevoir des Petits-Pères Je m'oubliai dans cet instant je devins encore une fois le rival du petit Jésus Elle était charmante grasse bien embonpoint Ah quel plaisir pour un mortel de croquer de si jolies épouses qu'il laisse morfondre dans son sérail

A nun with the eyes of a woman of the world – a prostitute, since she was eyeing religious men – was apparently an easy prey, if the entire episode was not just a stylised manifestation of the glass worker's erotic fantasies.[93] What actually happened does not really matter, since the issue here is to trace what is recognisable from Enlightenment in Ménétra's attitudes. Enlightenment scorn is found here, a derision as essential to '*les philosophes*' as it was repellent to its opponents. In the Swedish debate on tolerance, several people were particularly offended by Voltaire's derisive attitude towards Christianity. For example, a writer under the pen name 'Laicus' says that one should not make use of violence 'nor ironies, defamation and biting jokes, in the manner of Voltaire'.[94] The anonymous pamphlet *Om tolerancen* described the religious criticism of Enlightenment as follows: '[t]hat thoughtless Intolerance, I admit, is milder in gesture and behaviour: fire, broadaxes and the rack are not its weapons, but simple derision, jesting and the grimaces of a self-imagined wisdom'.[95]

A typical example of this is the 'physicalistic' criticism Ménétra levelled at the ritual of holy communion. How, he asked, could it be possible for a person to swallow and digest God without developing stomach pains? And how could it be possible even to get God down to the church altar? Any sensible person must realise the unreasonableness of such folly.

Perhaps Ménétra's attacks can be regarded as being more pre-Christian than secularised, ignorant rather than enlightened. The fourteenth-century villagers in Montaillou, for example, confessed how hard it was for them to accept that Christ would pass through 'the shameful parts of the human body if he really was present in the flesh during communion'.[96] In medieval Sweden, too, people seemed to have pondered the mystery, and whoever dared to reveal any doubts about the possibility of this holy metabolic feat could even be burned at the stake – that was the fate of Botolf in Gottröra.[97]

But Enlightenment philosophers also vigorously made fun of Catholic doctrines; in fact in his philosophical dictionary Voltaire joked about the doctrine of transubstantiation in phrases as biting as those Ménétra used in his book of travels. The similarity is striking:[98]

Ménétra	Voltaire
Jamais je ne fus fanatisé et n'ai jamais (crue) et ne croirai jamais qu'aucun être sur la terre soit en état de faire descendre un Dieu sur l'autel à sa volonté et de l'avaler de même de le donner à qui le gosier assez fort pour digérer leur Dieu Cela passe à tout homme censé l'imagination Aussi ont-ils raison d'avoir toujours ces paroles dans la bouche	Les protestants, et surtout les philosophes protestants, regardent la transsubstantiation comme le dernier terme de l'impudence des moines, et de l'imbecillité des laïques [...] Leur horreur augmente, quand on leur dit qu'on voit tous les jours, dans les pays catholiques, de prêtres, des moines qui, sortant d'un lit incestueux, et n'ayant pas encore lavé leurs mains souillés d'impuretés, vont faire des dieux par centaines, mangent et boivent leur dieu, chient et pissent leur dieu.

For both men, the central absurdity seems to have been God's passage through the stomachs of men, and even if Ménétra and Voltaire poked fun at somewhat different stages of the communion, their attitudes were very similar. Their venomous and mocking attack on communion was a materialistic or physicalistic rational criticism, difficult to contradict for anyone who was unwilling to reject rationality as such.

However, a difference still lurks between the ideas of the master glass

worker and the philosopher: Ménétra was probably not clear about the epis-
temological terms of the discussion, although these had been known and
recognised by thinkers on both sides of the argument for a long time. Voltaire
knew that religious belief 'did not consist of believing in what appears true,
but rather in that which to our reason appears false'.[99] It was the same –
though in reverse – for Luther, who argued that reason must be drowned in
the Christian baptism, that only credulity filled with implicit faith could be a
defence against rational doubt, for example in transubstantiation. Or, as he
said in a sermon:[100]

> [...] if you hear God's beloved Son say, Take this and eat, this is my body
> which has been sacrificed for your sake [...] If I hear this and accept it, then
> I trample reason underfoot and say, Silence, damned whore. Are you
> trying to seduce me into fornicating with evil? So can reason be punished
> and liberated through the Word of Jesus.

Ménétra also had his own views when it came to the Jews. He criticised the
Church for inciting opinion against the Jews despite boasting of its tolerant
principles; and for forcing them to wear stigmatising apparel and to listen to
the nonsense of the monks. And, he argued, the Church did this without
taking into consideration the fact that the Jews were everyone's fathers, that
it was the Jews who must be thanked for everyone's existence.[101]

Ménétra may have taken the principle of tolerance directly or indirectly
from Voltaire. It is less clear where he found his solemn attitude towards
Jewish culture, even if he must have been very familiar with the biblical
teaching in which Jewish culture had for generations appeared as the origin
of everything. Voltaire was not consistent on this issue. In his dictionary he
portrayed 'the Hebrews' as a fairly insignificant Arab tribe, which had tried to
incorporate very old traditions of the great nations into its own very young
culture,[102] quite contrary to Ménétra's opinion. Nonetheless, elsewhere he
had appealed, as Ménétra had done, to the Christians to stop their persecution
of the Jews, because as people they were the Christians' brothers, as Jews,
their 'fathers'.[103] In the eyes of his contemporaries it seemed quite clear that
Voltaire was for the most part anti-Semitic.[104]

Whatever the case, the similarities between the philosopher and the glass
worker were otherwise so great that one suspects the existence of an influence
between Voltaire and the social group represented by Ménétra, an influence
whose direction is not so easy to determine. Roche has tried to analyse Ménétra's relations with Enlightenment, but has not taken into account any
upward influence, only a disrupted downwards movement which had little
to do with the dissemination of published texts or articulated ideas. Voltaire
justified the publication of his own pocket dictionary as an alternative to the
Encyclopaedia as follows: 'Twenty folio volumes will never make a revolution.

It's the small portable books of thirty sous that are dangerous. If the Gospel had cost 1,200 sesterces, the Christian religion would never have been established.'[105] Judging from Robert Darnton's examination of forbidden literature in pre-revolutionary France, Voltaire also had some success. His pocket dictionary was a bestseller.[106]

Roche may be right, but I do not believe it was that simple, and shall therefore express some as yet unconfirmed hypotheses to complicate the issue. On the one hand, Voltaire acted in a premeditated way to make his ideas accessible to a broad-based bourgeois public. That is why he chose to publish his dictionary in a small format, in contrast to the large and heavy *Encyclopaedia*. On the other hand, it was not Voltaire who had invented these ideas; they already existed among people, and had done so for a very long time. Enlightenment mockery of religion suited the remnants of a partly pre-Christian dislike of the clergy's preaching, and modern paganism could now enter into an alliance with ancient heathendom within the context of the on-going secularising process. Drastically expressed, the circle of philosophers and other intellectuals overcame a worn-out Christian intellect at which artisans and farmers had not yet completely arrived. What one group had endured, the other could therefore escape: what was secularisation for the one group was a kind of redress for the old values of the other, however badly Enlightenment philosophers themselves regarded all things primitive.

Despite the fact that it is possible to see traces here of ideological convergence between two cultural spheres, there still remained at least one significant and profound difference between them: in their secularising criticism of religion, Enlightenment philosophers developed a self-reflexive cultural relativism which, despite certain superficial resemblances, possessed fundamentally different qualities from the old heathen values which were in the process of being restored within the popular cultural sphere. And, in my view, relativism was a more fundamental change in intellect than secularisation, despite the fact that not even Enlightenment philosophers managed to maintain such an attitude more than temporarily.

The presence of old inversion rites – rites in which normal relationships were turned upside down – in many of the French Revolution's activities may be regarded as a manifestation of this unholy alliance between heterodox attitudes each on its own side of the Christian culture of unity.[107] As far as Sweden is concerned, an analogous example is Swedenborgianism. This involved a strongly intensified piety, but it also combined both very old notions about demonic possession and advanced criticism of the doctrine of the Trinity, as well as Enlightenment's belief in a benevolent God and its demand for freedom of thought and the press.[108] This is not altered by Sweden's prominent and high-church friends of Enlightenment mocking the

Swedenborgians as a group of mad dreamers, and even inciting religious censorship of them. It only shows that both these competing systems of ideas were comprised of conflicting elements.

It is, of course, possible to imagine a series of reasonable objections to my hypothesis. Maybe peasants and artisans were no more pre-Christian than anyone else who allows old gods to survive beside the new ones, and who allows himself to be governed by very broad and contradictory rules of behaviour. Perhaps the wide-spread mockery directed against the clergy was more a parody about what is holy than about what is ridiculous. And perhaps people had for centuries been the unresisting target of a Christian rhetoric, which for the first time they could, with the spread of literacy towards the end of the eighteenth century, regard with a critical eye.

The second theme: the world around us

Enlightenment and the world around us

Voltaire's attempt to deprive Judaism of its own distinctive character was a way of defending 'ancient' Chinese culture, and this defence was in turn a method of attacking his own culture.[109] In this way, a passion for China was of strategic importance to Enlightenment philosophers in their endeavours to reform their own society.

We now arrive at another central theme of Enlightenment: its view of the world around us, or of 'the world beyond the West', as the Swedish historian Åke Holmberg described it.[110] There are several reasons to be brief here. One is that I have just discussed the issue, as it is hard to distinguish it from the question of religion; another is that Hjerpe had little, and Ménétra nothing, to say about the most distant parts of the world around them. It is true that Hjerpe wrote something about the subject, and seems to have been very well-up on contemporary world events, but it is impossible to find a single word by Ménétra about events outside France, or even about things that happened outside the route of his travels as a journeyman.

In general, Enlightenment philosophers were prepared a priori to accord an equal value to all peoples,[111] even if China was used as the supreme illustration of an advanced culture, and indeed was portrayed as 'the most cultured' nation.[112] Here it is possible to discern an attitude which has overcome a restricted conventionality, an enlightened reason which embraced all humanity in its moral obligations.[113]

Similarly, the Encyclopaedists' assertions were reflected in the Swedish Enlightenment debate. For example, referring to the contempt felt by many Swedes for 'our Brothers here, the Turks', Kellgren criticised 'the pride, which drives one people, to entertain [...] false and unjust ideas about another'. For him, the reason behind such a restricted attitude was a kind of socio-centric lack of relativism, or, as he put it: 'We almost never like or reject something, by virtue of our own investigation into its worth, but merely with respect to its relationship to us'.[114] In the newspaper debate, it was argued that a general love of mankind must embrace all nations. It was a kind of 'abstract emotion', superior to the love both of individuals and of a particular people, although it was an emotion that only men – and among them philosophers in particular – could attain.[115] In this discussion, a linkage was also made between the principle of tolerance and that of global brotherly love. Under the pen name 'Hilarius', a writer argued that even if people did not agree about absolutely everything, they ought to be able to put up with each other anyway. It would not therefore be dangerous to the social order to allow differing opinions to meet in a public exchange of views, because 'despite this, people could and should love each other all the same, and live as brothers on this earth'.[116]

Nevertheless, there were several contributions to Enlightenment discourse which marred the global broadmindedness. A radical materialistic Enlightenment figure such as Baron d'Holbach, for example, expressed precisely the ethnocentric European attitude which Kellgren regarded as being alien to enlightened thought.[117] Further, the liking of China was due to special motives, and was not universal. It is true that in their praise of Chinese culture, the men of Enlightenment passed on an inheritance from the Jesuits. But whereas the Jesuits sought traces of an archetypal Christianity, Enlightenment debaters looked for support for an attack: only here did they find a religion which was free from fanaticism and a culture which must have been more than six thousand years old. The Christian culture was inferior in all respects.[118]

At the same time, the Encyclopaedist body of thought was profoundly contradictory when it came to the question of attitudes towards the peoples of the world. All peoples were equal, but the blacks ranked below the whites. This was Voltaire's view, and it was a modern, 'progressive', poly-genic conception, not the remnants of an outmoded way of thinking. It was an integral element in the biblically-critical Enlightenment dispute with monogyny – the belief that all peoples had a common origin in Creation's first couple.[119]

In this respect – that is, through its secularising argument in favour of polygeny – Enlightenment helped to replace a cultural-religious division of mankind with a biological one. Here we find one of the foundations of a racist condescension towards foreign cultures. During the nineteenth century, this attitude was fuelled by new arguments stemming from the development of evolutionary biology, itself also an inheritance from

Enlightenment's Lamarckian sensationalism within the discipline.[120] In addition, the contempt gradually became more widespread as Europeans became acquainted with foreign cultures through successful European attempts to colonise them.[121] In the end, the East could not measure up to the old world in the West. It was true that China had a high level of culture, but it was a culture which seemed to stand completely still in comparison with the technologically expansive Europe.[122]

Hjerpe and the world around him

Johan Hjerpe was tolerant of fantatics nearer home, and in this respect he was hardly Gustavian, despite his many declarations of love for the king. But in his notes on world history, there is no sign of a corresponding disdain for ideologically and geographically distant cultures, despite the fact that he based much of his writing on work which was carried out in a disparaging manner.[123] I venture to interpret this silence, although I am aware of the risk of attaching oneself to something which is supported by the absence of indicators. The silence resembles the gaps in a censored piece of writing, because when one compares the traces of Hjerpe's way of thinking with what he based his writings on, one discovers a system in the omissions.

For all that, Hjerpe certainly had no thought-out programme based on principle when he cleared out the Eurocentric contempt in his calendar notes of world history. His liberal attitude was something more of a lack of wider perspective: it had simply not occurred to him that the West should be singled out as the jewel of Creation and the measure of all things. He had another pattern of recognition for assimilating exotic information. It was simple, conventional, and down to earth, and it meant that the cultural divisions between different civilisations were filtered away as being irrelevant. What was important and globally unifying was the identification, all over the world, and for every historical epoch, of the legitimate father of the nation, he whom the people could love without reservation, irrespective of whether he was a Swedish king, a Turkish sultan or an Indian emperor. Against these figures, he always contrasted evil and false usurpers, who sought power for its own sake, without a thought for their subjects' need of paternal protection.

Hjerpe also drew the same line between good and evil when the interests of the Western world were at stake. In one of his notes about world history, he lamented the conquest of Mexico by the Spaniards, admittedly in phrases very similar to those in the source to which he referred.[124] But we have already seen that Hjerpe's faithfulness to his material was only conditional, and in another note he lamented the English penetration into India in a way that lacked support in the alleged source, even though it would seem certain that he did in fact take his information from that particular source:[125]

Hjerpe

There occurred one [of] the most remarkable Conquests in India, in that the English under Generals Harris and Stuart by means of a General assault captured the Rich Emperor of Mysor's Residence city Siringapatman. Emperor Tippo Saib who had always sided with the French, had through them made war on the English possessions in that country, and now stood without the help of his Ally, who had lured him to this dangerous enterprise. most immense treasures in Gold and precious stones, the whole imperial Family were taken – and the Army; after Tippo himself fell as a hero with his bravest Friends at one of the gates of the town.

Stockh: Post Tidn N 111, 3 Oct 1799.

Stockholms Posttidningar

London, 13 Sept.
For the past 10 days here, one victory newspaper has followed close upon the other [. . .] Today they [the canons, *AJ*] were again fired as an expression of joy over the complete victory our Troops obtained over Tippo Saib and the French in East Indian [. . .] took Seringapatnam by storm, when The Tippo himself fell and all his family became prisoners of war [. . .] One does not doubt, that the entire Land of Mysore will come to belong to England [. . .] since Buonaparte and Tippo's great project came to nothing. Private letters assure us, that in Seringapatnam they have found immense treasure.

It is true that one fails to find any clearly Euro-centric negative comments about the Indians or about Emperor Tippo in *Stockholms Posttidningar*, even if the joy at England's victory is obvious. But there is still a subtle yet important difference between the 'transcript' and the original: for Hjerpe, the defeated emperor was a hero; for the newspaper's correspondent, he was only a defeated king.

In Hjerpe's calendar of world history, there is a note for 29 May about the 1807 coup d'état in Turkey. It contains some dry details about the dramatic event: the janizaries had deposed Selim II, taken him to the old seraglio and proclaimed Mustapha IV as the new sultan. In addition, the calendar states that Selim II had been much loved.[126] The reference is to *Stockholms Posttidningar*, No. 82, 1807, where it is not possible to find one word about the people's supposed love for the deposed sultan, although there are several passages about his improprieties, for example that he had broken the laws of Islam, and, worst of all, tried to avert the danger by sending his opponents 'the heads of several Ministers'.[127]

Hjerpe, as usual, added some things and took others away: the sultan he had chosen to praise could not have any flaws. Everything had to suit the given pattern, which did not include any reproach of a king, nor did it include the 'progressive' concept that some cultures had come further along the path of development than others. In his view of the passage of time, there was no room for development or cumulative progress, but that issue falls under the next thematic heading. It is thus time to move on, even if the examples of Hjerpe's views about the world around him are far from being exhausted.[128]

The third theme: the idea of progress

Enlightenment and the idea of progress

According to the standard reasoning of the first generation of Enlightenment thinkers, the world was organised according to rational, God-given laws which could be unveiled by using empirical methods. The more laws that were revealed behind life's confused façade, the more enlightened the world would become. For some of 'les philosophes', the growth of knowledge was also the way to human progress in general, and they could therefore be optimistic about development to the same extent that they credited science with having unlimited possibilities.[129]

Thus, the world did not have to stand still because its laws were laid down once and for all, but neither was the reverse of a foregone conclusion. The common points of departure provided openings in several directions, and, as the advocates of Enlightenment alternated between empiricism and rationalism, or between 'activism' and determinism, they also moved between belief and disbelief in society's continued development.[130] Enlightenment can not be described as a movement unified in being optimistic about development, and even less can it be described as an evolutionary movement, however eagerly and harmoniously its representatives proclaimed their own age as the spiritual summit of history.[131] In my view, the concept of development only becomes an evolutionary idea when it has both a cumulative perspective, in which history has a direction and the past does not repeat itself, and when it is based on the perception that the process is regulated by laws. This was not common to Enlightenment thought. Nonetheless, with d'Alembert, it is possible to see a clear link to evolutionism within contemporary biological science.[132] At the beginning of the nineteenth century, the Romantics who spoke about progress often used the term to mean a 'happy' return to the situation which prevailed before the French Revolution. Therefore, they were not evolutionists.

And vice versa, the idea of progress is older than Enlightenment and can also be found among the nineteenth-century Romantics, even in a form which is optimistic about development. On the one hand, there is Jean Bodin, among others, who as early as the mid sixteenth century, objected to contemporary pessimism's many retrospective myths about the golden age, and attributed to history the power to bring about at least recurrent phases of human progress.[133] On the Romantic side of Enlightenment, Lorenzo Hammarsköld asserted how unfamiliar and unreasonable it would be 'to want to see only an eternal circular motion in world events, which constantly revolves around the same point'. On the contrary, every experience suggested that in the long run, human spirit distanced itself from a primitive past, even if, for example, the French Revolution had shown that this must happen via painful but purifying retrogressions.[134] In the introduction to his historical manual for women, Becker addressed his 'Female Readers' with the hope that it would, 'at the end of its reading, become fairly comprehensible, how these crude peoples of the Middle Ages, at the beginning of the nineteenth century, had been able to attain the degree of good manners and refinement, which we now admire in them'.[135] Even Leopold von Ranke formulated a historical credo with clear traces of a hopeful attitude towards the idea of stages of historical development.[136]

However, we should not go too far in removing from Enlightenment all its distinctive characteristics as regards the issue of history and development. The idea of continuous moral and scientific progress was in reality Enlightenment's own original contribution, despite the fact that many within the circles of the Encyclopaedists doubted its prospects, and even if its invention was also clearly spread to the opponents of Enlightenment. Even H. Vyverberg, who has particularly stressed the element of pessimism among Enlightenment philosophers,[137] argues that optimism was still typical: 'Certainly the prevalence of optimism in the French Enlightenment cannot be denied'.[138]

What was decisively new in this was not, perhaps, how change should be evaluated, but the less provocative theory of history's cumulative course: the idea that in its development, society never returns to its starting-point.[139] Still, the idea of progress was sufficiently prominent, and therefore sufficiently provocative to those who maintained that people of all physical ages and all historical epochs found themselves at the same distance from God.[140] This was, however, a point of view which would become increasingly hard to maintain, the more the ground gained by biology and economy during the nineteenth century appeared to show that the obstacles to development were being surmounted.[141] Nonetheless, many Christians managed to assimilate Lamarckian evolutionary biology with the doctrine of original sin: he who did not take care of his body and refrain from excesses would not only be destroyed himself, but would also pass on a degenerative inheritance to future generations. They inverted Spencer's perspective, which involved a belief in genetically determined progress.[142]

It is very likely that the expansive nineteenth century lay beyond the conceptual horizons of both Johan Hjerpe and Jacques-Louis Ménétra; they had nothing to say about the idea of progress, nor about objections to it, and it is precisely this silence which will now be considered.

Hjerpe's relative silence, plus a little about Ménétra's

No doubt Hjerpe vehemently disapproved of Enlightenment and all its objectionable leaders. He regretted the contemporary way of thinking, when no one wanted to take orders, when 'Modern Friendship' made people indifferent to one another and when everything else that could possibly be worthwhile was swept away by the course of progress.[143] Nevertheless, he did not go through life completely unaffected by the general change in outlook of which Enlightenment was a part. Something of a cumulative perspective crept up on him at last, and with this an enlightened disdain for reactionary people who clung stubbornly to their superstitious old ways of doing things. Hjerpe, too, was infected by the scientific spirit.[144]

In the surviving examples of Ménétra's writing, by way of contrast, no statement of opinion on this issue can be found. He neither praised nor regretted development in general terms, and made no such comments about the French Revolution. On the contrary, in his definite but changing perceptions, he closely followed the phases of the revolution. First, he was a royalist revolutionary, then a Jacobin and finally a relieved man when the reign of terror was over. The revolution did not form part of his plans, it only got in his way in the form of a now gratifying, now disturbing element in daily life.[145]

The real question is how much Ménétra planned at all. He does not appear to have been in a particular hurry. For a long time – indeed, for far too long a time to be an economically responsible self-employed artisan – he squandered money in taverns and on his amorous adventures in France. That is why it took so long before he had saved enough money to set himself up as a master craftsman in the guild where he had received his education.[146]

However little Ménétra regarded the revolution as an epoch-making event in French history, some kind of milestone in the course of development, he seemed to have just as little regard that his energetic intervention into his social microcosm was governed by any more long-term aims in life. Nothing in his autobiography is described in progressive terms, and his account is therefore punctuated by neither specific references to time nor grammatical punctuation marks. Everything seems special; hardly a date or a year is given in his account. The hypothesis is that Ménétra saw the world as he described it, even if the detail in his account could, of course, be connected more with the epic structure of the genre than with the narrator's personal perspective.

However, despite the fact that Hjerpe made use of completely different genres from Ménétra, his perception of history did not contain much of a development perspective. Instead, it consisted mostly of repetition. The battle between the good princes and the evil usurpers had to be fought, a battle interspersed with fires, plagues and destitution, to which anything really new is seldom added.[147]

Nonetheless, Hjerpe based his calendarial depiction of history on modern writers who were optimistic about progress – historians who had clearly been influenced by 'les philosophes'. He gave an account of what they had said about history, but there is still very little in his notes that shows the historians' message had reached him. Hjerpe ranked some kings above others, and at the top, of course, was Gustavus III. But most often he saw no development, no cumulative change of attitude which would have made different generations of people unfamiliar with each other's way of thinking. As a result, he respected earlier generations. In this he was, therefore, not a man of Enlightenment.

Both parties – Hjerpe and the historians – dealt with the same everlasting themes: war and death, kings and their peoples. But for the one party, history was a calendar where everything should repeat itself, whereas for the other party, time was instead accompanied by a continual drift away from all that was old. Hjerpe's dislike of development and his hopes for a rehabilitation of old values appear most clearly in his notes on the French Revolution. They therefore deserve separate treatment.

On 27 May 1788, Johan Hjerpe, still a young linen shop assistant, noted in his diary:

> The dispatches say that the night between the 8th and 9th of May, the king of France ordered the arrest of his Parliament in Paris. In that country, things are beginning to look grave. The Crown has fallen into terrible debt due to the power which has accrued to the king to far too great an extent. Louis XVI is a gentleman of small capacity [. . .] Things have now gone so far that the French Nation shall be compelled by violence at the discretion of several unworthy Ministers. Levies are imposed without any order, and take the place of justice [. . .] The Nation asserts the law of the People, but the court does not want to understand anything other than what they say shall happen.

As has already been mentioned in Chapter 1, Hjerpe kept a diary at least between the years 1788 and 1792. Most of the contents concern Gustavus III and the war against Russia. But now and then he reflected upon the events in

France. The diary therefore gives a unique testimony about the impression made by the French Revolution on a contemporary artisan's son, a simple man, a man of the people.

'The Nation asserts the law of the People', Hjerpe said with a nod of assent. It is thus not hard to imagine the enthusiasm such a man must have felt for the news about the storming of the Bastille, the new constitution, the king's capture in Varennes, the establishment of the republic in September 1792 and other things that would raise the yoke of repression from the shoulders of the poor. As early as 1788, Hjerpe had lamented over 'the Bastille, that prison due to pure arbitrariness where many sit until their death'.[148] And the *sans culottes* – the key troops of the revolution in the French capital – were of the same rank as he: small businessmen, master craftsmen and journeymen.[149] But no. As early as the beginning of 1789, he had become guarded. Now the diary reads: 'Feelings are so agitated that much evil is feared', and France's political crisis no longer stemmed, as it had a year earlier, from a royal power that was too strong, but from 'a weak Louis'.[150]

It is true that the king's power 'had been too overbearing', but 'what will he become now?' Hjerpe regretted that France did not have a 'Gustavus instead of a Louis XVI'. He regarded it as a bad sign that the king was forced to summon the National Assembly, because now 'the king's power ... [would] in consequence finally fall'. 'Can France then be happy?' he asked himself anxiously.[151]

In *Dagligt Allehanda* of 12 August 1789, one can read that the people of Paris had torn down the Bastille, 'that hateful monument to Despotism'. *Stockholms Posttidningar* also rejoiced that the fortress had fallen, and praised 'the happy revolution, which forestalled much greater acts of violence'.[152] But in the diary there was no trace of the delighted remarks in the press about the fall of the Bastille. Perhaps the news did not immediately reach Hjerpe; when it appeared in the Swedish newspapers he was still travelling home from a fair in Karlstad. But when he heard what had happened, he was appalled:[153]

> there came through the Dispatches the remarkable news that the French Nation has taken power from its King, and instead of Sovereignty which the kings there abused have made themselves completely free. Unhappy country, where due to internal disagreement more than 1000 have sacrificed their Lives – the Nation loves its weak king ... what now is the great France which gave Europe laws – how does one now look upon this previously so splendid nation, yea, with contempt – and that is what it is worth.

In April, the wallpaper manufacturer Reveillon made a fool of himself in the National Assembly: he said that the workers could not be poor because they had gold watches. The people of Paris answered with a riot and were met by cannons and rifles. More than 130 'remained on the spot', as *Stockholms Post-tidningar* described the deaths, and 350 wounded were taken away. The event caused Hjerpe to express dislike for the people's desire to 'free themselves from the power of the sovereign king'. Nonetheless, he maintained a disapproving distance from the holders of power who he felt had used excessive force against 'the mob', a violence which affected both 'the guilty and the innocent'.[154]

However, from the autumn of 1789 and onwards, Hjerpe's flirtation was over; he could no longer find anything extenuating about the French Revolution. He felt that 'through internal unrest, France has come so far off course that it seems to disappear in Europe',[155] that 'this Absurd nation! which before was noble in freedom [commits] the greatest follies'.[156] He lamented gloomily that France could no longer lead the world: 'This remarkable Realm which has governed Europe cannot now govern itself'.[157] And the reason was that it was to be governed by the people.

Johan Hjerpe gave nothing for 'Freedom' and nothing for the rule of the people, although he had done in 1788, when the aristocracy appeared to threaten it. But now that the people themselves had seized this right, things were different, because what would happen 'after the Aristocracy has been abolished and everyone made equal?' He continues:

> Civil war will be unavoidable – the Realm can never be governed by the Mob, however Philosophically Voltaire and Rouseau [*sic*] paint freedom [. . .] the one Party destroys [things] for the other and it never goes well.[158]

And further:

> oh! when a nation so badly estimates its Powers/Authorities! how shall it be governed by the Mob?[159]

Hjerpe found the power of the people to be unacceptable despite the fact that he was a man of the people. One wonders: are these diary notes evidence of an opinion that generally prevailed among the bourgeoisie or petit bourgeoisie in Gustavian Stockholm, or was Hjerpe simply the odd man out?

It is clear that he was out on his own; his extraordinary diligence with the pen is proof of that. His diary is very comprehensive – about 650 handwritten pages in all, not counting the interleaved newspaper clippings! By carefully following the foreign news in the newspapers, he kept himself extremely well informed about daily political events both in Sweden and abroad. That was how he learned about the tumult in Paris. Sometimes it was *Stockholms Posten* which caught his attention, at other times it was *Stockholms Posttidning-ar*. But he probably preferred, above all, to read *Dagligt Allehanda*, which appealed in particular to ordinary people, and which also most strongly repudiated the French Revolution throughout.[160]

Although one can clearly see traces of Hjerpe's sources in the diary, his notes are not purely transcripts; in fact they are less so here than elsewhere. He was indeed an unusual man, but not a hermit. We already know that he had his own opinions about what he could glean from the newspapers.

On 25 February 1790, the newspapers reported that at the beginning of the month, Louis XVI had paid a visit to the National Assembly and there vowed his support for 'the system that now prevails'. Indeed, the king had actually called himself 'the head and Protector of the Revolution'. Everyone was moved, tears flowed and the king received tributes from the members of the assembly. The newspaper correspondents do not appear to have found grounds to doubt Louis' sincerity. *Stockholms Posttidningar* even wrote that the king 'made so much more of an impression that it appeared to be a pouring out of the Monarch's innermost feelings'.[161]

In Hjerpe's diary there is a note about the event. It is obviously based on the newspaper reports. It is equally clear that Hjerpe gave the event his own – let us say, royalist – interpretation: the king was out of the running, a prisoner in his own palace, and against his own convictions had to pay lip service to the revolution:[162]

> It is deplorable with the king in France; what now is his power, when the people have taken it? when he wanted to leave several 1000 escorted him as a guard; is not he then a prisoner! [the specific date not supplied] He had to go before the National Assembly and explain himself to the leaders of the Revolution, but how satisfied he was about accepting everything, time will show, when he receives a freer hand. Over this, there were Illuminations and Te Deum – they got just what they wanted.

Hjerpe was unusual, but for all that, he was not alone among Stockholm's lower bourgeoisie in disliking the development of the French Revolution. There were many who felt sympathy for the increasingly powerless king 'of the French'. It was only natural that *Dagligt Allehanda* criticised the new régime in France more than the other newspapers – natural, bearing in mind its readers were ordinary people.

In Sweden the nobility disliked kings, not the people. And it was the king who carried out revolutions against the aristocracy who guarded the rule of the estates of the realm and its right to deny the king money for silly heroic wars. Gustavus sought his support among the bourgeoisie; he appealed to them, flattered them, and raged against the aristocracy. So the capital city's journeymen – master craftsmen and tradesmen – liked their own king, the great Gustavus, their fatherly protector against the rule of the noble few.[163]

Seen from this perspective, it becomes possible to understand Hjerpe's attitude – one which he shared with his fellows, however unlike them he was in other respects. He found himself between the opposing pressures of two revolutions: an old kind and a new one. In a broad sense, one could say that until then, revolutions had been the prerogative of those in authority and, in particular, of kings. Making a revolution meant restoring legitimate power. In the spring of 1788, the Parisian bookseller Sébastien Hardy made notes in his diary about the 'coming re-volution'. What he envisaged was not the people settling their score with the monarchy, but rather Louis XVI planning to abolish an obstructive parliament.[164] But the revolution the following year made the king the object of attack and also caused the concept of revolution itself to be re-defined: revolutions no longer led back to the past, but away from it.

This was part of Hjerpe's dilemma; it can be seen from another point of view. Hjerpe was a bourgeois man and at the same time a kind of pre-industrial universalist. That is to say, he felt a sense of affinity with the bourgeoisie in all countries, including France. But whereas Stockholm's journeyman artisans took part in a royalist uprising towards the end of the 1780s, the Parisian bourgeoisie prepared to take power from their king. How would Hjerpe make sense of such a contradictory world?

He tried to make Sweden into a model for his interpretation of the events in France. Just like the Swedish aristocracy, the French nobility did everything it could to avoid contributing to the state's finances, and the bourgeoisie in France were left to carry the debt burden – as they would have been forced to do in Sweden, but for Gustavus III Hjerpe wrote in his diary on 27 June 1788:[165]

> there, a general insurrection is feared. the Crown is in debt, it shall be paid. The Nobility and the Clergy who have the greatest incomes are friends of the Ministers and have evaded the expenses. The Burghers shall then get the largest which are not cheap.

In the beginning, the re-interpretation moved apace, and with this scenario before him it was not difficult for Hjerpe to reconcile himself with the French nation's demand for 'the law of the People'. Moreover, it was not until 1792 that the Parisian Jacobins made it clear – to themselves and the rest of the world – that the king had no place in the revolution, other than as suspended (August), deposed (September), and beheaded (January 1793). He very soon became powerless, and that gave Hjerpe problems with his world-view. If, in 1788, he had regretted the plight of the French bourgeoisie and blamed the nobility, he soon stopped speaking in class terms about what was happening in France. What for him had been the victimised bourgeoisie, soon became the evil people or the mob. The word bourgeois was removed from the vocabulary of the introspective discussions in his diary.

For Johan Hjerpe, the people's rights rested on the king's sovereignty. They had always done so, and should continue to do so. But in all ages, legitimate monarchs had been threatened by aristocratic usurpers. Nonetheless, there was perhaps a worse threat: from within, from the king's consorts. These scheming women were constantly turning up – women from King Birger's Märta to Louis XVI's Marie Antoinette.[166] 'The Nation loves its weak king', Hjerpe wrote in his diary, and continued: 'but they are very embittered about the queen; she has also to a great extent caused much harm'.[167]

The thought of a people's democracy was far too mind-boggling for Hjerpe, and he had even greater difficulty imagining women holding the reigns of power. As a young shop assistant, he had already repudiated the French Revolution. Nothing in his attitude had changed when he touched upon the theme again many years later.

Despite his life-long aversion to change, Hjerpe was conservative in a different way from a Romantic like Lorenzo Hammarsköld, in whose conservatism there was still room for a kind of evolutionary determinism. At the same time, both men regarded Enlightenment, the French Revolution and Napoleon's rule as disturbances in a natural state which should be restored. So when Napoleon had finally been deposed and Louis XVIII was reinstated, Hjerpe could relax after decades of distress. In the following note, as in most of his many references to the events in France, he lets his heart rule his pen. By and large, only the actual dates have anything to do with his source material; in fact, from the words 'most ceremonious' onwards, nothing else he says can be found in the source:[168]

1814. France's King Louis 18th arrived at Calais aboard an English royal Yacht. There he was received in the most ceremonious manner by his Subjects, after he had been in exile for 20 years and had not received any safe haven before he arrived in England. Called by the French Senate last month, to ascend his Ancestors' Throne, he arrived to heal the deep wounds that the Tyrant to the people's happiness Napoleon Bonapart [sic] so deeply carved in the previously happy France. The Nation celebrated Louis' arrival with enthusiasm, and his entry into Paris the 3rd May thereafter was one of the happiest days of the redeemed Fatherland.

Although relieved, Hjerpe was still angry and unforgiving, far more so than the press from which he so diligently took his information. When *Stockholms Posttidningar* reported in neutral terms about the restored king's general amnesty, that no one would be 'persecuted for his political beliefs or conduct, for his attachment either to any of the Contracting Parties, or to any Government which has ceased to exist',[169] Hjerpe made the following remarks:[170]

France's King Louis 18th signed in Paris the remarkable Peace with all of the Powers united against France, and the bloody 22-year war which had broken out due to the French revolution ceased. France which had tormented Europe returned to within the borders it had had the first of January 1792. A complete Pardon was given to all the murderers of Louis 16th, and to others who had made themselves renowned during this bloody time. Everything that has happened has been forgotten by the good Louis 18th, who with that wishes to make everyone his ally; but time showed that Villains never stop being so as long as he has power.

Johan Hjerpe and Jacques-Louis Ménétra had very different personalities: the one deeply pious, accepting royal power and the obedience of the people, the other a hater of the clergy and their teachings, and a supporter of his country's great revolution, albeit with an unclear attitude towards his king. But in these very differences, they were both loyal to the mentality of their own local social environment. And although one of them was an opponent of development while the other accepted it, both lacked a well-considered developmental perspective on what they wanted to oppose or support. For neither of them did history have any definite direction, and yet both belonged to the educated part of their social class.

*

Less than a hundred years after the deaths of the silk manufacturer and the master glass worker, the sawmill workers in Holmsund, a small community on the top corner of the Swedish map, founded a teetotallers' lodge. The lodge's members would come to belong to an educated élite within the working class. For these people, optimism about the future was self-evident and one of the cornerstones of their social and political project. Where Hjerpe and Ménétra had been naïvely unaware of the possibilities of development, these people, the modern workers of the capitalist age, were confidently optimistic about the future. It was these late nineteenth-century workers who first consciously adopted the Enlightenment project, which Hjerpe and Ménétra, the project's contemporaries, were only vaguely aware of.[171] In this way, the differences between the two men who have been the main objects of comparison in this chapter are made even more obscure in time's retrospective mirror.

Enlightenment reflections

In the next chapter I shall try to fulfil the promise made in the introduction to discuss, to some degree, the issue of the value of studying individual people from the past. First let me give a short, analytical résumé of what has been said in this chapter.

With Enlightenment, a series of spiritual processes came to light with unique clarity, processes that subsequently left their mark on the development of thought in our part of the world. What was new and central was the Enlightenment philosophers' energetic attempt to strip authorised ideological and cultural attitudes of their general, timeless validity. Knowledge had also to be supported by experience, but experience was limited and particular; truth was therefore relative and not absolute. This was the reason why Enlightenment philosophers chose foreign cultures as viewpoints from which to regard their own. They could cultivate the self-reflective relativism that was the basis for the concept of tolerance for which they fought and which aimed at dismantling values which had hitherto been regarded as eternal. This relativism – sometimes a distinct docrine, sometimes an indistinct way of thinking – was a kind of fundamental concept of Enlightenment thought, despite the fact that 'les philosophes' often fell back on absolute values.

Out of this relativism, some connected sets of themes emerged more than others: a secularised deism or atheism, an expanded consciousness of the value of foreign cultures, and the transformative thought that history never returns to its starting-point, a thought which for some was elevated to a belief in progress. These complexes of ideas can either be regarded as being constituent elements in the informal Encyclopaedist programme, as being part of spontaneous intellectual changes, or as both.

The task of this chapter has been to search for reflections of Enlightenment thought in samples of the writings of Johan Hjerpe and Jacques-Louis Ménétra, two members of the petit bourgeoisie in eighteenth- and early nineteenth-century Europe, one of them from Stockholm and the other from Paris. The two men have been compared with one another, with the central themes of Enlightenment and with self-reflective cultural relativism which was a common basic theme in the spiritual renewal towards which the Encyclopaedist philosophers worked.

In general, both these men showed examples of a kind of religious tolerance. Ménétra was an outspoken enemy of the clergy and of Christian teaching, and spoke about the need for tolerance of Jews and others. In contrast, Hjerpe was a devoutly Christian man who, it is true, displayed severity in his judgement of religious zealots close to home, but who at the same time refrained from making any condemnatory statements about Jews, Muslims and others of exotic faiths in other parts of the world. He was also very well-oriented both in terms of contemporary international politics and world history. Yet, he still did not place either his own time or Europe and Sweden above the past or above the contemporary world beyond the West. What is also striking in this context is the complete lack of a Eurocentric disdain for foreign (and, in time, colonised) cultures. Hjerpe's way of describing Selim II of Turkey or the Indian emperors was the same as his way of describing power struggles in Europe. This can also be linked to the almost total absence of a cumulative perspective on social development, an absence which is striking in both Hjerpe and Ménétra. Nonetheless, in contrast to Hjerpe, Ménétra said nothing at all about foreign worlds, but was completely preoccupied by events in his immediate environment.

Compared with the enlightened ideological debate, it is possible to recognise some things in the lines of thought of Hjerpe and Ménétra, even if a cumulative perspective was as absent in both these men as it was present in the ideological debate. However, the similarities that one does find, in my opinion, were not related via influences from above. It was more a question of a kind of 'convergence': Enlightenment arrived at a tolerance on matters of faith which many people had not got as far as 'transgressing'.

There still remained at least one important and major difference between the different cultural spheres: with their secularising criticism of religion, Enlightenment philosophers developed a self-reflective cultural relativism, which was not innate to the rehabilitation of old heathen values in the sphere of popular culture. Such a relativism is not to be found in Hjerpe or Ménétra, despite the fact that these men were very unlike each other and despite the fact that both in their educated or semi-educated ability to put down their own ideas on paper differed from their social equals. And, in my view, this relativism was a more fundamental change of intellect than was secularisation, even if the Enlightenment philosophers did not have the strength to sustain such an attitude more than temporarily.

Notes

1.   Hjerpe has appeared sporadically in historical research. See Boberg, *Kunglig krigspropaganda*, pp. 11–14, 32, 38, 43, 50, 76; Lönnroth, *Den stora rollen*, p. 182. Someone who has been particularly interested in Hjerpe is R. Liljedahl, who published an article on him back in the 1940s, entitled 'En gustaviansk handelsbetjänt'. See, too, his 'En märklig auktion i Skara', 'Samtal med en 1700-talsmänniska', 'Att umgås med en 1700-talsmänniska'. Finally, Johan Hjerpe was to be found in an exhibition on the French Revolution at the Uppsala University Library. See the catalogue for this, *Med tryckpress och giljotin: en utställning om franska revolutionen*, p. 47.

2.   In 1982, D. Roche published Ménétra's autobiography, for which he wrote a long commentary: J.-L. Ménétra, *Journal de ma vie: compagnon vitrier au 18e siècle*. It was subsequently published in English under the title *Journal of My Life*, this time with a foreword by Robert Darnton as well. See also Chartier, 'Les pratiques de l'écrit', pp. 157–58; Chartier, *The cultural origins of the French revolution*, pp. 83, 122–24; A. Farge, *Livets sköra tråd: våld, makt och solidaritet i 1700-talets Paris*, pp. 59, 74; G. Lévi, 'Les usages de la biographie', p. 1331; D. Roche, 'La violence vue d'en bas: réflexions sur les moyens de la politique en période révolutionnaire', pp. 50f. Menocchio is the central figure in Ginzburg, *The cheese and the worms*. The same applies to Martin Guerre in Davis, *The Return of Martin Guerre*, and Pierre Maury plays a prominent role in E. Le Roy Ladurie's *Montaillou*.

3.   Ménétra has previously been compared with another contemporary of his, the

woollen-miller and innkeeper Louis Simon, in Roche 'La violence vue d'en bas', pp. 50ff. But that concerned the views of two artisans of the violence in the French revolution.

4. The idea is eventually to extend the analysis to other writing representatives of the common folk. Some exploratory work has already been done to that end. Random volumes for each letter in *Otto Waldes register över enskilda arkiv* (alphabetically organised), the Royal Library edition, has been sorted through and popular, personal material has been catalogued. Börje Bergfeldt should be thanked for his work with this cataloguing as a doctoral student at the Stockholm University Department of Economic History. I myself have gone through selected parts of the unpublished papers left by Christian Johansén, a sanctuary artisan from Eskilstuna at the end of the eighteenth century and the beginning of the nineteenth century. It has not been impossible to fit this work into this chapter, however. See Eskilstuna stadsarkiv (*ESA*), *Handlingar rörande Christian Johansén*, vol. 1: diaries and accounts books 1765–77; vol. 4: miscellaneous documents; vol. 5: on Swedenborgianism (containing mostly translations of Swedenborg from Latin to Swedish). My thanks to Lars Magnusson of the Department of Economic History, Uppsala University, for the tip about Johansén's paper. Attention has previously been drawn to Johansén in connection with Swedenborgianism. See H. Lenhammar, *Tolerans och bekännelsetvång: studier i den svenska swedenborgianismen 1765–1795*, p. 255ff.

5. *Förteckning på Johan Hjerpes boksamling*; Liljedahl, 'En märklig auktion i Skara', in which the author assumes that Hjerpe's diary actually covered many more than the five years (1788–92) which have been preserved. In Hjerpe's estate inventory, the only thing mentioned is 'Diverse Manuscripter', Göteborgs landsarkiv (*GLA*), the estate inventories of the district of Skåning 1808–30. See also A. Jarrick, 'Framstegstanken i den historiska texten: några uppslag om fiktion och forskning'.

6. Hjerpe seems to have been a rather solitary man, even if he was not without friends. He remained unmarried. See *LSB*, J. Hjerpe, Berättelse om en lustresa . . . , especially p. 307; in *UUB*, JHJ, there are also references to socialising, although rather modest ones. At the same time there is obvious testimony here to his aloofness: 26 July 1789, 28 July 1789, final entry in December 1789 (undated), final entry in December 1790 (undated).

7. *UUB*, JHJ, 19 July 1789.

8. *Förteckning på Johan Hjerpes boksamling*: *UUB*, JHJ and Merckwärdige händelser för alla årets dagar.

9. The assessment is based on a thorough survey of his historical accounts. His calendar of world history contains approximately 1,800 entries. These were first divided into eleven subject headings, in which items on war, kings and the fate of other men and women of note dominate entirely. I have subsequently studied 160 items closely, and of these I have compared 90 with the data referred to. I have also divided items on the history of Stockholm into subject categories, this time under 19 headings for the years between 1649 and 1792. Previous years, i.e., from 1552 onwards, have not been divided into subjects. As Hjerpe only cited references for four of all his items on the history of Stockholm, it has been very difficult to trace his material here. Several attempts have, however, been made, and I have gone through some twenty works altogether, including a good number of volumes of *Stockholms stads kalendar*, probably Hjerpe's most important source. An account of this derivation work has not been included here due to space.

10. Hjerpe's histories of Stockholm and the world are both largely concerned with kings and wars, interspersed with disasters and epidemics. Other sorts of events took up very

little space. *KB*, J Hjerpe, *Kong residensestaden Stockholms* . . . ; *UUB*, Johan Hjerpe, *Merckwärdige händelser* . . . See Nyman, *Press mot friheten*, p. 116.

11. *Allmänna journalen* is an example. The newspaper had, as a permanent feature, reports from the history of the world on curious events. See also *Märkvärdigheter utur äldre och sednare tiders Mennisko- Folkslags- och SedeHistorie.*

12. *Allmänna journalen* number 31 (1818); *UUB*, Johan Hjerpe, *Merckwärdige händelser* . . . , 7/2.

13. Lindroth, *Vetenskapsakademiens historia I:2*, pp. 862–63; *Historisk almanacka* for the years 1750–54 and 1780–84. Even during the Period of Liberty, it had become fashionable to organise historical material thematically. On this, see N. Eriksson, *Dalin–Botin–Lagerbring: historieforskning och historieskrivning i Sverige 1747–1787*, pp. 31–32; Jarrick, 'Framstegstanken i den historiska texten', p. 243. An exception to the calendarial principle in the almanacs is Pehr Wargentin's feuilleton on Swedish history in *Stockholms stads (historiska) calender, 1761–1777*, in which a chronological principle is followed. The items quoted are from *UUB*, Johan Hjerpe, *Merckwärdige händelser* . . . , 7/2. For the lack of agreement in historical research, see H. Horstbøll, 'Tingenes natur er ikke en roman: om historieskrivningens tider og rum', pp. 107–10.

14. J.-L. Ménétra, *Journal de ma vie*, Roche's introduction, pp. 19, 21.

15. Ibid., pp. 21, 25.

16. Ibid., pp. 138, 204–05, 207–08.

17. See, for example, *LSB*, J. Hjerpe, *Berättelse om en lustresa* . . . , pp. 47, 62, 71–72.

18. Ménétra, *Journal de ma vie*, Roche's postscript, pp. 300–01.

19. *UUB*, JHJ, 17 May 1789; Ménétra, *Journal de ma vie*, p. 37.

20. *UUB*, JHJ, 24 December 1790.

21. By conventional I mean here the same as Jürgen Habermas in his book *Communication and the evolution of society*, p. 80, in which, referring to Lawrence Kohlberg, he writes about a 'phase' of the conventional moral level in the following way: 'There is orientation toward authority, fixed rules, and the maintenance of the social order. Right behavior consists of doing one's duty, showing respect for authority, and maintaining the given social order for it's own sake'. Habermas and Kohlberg contrast this with pre-conventional and post-conventional; the post-conventional moral 'is a clear effort to define moral values and principles which have validity and application apart from the authority of the groups or persons holding these principles' (p. 80).

22. One such example is the tale of the execution in 1707 of Pajkull and Patkull. On this, compare *KB*, J Hjerpe, *Kong residensestaden Stockholm* . . . , 1707 with S. Lagerbring, *Sammandrag av Svea rikes historia*, pp. 35–41.

23. Habermas, *Communication and the evolution of society*, p. 80.

24. Ibid.

25. *LSB*, J. Hjerpe, *Berättelse om en lustresa* . . . , p. 128.

26. Ménétra, *Journal de ma vie*, for example pp. 147–49, 152, 161 and 278. The difficulty with placing Ménétra morally exists in relation to different stages of development psychology, as in the psychology of Habermas and Kohlberg. See Habermas, *Communication and the evolution of society*, p. 80, in which all three stages could be placed: 1) the pre-conventional, with reference to its reliance on its own strength to achieve its desires; 2) the conventional, with reference to its normative anchoring in certain social groups; and 3) the post-conventional, with reference to its programmatic defence of universal values.

27. Breisach, *Historiography*, pp. 205, 210; P. Gay, 'Editor's introduction' to Voltaire, *Philosophical dictionary*, p. 14; A. Hertzberg, *The French Enlightenment and the jews*, p. 282; J. McManners, *Death and the Enlightenment: changing attitudes among christians and unbelievers*

in eighteenth-century France, pp. 123, 151, 154, 160–73; Voltaire, *Philosophical dictionary* (1988), for example p. 208; H. Vyverberg, *Historical pessimism in the French enlightenment*, pp. 211-12, 219. One always suspects a sort of ironical undertone in Voltaire.

28. McManners, *Death and the Enlightenment*, pp. 178, 181, 184.

29. P. Gay, 'Editors's introduction', p. 17; Gay, *The Enlightenment* 1, pp. 5-18; J. McManners, *Death and the Enlightenment, pp. 165, 172–73; M. Ozouf, Festivals and the French revolution*, p. 273; Voltaire, *Philosophical dictionary*, pp. 173, 206, 236–37; *Encyklopédie ou dictionnaire raisonné des sciences . . .*, Vol. 28, p. 248: 'Ces hommages dûs à Dieu, font ce qu'on appelle autrement culte ou religion. On en distingue de deux fortes, l'un intérieur, & l'autre extérieur. L'un est l'autre est d'obligation. L'interieur est invariable; l'extérieur dépend des mœurs, des temps & de la religion'.

30. *Encyklopédie*, p. 246.

31. On this, see Lenhammar, *Tolerans och bekännelsetvång*, pp. 151–58, 192–97; Nyman, *Press mot friheten*, pp. 154–55; *Anmärkningar vid den gamla Folks-maximen . . .*; *Om tolerancen*. The tolerance debate in *Stockholms Posten* in 1784 has been commented on previously, but usually only superficially. I have thus gone through it myself. An account of this survey will be presented elsewhere. For commentaries on Voltaire, see *Stockholms Posten* numbers 24, 28, 34, 55, 61, 72, 199. See also numbers 22, 74, 76, 92, 93, 95, 96, 192–95, 200, 203, 204, 215, 216, 221, 226 (1784). See also *Dagligt Allehandla*, number 136 (1784).

32. On secularisation in France, see Vovelle, *La mort et l'Occident . . .*, pp. 416ff; Vovelle, *La mentalité révolutionnaire*, pp. 43–48; A. Pardailhé-Galabrun, *La naissance de l'intime: 3000 foyers parisiens XVIIe–XVIIIe siècles*, pp. 402–19. For the secularisation under way in contemporary Sweden, see E. M. Hamberg, *Studies in the prevalence of religious beliefs and religious practice in contemporary Sweden*, pp. 31–32, 55.

33. M. Ozouf, *Festivals and the French revolution*, p. 197; Vovelle, *La mentalité révolutionnaire*, p. 166.

34. Vovelle, *La mentalité révolutionnaire*, pp. 170–72. See also Ozouf, *Festivals and the French revolution*, Chapter 4. She has a different perspective on the carnivals from Vovelle, however, and argues that these festivities were 'atypical' (p. 89). But they occurred in any case, often had an inversion character (pp. 91, 94) and 'in certain regions and at certain times, cultural archaism was stronger than revolutionary innovation', (p. 91).

35. See, for example, A. Farge, *Livets sköra tråd*, p. 252. For an example of a Danish clergyman of this sort, see H. Horstbøll, 'Cosmology and Economics', p. 33.

36. Hammarsköld, 'Teleologiska betragtelser öfver verlds-historien', p. 32.

37. Hammarsköld's model was, perhaps, La Mettrie, who claimed, to a considerable degree, precisely that with which Hammarsköld burdened the entire Enlightenment. See, for example, Vyverberg, *Historical pessimism in the French enlightenment*, pp. 219–22. However, there were advocates of a sort of moderate Enlightenment in Sweden in the early nineteenth century, which associated this with a defence of a tolerant protestantism, for example, J. F. Eckerlund, *Tal om Upplysningens förmånliga följder, i anledning af reformationsseclet; Anmärkningar vid den gamla Folks-maximen . . .*, pp. 10–17.

38. Nyman, *Press mot friheten*, pp. 158–64.

39. *Prästeståndets riksdagsprotokoll 1778–1790*, memorandum concerning the proposed restrictions on religious freedom for Jews and Catholics, pp. 200–24; Anders Chydenius's memorandum, p. 203.

40. The father, Anders Hjerpe (1712–91), was a member of the Moravian Brethren from 1760 onwards. *SSA*, Nicolai parish register of births and baptism, p. 354 and record of deaths, pp. 447–48; *EBAS*, Catlog över Ev Brödrasocieteten i Stockholm 1761–1770.

41. On this, see Jarrick, *Den himmelske älskaren*.

42. See, for example, *UUB*, JHJ, 1/1, 12/5 1788; May, 4/8 1789; 14/2, 2/4, 17/6 1790 among

many other diary entries. I have only found one place in which Hjerpe testifies to a sort of heightened religious feeling. It concerns a sort of physico-theologically reported experience of nature during the summer at Visingsö in 1810. *LSB*, Berättelse om en resa . . . , p. 201.

43. *UUB*, J. Hjerpe, Merckwärdige händelser . . . , 20/2.

44. J. J. Björnståhl, *Resa till Frankrike, Stockholm 1780–1784*, pp. 68–70.

45. For Hjerpe's love for Gustavus III, see Boberg, *Kunglig krigspropaganda*, p. 76, n. 4; *LSB*, Johan Hjerpe, Samlingsbok . . . för diktavskrifter o.d., 'Wid Konung Gustaf 3^{dies} återkomst från Finland'; *UUB*, JHJ, 28/8 1790. On Gustavus III and Voltaire, see B. Hennings, *Gustav III*, p. 36; Lindroth, *Svensk lärdomshistoria: gustavianska tiden*, pp. 171–72, 175. For Voltaire's influence on the penal law reforms of Gustavus III, see E. Anners, *Humanitet och rationalism: studier i upplysningstidens strafflagsreformer med hänsyn till Gustav III:s reformlagstiftning*, pp. 7–8, 185, 204–05.

46. J. C. Bauer, *Adertonde århundradets märkwärdigaste händelser*, pp. 166, 178.

47. *UUB*, J. Hjerpe, Merckwärdige händelser . . . for example 11/1, 1/3, 1/5, 2/6, 5/8, 18/9 and 6/10.

48. On the persecution of the Moravians, see Jarrick, *Den himmelske älskaren*, p. 37. On the clergy's continued association of the Moravians with other sects at the end of the 1770s, see *Prästeståndets riksdagsprotokoll 1778–1779*, p. 97.

49. M. Lamm, *Upplysningstidens romantik II*, pp. 61–63; Lenhammar, *Tolerans och bekännelsetvång*, pp. 219–28.

50. *SSA*, Population register for Anders Hjerpe 1780, p. 30 and for Anders Kjellstedt 1790, p. 83.

51. *KB*, J. Hjerpe, Kong residensestaden Stockholms . . . on the year 1780.

52. *RA*, Acta Ecclesiastica, religion cases; Jarrick, *Den himmelske älskaren*, pp. 70–72; Nyman, *Press mot friheten*, pp. 31, 255 n. 349.

53. See *Stockholms Posten* numbers 34, 55, 192 (1784).

54. This inclination is particularly prominent in the feuilleton contribution by 'Archaicus', *Stockholms Posten* numbers 192–95, 198–200 (1784).

55. *Anmärkningar vid den gamla Folks-maximen: 'Det är bättre att tro för mycket än för litet' helgade åt Upplysningens vänner*, p. 9.

56. Lenhammar, *Tolerans och bekännelsetvång*, pp. 221–22; *Prästeståndets riksdagsprotokoll 1778–1779*, p. 97.

57. Lamm, *Upplysningstidens romatik II*, pp. 61–63; Lenhammar, *Tolerans och bekännelsetvång*, pp. 222–26.

58. *SSA*, Södra förstadens kämnärsrätts kriminalmålsprotokoll 1780. See also A. Jarrick and J. Söderberg, *Empirisk civiliseringsforskning*, p. 37–40.

59. Voltaire, *Philosophical dictionary* (1988), p. 220; Voltaire, *Traktat om toleransen*, pp. 82–84, 122–23; Nyman, *Press mot friheten*, pp. 108, 117, 125, 126, 131, 257–58 n. 37. In this note, Nyman discusses the different views of Enlightenment stances on the Jews.

60. On the size of the changes in immigration, see J. Zitomersky, 'The jewish population in Sweden 1780–1980: an ethno-demographic study', p. 122.

61. *KB*, J. Hjerpe, Kong residensestaden Stockholms . . . , 1782.

62. Nyman, *Press mot friheten*, p. 149.

63. *EBAS*, syster Arnelles levnadslopp, levnadslopp vol. 91, pp. 5–6.

64. *UUB*, J. Hjerpe, Merckwärdige händelser . . . 22/2.

65. Ibid., 3/9.

66. See *SSA*, Handelskollegiet, förteckning på judar 1806–1837, in which the Jews are referred to as a nation. Cf. K. Johannesson, ' "Schene Rariteten": antisemitisk bildagitation i svensk rabulistpress 1845–1860', p. 183.

67. Nyman, *Press mot friheten*, p. 126; cf. Johannesson, ' "Schene Rariteten": antisemitisk bildagitation i svensk rabulistpress 1845–1860', p. 183.

68. Burke, *Popular culture* . . . , pp. 192–94.

69. *LSB*, J. Hjerpe, Berättelse om en lustresa . . . , p. 189.

70. *Stockholms Posten* number 55, 1784.

71. Jarrick, *Den himmelske älskaren*, pp. 74–75.

72. Zitomersky, 'The jewish population in Sweden 1780–1980', p. 122.

73. See, for example, *SSA*, Handelskollegiet, Förteckning på judar 1806–1837.

74. In *Stockholms Posten* number 200 (1784) I have, however, stumbled across the claim that the Jews 'have an inherited hatred of Christ and his teaching'. But this must be among the exceptions, and has to do with their religious characteristics.

75. Johannesson, ' "Schene Rariteten": antisemitisk bildagitation i svensk rabulistpress 1845–1860', p. 183.

76. Ibid.; Nerman, *Crusenstolpes kravaller*, pp. 265–89; H. Valentin, *Judarna i Sverige*, pp. 56, 62–63, 65–66, 72, 78–79.

77. Hertzberg, *The French Enlightenment and the jews*, p. 276. Cf. also E. Lönnroth, 'Europa, Norden och judarna', p. 10, in which the author claims that in the nineteenth century, both Indians and Negroes could be adopted as valid members of Swedish culture if they converted to the Lutheran faith.

78. R. J. Richards, *Darwin and the emergence of evolutionary theories of mind and behavior*, p. 286. It should be noted that Darwin did not deny the thesis that acquired traits could be inherited. Spencer and Darwin were influenced by each other. See Richards, pp. 64, 90–94, 292–93.

79. *UUB*, Johan Hjerpe, Merckwärdige händelser . . . , 9/6; *Allmänna journalen* number 128 (1818). Hjerpe's attitude should be contrasted with the fact that Muslim Turks have always had an unclear relationship with European culture, and since the Middle Ages have been thought to threaten Western civilisation. On this, see Delumeau, *Sin and fear*, p. 119; V. G. Kiernan, *The lords of the human kind: black man, yellow man, and white man in an age of empire*, pp. 8, 15, 108–15, 139.

80. Johan Hjerpe, Kong residensestaden Stockholms . . . , 1676.

81. Per-Anders Fogelström, 'Häxorna i Katarina', pp. 90, 108–15.

82. Lagerbring, pp. 129–33.

83. Ménétra, *Journal de ma vie*, for example pp. 48–49, 54, 92–93, 99, 117ff, 135–36, 146, 160–61, 193, 207, 214. See also postscript by Roche, p. 405.

84. *UUB*, J. Hjerpe, Merckwärdige händelser . . . , 21/1.

85. *LSB*, J. Hjerpe, Berättelse om en lustresa . . . , p. 128.

86. Ménétra, *Journal de ma vie*, pp. 93–94.

87. See, for example, Farge, *Livets sköra tråd*, pp. 249–50.

88. Ménétra, *Journal de ma vie*, postscript by Roche, pp. 299–300. See also Chartier, 'Les pratiques de l'écrit', pp. 119–20; Vovelle, *La mentalité révolutionnaire*, p. 37.

89. Pardailhé-Galabrun, *La naissance de l'intime*, p. 416.

90. Ménétra, *Journal de ma vie*, postscript by Roche, p. 300.

91. Ibid., p. 409.

92. Ibid., p. 118.

93. Cf., preface by Darnton in Ménétra, *Journal de ma vie*, p. ix.

94. *Stockholms Posten* number 55, 1784.

95. *Om tolerancen*, p. 5.

96. Le Roy Ladurie, *Montaillou*, p. 119. See also pp. 193 and 401.

97. E. Silvén and I. Söderlind, *Ett annat Sverige: dokument om folkets kamp 1200–1720*, pp. 42–44.

98. Ménétra, *Journal de ma vie*, p. 193.
99. Voltaire, *Philosophical dictionary*, p. 208. However, among Christian adherents of Enlightenment one occasionally encounters the view that only reason leads to true fairness. See, for example, *Anmärkningar till den gamla Folks-maximen . . .* , pp. 13ff.
100. Martin Luther in a sermon given in Wittenberg, cited in J. Delumeau, *Sin and fear: the emergence of a Western guilt culture 13th–18th centuries*, p. 152.
101. Ménétra, *Journal de ma vie*, p. 94.
102. Voltaire, *Philosophical dictionary*, p. 217.
103. Hertzberg, *The French enlightenment and the jews*, p. 28.
104. Ibid., pp. 286–99.
105. Cited by Peter Gay, editor's introduction, in Voltaire, *Philosophical dictionary*, p. 28.
106. Darnton, *The Forbidden Best-Sellers . . .* , p. 64; Robert Darnton, *The corpus of clandestine literature in France 1769–1789*, p. 195.
107. Ozouf, *Festivals and the French revolution*, Chapter 4; Vovelle, *La mentalité révolutionnaire*, pp. 172–76; 186–98.
108. Lenhammar, *Tolerans och bekännelsetvång*, pp. 16–20, 186–97, 228–29, 243–50, 263–64, 276–95, 302–06; Lindroth, *Svensk lärdomshistoria: gustavianska tiden*, pp. 166–70, 177–87; Segerstedt, *Nils von Rosenstein*, p. 223.
109. Vovelle, *La mentalité révolutionnaire*, p. 113; Holmberg, *Världen bortom västerlandet*, p. 83.
110. Holmberg, *Världen bortom västerlandet*.
111. Kiernan, *The lords of the human kind*, p. 20: 'One feature of it [the Enlightenment, *AJ*] was a willingness to recognize civilizations outside Europe as fellow-members of a human family, equal or even superior to Europe in some of their attainments. The Philosophes thought, or liked to think they did, as citizens of the world . . .'.
112. Kiernan, *The lords of the human kind*, p. 146; *Encyklopédie . . .* Vol. 7, p. 748: 'La Chine [. . .] C'est le pays le plus peuplé & le mieux cultivé qu'il y ait au monde [. . .] Les Chinois sont fort industrieux; ils aiment les Arts, les Sciencies & le Commerce; l'usage du papier, de l'imprimerie, de la poudre à canon, y étoit connu long-temps avant qu'on y pensât en Europe. Ce pays est gouverné par un empereur, qui est en méme temps le chef de la religion, & qui a sous ses ordres des mandarins qui sont les grands seigneurs du pays: ils ont la liberté de lui faire connoitre ses défauts. Le gouvernement est fort doux. Les peuples de ce pays sont idolâtres: ils prennent autant de femmes qu'ils veulent'.
113. Cf. Habermas, *Communication and the evolution of society*, on the post-conventional stage, p. 80. See also p. 89.
114. Cited in S. Ek, *Skämtare och allvarsmän i Stockholms Postens första årgångar: studier i tidningens prosainlägg och Kellgrens utveckling 1778–81*, pp. 308–09.
115. *Stockholms Posten* number 214 (1784), continuation of a contribution from number 213 entitled 'Om Wänskapen, Kärleken, Patriotismen hos Fruntimmer'.
116. Ibid., number 61 (1784).
117. Hertzberg, *The French enlightenment and the jews*, p. 310.
118. Voltaire, *Philosophical dictionary*, pp. 113, 203 and 390: 'There is only one religion in the world that has never been sullied by fanaticism, that of the Chinese scholars. The philosophical sects were not only free from this pest, they were its remedy'. See also Kiernan, *The lords of the human kind*, p. 146. The Jesuits were not, however, narrowly concerned with China, as Enlightenment eventually transferred its interest to Indian culture. On this, see Paz, *Sor Juana or the traps of faith*, pp. 34–43; Holmberg, *Världen bortom västerlandet*, p. 103.
119. Holmberg, *Världen bortom västerlandet*, pp. 104–06; Thomas, *Man and the natural world*, pp. 151–52. Cf. Kiernan, *The lords of the human kind*, pp. 194ff.

120. Richards, *Darwin and the emergence of evolutionary theories of mind and behavior*, pp. 27–28, 47–57, 244, 285–86.
121. Å. Holmberg, 'Att omvärdera omvärlden – synen på exotiska folk i svenska historieböcker', pp. 97, 99, 101–03; Holmberg, *Världen bortom västerlandet*, pp. 28, 87ff, 107; Kiernan, *The lords of the human kind*, pp. 21, 160.
122. Kiernan, *The lords of the human kind*, pp. 23, 149.
123. C. F. Becker, *Handbok för fruntimmer i äldre och nyare historien 1–10* was such a book. On this, see Holmberg, 'Att omvärdera omvärlden', pp. 101–02; Holmberg, *Världen bortom västerlandet*, pp. 87–88. In *UUB*, Johan Hjerpe, Merckwärdige händelser ..., there are many references to Becker's book: 30/1, 18/2, 28/4, 1/6, 7/6, 7/8, 29/10.
124. *UUB*, J. Hjerpe, Merckwärdige händelser ..., 13/8; *Allmänna journalen* number 185 (1818).
125. *UUB*, J. Hjerpe, Merckwärdige händelser ..., 4/5; *Stockholms Posttidningar*, number 111 (1799).
126. *UUB*, J. Hjerpe, Merckwärdige händelser ..., 29/5.
127. *Stockholms Posttidningar* number 82 (1807).
128. In *KB*, Johan Hjerpe, Kong residensestaden Stockholms ..., which was written several decades before the calendar of world history, there are several examples of this.
129. Condorcet is usually pointed to as the 'ideal type' for this attitude. On this, see Frängsmyr, *Framsteg eller förfall*, p. 122; B. Mazlish, *The riddle of history*, pp. 77, 82, 85; Vyverberg, *Historical pessimism in the French enlightenment*, pp. 45, 67–72, 230–31.
130. Breisach, *Historiography*, pp. 209–10, 220–21; Frängsmyr, *Framsteg eller förfall*, pp. 112–13: Gay, 'Editor's introduction', p. 14; S. Nordin, *Från tradition till apokalyps: historieskrivning och civilisationskritik i det moderna Europa*, pp. 51-54; Voltaire, *Philosophical dictionary*, pp. 172–73, 205–07, 275–78; Vyverberg, *Historical pessimism*, pp. 83–85, 99–108, 172, 187–88, 198–99.
131. This is, however, no newly acquired insight, but has rather been the standard view for decades. See Frängsmyr, *Framsteg eller förfall*, p. 110; Breisach, *Historiography*, p. 207; Gay, *The Enlightenment 2*, pp. 107, 117, 124; Nordin, *Från tradition till apokalyps*, pp. 51–54; Vyverberg, *Historical pessimism* ..., as Frängsmyr finds support in the criticism of the Enlightenment-development optimism linkage, which first appeared in 1958.
132. On this, see Richards, *Darwin and the emergence of evolutionary theories ...*, pp. 27–28.
133. Delumeau, *Sin and fear*, p. 125.
134. Hammarsköld, 'Teologiska betragtelser ...', p. 40.
135. Becker, *Handbok för fruntimmer i äldre och nyare historien*, part 5, p. 3.
136. Ranke has certainly been judged in very contradictory ways on this matter, even by one and the same author. Compare, for example, G. G. Iggers and H. T. Parker (eds), *International handbook of historical studies*, p. 6 with G. G. Iggers, *New directions in European historiography*, p. 23. But in my view, the following description by R. Torstendahl, 'Leopold von Rankes historiografiska betydelse', p. 32 is more convincing: 'In the medieval part of Weltgeschichte, the linkage element took to the fore. The Islamic world became an important link between Europe and the Orient and between antiquity and the new period. In that way, the perspective remained both there and otherwise Eurocentric and evolutionist. World history ultimately came to concern the emergence of Europe: it was to Europe that the future belonged; this was Ranke's religiously universalistic image of history'.
137. H. Vyverberg, *Historical pessimism*, pp. 84–85, 125, 151.
138. Ibid., p. 151.
139. Vyverberg, *Historical pessimism*, Chapter 9, p. 107. Once again, this does not keep one from also finding cyclical theories within Enlightenment, but they were not 'modal'

here. On this, see Frängsmyr, *Framsteg eller förfall*, p. 116; Nordin, *Från tradition till apoka-lyps*, pp. 38–41.

140. Breisach, *Historiography*, p. 223.
141. Many Christians in the USA succeeded, however, in assimilating Lamarckian evolutionist biology with the teaching on original sin: he who did not take care of his body and refrain from excesses would not only become depraved himself, but would also pass on a degenerate inheritance to coming generations. But they turned Spencer's perspective, which entailed a belief in genetically conditioned progress, on its head. On this, see Peter Gardella, *Innocent ecstasy: how Christianity gave America an ethic of sexual pleasure*, p. 49; Richards, *Darwin and the emergence of revolutionary theories* . . . , pp. 246, 261.
142. Peter Gardella, *Innocent ecstasy*, p. 49; Richards, *Darwin and the emergence of evolutionary theories* . . . , pp. 246, 261.
143. *LSB*, J. Hjerpe, Berättelse om en lustresa . . . , pp. 128, 140.
144. Ibid., pp. 58–59, 100.
145. Ménétra, *Journal de ma vie*. On his view of the revolution, see postscript by Roche, pp. 395–401.
146. Ibid. Cf. Magnusson, *Den bråkliga kulturen*, pp. 337–45, who claims that the extravagance of the poor artisans in the taverns had an economic rationality: it was a sort of insurance system, whereby whoever had a bit extra at the moment could, by treating the others, ensure himself returned favours in times of need. There is a conflict of goals here, however, at least for the journeymen who needed to scrape together the costs of becoming established in the guild. This is something which can call the economic rationality of pub life into question.
147. This applies to the subject classification in *KB*, Johan Hjerpe, Kong residensestaden Stockholms . . . and in *UUB*, Johan Hjerpe, Merckwärdige händelser . . .
148. Ibid.
149. A. Soboul, *The Parisian sans-culottes and the French revolution 1793–94*, Chapter 1; Vovelle, *La mentalité révolutionnaire*, pp. 70–81, 115–22.
150. *UUB*, JHJ, 3/2 1789.
151. Ibid., May 1789.
152. *Dagligt Allehanda* 12/8 1789 (number 184); *Stockholms Posttidningar* 6/8 1789 (number 61). *Stockholms Posten* 6/8 1789 (number 180) was, however, negative.
153. *UUB*, JHJ, August 1789. *Stockholms Posttidningar* 28/5 1789 (number 42). See also *Stockholms Posten* 18/5 1789 (number 113); *Dagligt Allehanda*, 18/5 1789 (number 113). The events are commented on many times. See, for example, Tilly, *The contentious French*, pp. 50–51.
154. *UUB*, JHJ, May 1789.
155. Ibid., 21/5 1790.
156. Ibid., 30/6 1790.
157. Ibid., March 1791.
158. Ibid.
159. Ibid., July 1791.
160. Nyman, *Press mot friheten*, pp. 41–49. In his diary, Hjerpe spells the word 'Parlement' with an 'e', as does *Dagligt Allehanda*, as opposed to *Stockholms Posten* and *Stockholms Posttidningar*.
161. *Stockholms Posten* 25/2 1790 (number 46); *Stockholms Posttidningar* 25/2 1790 (number 16); *Dagligt Allehanda* 25/2 1790 (number 46).
162. *UUB*, JHJ, March 1790.
163. See, for example, Boberg, *Kungliga krigspropaganda*, pp. 32ff; Lönnroth, *Den stora rollen*, pp. 51ff and 161–66; Staf, *Polisväsendet i Stockholm*, pp. 133–38.

164. Tilly, *The contentious French*, p. 228.
165. *UUB*, JHJ, 27/6 1788.
166. On Märta, see *KB*, J. Hjerpe, Kong residensestaden Stockholms . . . , for example 1298; Lynn Hunt, *The family romance of the French Revolution*, passim.
167. *UUB*, JHJ, August 1789.
168. *UUB*, J. Hjerpe, Merckwärdige händelser . . . , 24/4; *Stockholms Posttidningar* number 53 (1814).
169. *Stockholms Posttidningar*, Number 69 (1814).
170. *UUB*, J. Hjerpe, Merckwärdige händelser . . . , 30/5.
171. Ambjörnsson, *Den skötsamme arbetaren*, pp. 86, 120, 126, 128–29.

Chapter 6
The individual and history

The preceding chapter focused its attention almost entirely on one person. Despite the insistent presence of Jacques-Louis Ménétra, it mostly concerned the world according to Johan Hjerpe, the artisan son alone with his thoughts, protected both from the throng of people and from statistical intrusions. And even if Hjerpe had also made an appearance in the second chapter, it was only in the last one that he was dealt with as the central personality.

Studying one individual is no easier and can be done no more quickly than research into many. Even if it is occasionally more entertaining, it produces more problems from a scholarly point of view. Moreover, to devote one's research efforts to such an insignificant man as Johan Hjerpe can seem a bit questionable, as one hardly feels the breeze from history's wings beating in his presence.

In my view, the undertaking can, nevertheless, be useful, but because of the complications and its arousing oppositon, it must be furnished with suitable explanations of the value of the biographical in historical research. This does not mean that the interpretation made of Enlightenment reflections in the spiritual microcosms of Hjerpe (and Ménétra) can be likened to a biography, even a pocket-sized one. The analysis is far too limited, the data too scanty and the object not attractive enough for that. Biographies being also about single individuals, the methodological problems are partly shared by the individual-historical approach which has been used here. It would also seem that interest in historical biographies in the field of historical research is once again on the rise, after having played a very minor role for several decades.[1] This, too, should be taken into consideration in this context, and I will start with this point.

In the 1960s, an increasing number of scholars were won over to the notion that history should be depicted as a social history, a history of the hardships, struggles and joys of ordinary people. History had not been made by kings, and grandiose politics was only a superficial flicker, which really changed nothing in the basic state of things. The consequence was that political historiography, like historical biography, found itself in difficulty, as it had until then always been about a prominent sort of person who was suddenly not the least bit interesting any more.

Indeed, this process had begun several decades – if not centuries – before the 1960s. But it was only then that modern social history experienced a breakthrough and began to set the tone in research communities throughout the West.[2] Since then, countless works have been produced on rural poverty or on the masses in pre-industrial cities, on changes in the population in general or, more specifically, on the development of childhood and the family, and so on.

Historians are currently occupied, as never before, with social history studies, usually based on comprehensive studies of national registration material, church records and other similar sources. But in the last few years, politics and biography seem to have been on their way back into historical research. The stubborn representatives of the renowned *Annales* school were long united in a common silence about the history of high politics. But now it seems that, one after the other, they have given up their reluctance towards politics. This also applies to leading figures such as Emmanuel Le Roy Ladurie.[3] Recently, the *Annales* journal has given column space to historians to plead for historical biography.[4] Moreover, judging from the flood of popular history books of recent years, heroic biography is making progress again. The real best-seller of recent years has not been about poor Stock-holmers, for example, but about Charles XII, albeit quite rightly placed in a social-historical context of human suffering.

A suite of popularly written, long-forgotten biographies of some of history's best known autocrats has also been reprinted in Sweden recently – biographies of Julius Caesar, Mary Stuart, Queen Christina and Gustavus III. And if interest is maintained, perhaps some others will appear. But these biographies have very little in common with the current, renewed academic interest in accounts of individuals. Their authors are, in the traditional way, far too confined by a royalist framework which presumably was so obvious that they did not see it themselves. They formulated no analytical questions about the monarch under scrutiny, or about his or her times. They were not primarily interested in knowing what sort of monarchs Mary Stuart or Christina or Gustavus had been, but whether they had been *good enough*.

Although they all encouraged themselves in a belief in their own objective matter-of-factness, theirs was more a moralistic than scholarly business. And even if the accounts are basically unreliable (with a few possible exceptions), there is nevertheless something pleasing in the authors having been so eager in their determined moral commitment.

It is for this reason that this suite of biographies seems old, which indeed it is. The book by Stefan Zweig on Mary Stuart was first published in Swedish in 1927, and Beth Hennings published her work on Gustavus III in 1957. In the interim came Py Sörman's biography of Christina. And even if these hagiographic biographies responded to demand from the reading public, they are hardly typical of the newly acquired interest of historians in biography.

In general, the old sort of biography is not, then, on its way back in. Instead, historical research has followed a path towards a new sort of study of individual human fates from the past. The gradual reorientation has followed a sort of inner logic which concerns the departure of social history from political history in the 1960s.

The pioneers of social history deflected interest from rulers' political intrigues and began instead to enquire into the attributes of everyday life. It was a short step from there to the study of mentalities, of the popular attitudes which had kept customs alive and handed them down from generation to generation. The researchers into mentalities were also social historians, even if they wanted to glean different insights from the common sources. Estate inventories, for example, were still interesting, no longer for their information about fortunes but because they bore witness to the spiritual life of departed souls, the mirrors, books, pictures and the like left behind by the deceased. And by studying thousands of wills from various times, recurrent and gradual shifts in the relation of people to God and heaven became apparent. Judgement books, Inquisition protocols, church books, population registers, guild protocols, icons and police reports – to name but a few of the old, well-known source groups – have also been exposed to a new sort of approach.

The problems were that the documentation of the lives of the people had not come into existence in order to answer the questions of the future and – above all – the bothersome silence of the mass of simple people in the sources. What the tavern wench, artisan or peasant may have had in his or her mind must therefore be surmised indirectly.

Now, there were scholars who were not content with this, and who therefore tracked down the remnants of more articulate representatives of the obscure multitude. They shed light on and saved from eternal oblivion one hand-written, hidden, never-published piece of writing after the other, left behind by people who had defied the social fate to which they had been born.

Interest in biography was thus rekindled, not in the old manner, but as a spin-off of the still predominant social-historical way of looking at what had been. The peasant or artisan who was attracted to learning and wrote diaries, tracts, historical accounts and the like was not interesting in his own right, but as an example of a widespread way of thinking. He may have been an eccentric, but in his manner of reading, he nevertheless revealed his simple background and that he was constrained by popular notions. His way of filtering élite culture bore witness to the existence of an independent popular culture. This was the message in Carlo Ginzburg's renowned study of the world-view of the Italian sixteenth-century miller Menocchio, a study which has virtually become a model for this sort of semi-biographical historiography.[5]

However, Ginzburg's cultural-historical approach has also been called into question by the advocates of an even newer cultural history, led by the historian Roger Chartier. I have touched on this in an earlier chapter, where it was evident that this is a cultural history which wishes to take yet another individualising step towards the biographical, which tends to deny that popular writing samples can be traced back to common culture symbols and which is suspicious of the possibility of discerning overarching cultural patterns at all. To overstate the case somewhat, nothing is representative of anything else, and every individual appropriates the variety of transmitted thoughts in his own way. The unique is, once again, unique.[6]

It is not possible to say that historians in general stand side-by-side with the representatives of the new cultural history. The research community is not an establishment in which everyone marches in step. But neither would a breakthrough for Chartier's perspective signify a return to traditional biography. Cultural artefacts and great thoughts, kings and artists lose their unique position with the new orientation, and so every person – from the philosopher to the artisan – becomes interesting to study. The unique is no longer to be found in brilliant work either, but in the person who makes use of it.

Parallel with this development, a discussion about biography has taken place along existentialist lines. For Jean-Paul Sartre, biography was a most essential concern, because every fate could be retold as an example of history's space for free action decisions.[7] Recently, the Italian historian Giovanni Levi has made a case for biography in *Annales* in a similar way. He maintains that historical biography is important above all for the sake of moral issues. Each norm system is built on irreconcilable moral imperatives, and this creates a space in which people can freely choose how they will act. Biographical historians should therefore faithfully reproduce the personal in human choices of action and not play it down, or consign it to some supposed social system of compelling and uncontradictory norms. According to Levi,[8] nothing like this has ever existed.

One could, perhaps, say that Levi's view of the value of the biographical converges with the high esteem in which Chartier holds the unique, and that both in turn could be linked with the heroic biographies of the olden days. But that would be too simple. It would be equally oversimplified to imagine the modern development of biography as history in refined stages. In different proportions, most types have always existed. As I see it, it is possible to distinguish at least four fundamentally distinct justifications, each of them tied to a special way of depicting the destinies of different people.

The first justification is the *idiographic*. Everything and everyone is unique, no-one is less interesting than anyone else, and no individual destiny can be simply – if at all – traced back to any general social structure. Such a view is not troubled by any representativeness problems.

The *heroic justification* is the second. In history's infinite throng of the unknown, a few have raised themselves to become particularly significant heroes or rascals, and they deserve a biographical study by virtue of that. Nietzsche's defence of 'monumentalistic' historiography is such a justification but, apart from most traditional biographies, Erik Homburger Erikson's biographies of Luther and Gandhi can be included here, as well as a number of other studies within the psycho-biographic genre. Compared with 'idiographical' biographies, heroic biography naturally entails a considerable curtailment of the area of interest.[9]

The third justification is the *existential* and the fourth is what could be called the *popular cultural justification*. The former can be associated with Sartre and Levi, the latter with Carlo Ginzburg, and because I have already mentioned these, they need no further introduction.

Naturally, objections can be made to each of the four arguments. They have also been exposed to caustic attacks, and because they are contradictory, they have occasionally been deployed against each other. As we have seen, Chartier has played the idiographic justification against the popular cultural one,[10] but it would also be possible to turn the popular cultural justification against the heroic justification: the legacy of a person of note cannot be assumed, a priori, to have been more representative for its contemporary surroundings than the property of a half-educated eccentric among common folk.

Let me to elaborate on this using Johan Hjerpe as an example. He was, without any doubt, a man of the people. Fortunately, he was also an unusually articulate man. Unfortunately, he was, perhaps for that very reason, also rather less common. This results in a dilemma for anyone who aims to achieve both depth and breadth in the interpretation of popular mentalities. Both cannot be achieved with the same measure. On the contrary, it would seem that one ends up further from the one objective when nearing the other. If one wants depth, an abundant wealth of personal material is required. There are a few people who reveal in this way that they have distanced themselves from the majority.[11] If one wants breadth, material which yields comparable details about many is required. But mass data is seldom available for such penetrating questions which can be posed to personal sources. Broadening an in-depth analysis thus also involves, of necessity, new questions, which can only partly shed light on what the old ones were seeking to answer.[12]

The problem, then, really has no solution. But it is possible to approach a solution. This can be done, first, through the identification of the *culture* in the social proximity of Johan Hjerpe, and of certain traits in the élite culture to which he aspired (Chapters 1 and 3). Second, it can be done through the partial analysis of what is accessible in the mentality of the simple bourgeoisie to which he belonged (Chapter 3). Third, one can address the problem from the opposite direction, by attempting to pick out the cultural restrictions in Johan Hjerpe's inner world (Chapter 5). How did he sift through the impressions made by the world and literature? What was culturally-bound in this filtering process, and what can be traced back to his personal destiny in life?

The three approaches belong together, and when it comes to the study of eighteenth-century processes of cultural change, they can also be used to give nuance to the meaning and effects of Enlightenment. My impression is that demands for representativeness are less often placed on biographies of famous women and men than on biographies of obscure people. And this is so despite a general scepticism within the social sciences about biography as a genre.[13] It can be assumed that prominent people have exerted influence over sufficient numbers of people, and such a test is thus considered unnecessary.[14] Obscure people are unnoticed, have meant nothing to history, and are thus interesting only insofar as it can be demonstrated that as individuals they shared essential attitudes with others, in effect with the majority of their own kind.[15]

What is to be said about such inequality 'before the law'? Several cultural-historical studies have shown that it was not easy to spread élite culture to the common folk. If, for example, the congregations in Europe of the modern era were able to resist (albeit to variable degrees) the spiritual influences of the authorities who were in the process of reorienting themselves in the world and the cosmos, the influence of prominent men would thus appear to have been less self-evident. If they represented their age, this must be demonstrated. In addition, the same research has claimed that people *remoulded* élite culture, which suggests that it was filtered through a folk culture which was, in certain respects, independent. There was a distance between the moral of a story the élite broadcast and the normative and cognitive reinterpretations which were made by those representatives of the simple people who had the greatest thirst for knowledge. This distance has, on the contrary, been interpreted as proximity to a folk culture, which appears in its distinctiveness through these very 'misinterpretations'. The peasant or artisan who was drawn to learning and kept a diary or wrote tracts was perhaps a half-educated eccentric among equals. But through his reading, he nevertheless revealed his 'simple' background and how he was constrained by popular conceptions.[16]

The occurrence of a distinctive folk culture thus follows only as an implication and is not confirmed by comprehensive, close observation of the mentality of the masses. But with reference to the results of research into cultural history, one does not have more a priori right to assume that a prominent person exerted influence over his age by virtue of his prominence than that the obscure individual was like others simply because he was close to them socially. As I see it, both of these assumptions are equally strong – or weak. The principle must therefore be that biographies of different sorts are treated alike, albeit for different reasons.

This argument entails an acknowledgement that the problem of representativeness is also relevant to historical biography, but here too lurks an implication – partially concealed – that the problem is unsolved. The negative argument thus needs to be balanced by a positive one.

Such an argument could look like this. Only with penetrating analyses of individuals does it become possible to create truly comprehensive and nuanced *models* for a more quantitatively-oriented survey of the mentality of the masses. On the other hand, the biographical study can mean a wholesome corrective to overly synthetic analyses of the intellect. Similar psychological or ideological elements which are found among the many can have taken on varying meanings in the individuals being studied. Perhaps no individual is suited to formulated synthesis, and the study of individuals becomes a test of this.[17]

Naturally, every additional piece of biographical material on new, comparable individuals would yield surer and more representative knowledge, and what is found in the many is more interesting than what is found in the few. The text-analytical interpretation I have made of Hjerpe (and Ménétra) can, indeed, be seen as a *model* for the continued analysis of other petit bourgeois from eighteenth-century Europe. Even in itself, however, this testifies to the complications in the transferral of thoughts between people, but also gives an intimation of precisely what Giovanni Levi called the main question in historical biography: the possibilities for varying moral choice.

The historical-biographical credo which I have formulated here could be seen as a composite fabric woven from idiographic, existentialist and folk-cultural justifications, although the heroic justification can naturally also be valid, albeit in a more restricted sense than Nietzsche had in mind. Whether these justifications can be reconciled or whether I really have dealt them a savage blow in the interpretation of Hjerpe and Ménétra is now up to the reader to decide.

Notes

1. Cf. K. Jonsson, 'Mellan den sociala determinismens Scylla och den psykologiska reduktionismens Charybdis: problem i den idéhistoriska biografins genre', pp. 17–20.
2. See, for example, Floto, *Historie*, Chapter 4.
3. P. Burke, *The French historical revolution: the Annales school 1929–89*, Chapter 4; U. Jonsson, 'Annales-traditionen: ett "paradigm" i upplösning eller förnyelse?', pp. 231–32, 235.
4. Levi, 'Les usages de la biographie'. Since 1978, a journal called *Biography* has been devoted to biography, but has not yet discussed the subject in relation to social history research.
5. Ginzburg, *The cheese and the worms*.
6. For a general discussion in this direction, see *The new cultural history*, pp. 7–22; Chartier, *The culture of print*, pp. 1–9.

7. Jonsson, 'Mellan den sociala determinismens Scylla och den psykologiska reduktionismens Charybdis', p. 20; D. LaCapra, *Rethinking intellectual history: texts, contexts, language*.

8. G. Levi, 'Les usages de la biographie', p. 1333.

9. Nordin, *Från tradition till apokalyps*, p. 118; Jarrick, *Psykologisk socialhistoria*, p. 39.

10. For a comprehensive critique of Sartre's perspective on biography, see LaCapra, *Rethinking intellectual history*, Chapter 6.

11. See, for example, Houston, *Literacy in early modern Europe*, p. 128; Spufford, 'First steps in literacy'; the seventeenth-century Puritan Nehemia Wallington analysed in P. S. Seaver, *Wallington's world: a puritan artisan in seventeenth-century London*; Edmond-Jean-François Barbier and Sébastien Hardy, who kept diaries on Paris in the years before the French Revolution, discussed in Tilly, *The contentious French*, pp. 217–44; Jacques-Louis Ménétra, discussed in Chartier, 'Les pratiques de l'écrit', pp. 157–59.

12. For a similar discussion, see Chartier, 'Intellectual history or sociocultural history?', pp. 30–32, 39; Chartier, *Cultural history*, pp. 61–63; C. Winberg 'Några anteckningar om historisk antropologi', pp. 16–22; C. Lévi-Strauss, *Det vilda tänkandet*, pp. 260–61.

13. Post-structuralism considers biography impossible because no individual is thought to have an inner integrity or a collected centre, and structuralism because the individual's structural attributes are considered more interesting than the unique remnants of each individual. On this, see P. Jay, 'What's the use? Critical theory and the study of autobiography' p. 45; K. Jonsson, 'Mellan den sociala determinismens Scylla och den psykologiska reduktionismens Charybdis', pp. 17–20.

14. As is well known, such a view has long been seriously questioned, but nevertheless persists here and there. See, for example, E. Lönnroth, 'Det biografiska synsättet', p. 293, which I interpret in this direction.

15. See, for example, Christiansen, 'Construction of the past', p. 18; K. Lunden, ' "Postmodernistisk" historie, eller systemhistorie', pp. 46–49.

16. Among the prominent are Bachtin, *Rabelais and His World*, pp. 33–34, 82, 101–02; Darnton, *The Literary Underground . . .*, Chapters 1 and 6; Davis, *The Return of Martin Guerre*; Davis, *Society and culture in early modern France*, for example p. 225; C. Ginzburg, *The night battles: witchcraft & agrarian cults in the sixteenth & seventeenth centuries*, pp. 9–12, 15, 17–19; Ginzburg, *The cheese and the worms*; Schmitt, *The holy greyhound*, pp. 7–8, 15–24. See also Chartier, 'Intellectual history or sociocultural history?', p. 30; Christiansen, 'Construction of the past', p. 17.

17. In Jarrick, *Psykologisk socialhistoria*, pp. 134–35, I conduct such a test of how synthetic Moravian faith profiles correspond to factual ones.

Epilogue:
In retrospect

Why write a book about Johan Hjerpe and Enlightenment when no successful meeting ever took place between them? It is easy to give an answer.

One reason is that Enlightenment had a very strong presence in the social debate of the Gustavian period, and that many of its ideas also experienced a breakthrough as a practical reform programme, within the spheres of, for example, the administration of justice and legislation on freedom of the press. Another reason is that Hjerpe could not side-step the notions of Enlightenment however much he disliked them: they challenged him as obviously and permanently as their mentality insidiously influenced the entire lower middle-class social stratum to which he belonged. Equally 'les philosophes' and their kindred Swedish spirits, merchants, artisans and people in general were drawn into a gradual civilisation process which was, among other things, making people less violent and more tolerant of each other. But by the end of the eighteenth century, these people were still royalist and anti-aristocratic in a pre-modern way, and they did not realise that they were in the midst of a cumulative social change which, in time, would come to make them look old-fashioned.

So much for the brutal summary. It is, in fact, overly brutal, so I will elaborate on it a bit. For this, I must repeat a number of the statements I have already made.

With Enlightenment, a number of spiritual processes came to light with a unique clarity, processes which subsequently left their mark on development of mentalities in Sweden and its environs. The central thing which was new was the energetic aspiration of the Enlightenment philosophers to strip authorised ideological and cultural positions of their general, timeless validity. Knowledge was to be supported by experience, but experience was limited and special, and the truth therefore relative and not absolute. This was why Enlightenment philosophers chose foreign cultures as their vantage points from which to reflect upon their own. In this way, they could cultivate the self-reflexive relativism which was the basis of the tolerance notion they fought for and which aimed at the demolition of values which had until then been taken to be eternal. This relativism – sometimes an articulated doctrine, sometimes an unarticulated intellect – was a sort of basic conception for Enlightenment thinking, although 'les philosophes' often fell back on absolute values.

From out of that relativism, some themes emerged more coherent than others: a secularised deism or atheism, an extended consciousness of the value of foreign cultures, and the revolutionising notion that history never returns to its starting point, for some became a belief in progress. This complex of ideas can either be seen as components in the informal encyclo-paedic programme, as part of the spontaneous intellectual changes, or as both. Whichever way it is viewed, Enlightenment reached Sweden, even if many people also turned away from it.

*

An event has served as a concrete point of departure: the artisan uprising of April 1789 for king and war (Chapter 1). Then I investigated a number of the external aspects of the cultural change (Chapter 3) subsequently to approach, step-by-step, one of its inner ones: the ideal meeting between the reader and the flood of disparate texts with which he acquainted himself (Chapter 5).

It seems quite clear that the eighteenth-century artisan journeymen in Stockholm were ardent royalists and supporters of Gustavus III's war efforts. They had that in common with Johan Hjerpe. But, more than he did, they showed an open hatred of the opposition of the nobility, not just as a consequence of the nobility's supposed treason, but also because a golden opportunity had been given them to utter that hatred without threat of rep-risal. For a brief moment, they had the chance of being both loyal and 'disloyal' to the authorities. That they were probably paid to demonstrate their attitudes changes nothing here; a number of other events in the years around 1789 strengthen the impression that the artisan journeymen really thought what they thought.

There were, naturally no areas in which the opposing views of the jour-neymen and nobility could be engaged in dialogue; such a possibility did not occur to the former. They condemned the nobility and simply wanted to force them to yield. Apart from society not having given them any other opportunity to exert influence, the artisan journeymen's irreconcilable, mili-tant performance accorded with their general outlook.

If the powerless people were, up to then, only thought able to work through militant, irreconcilable and intolerant means – or not at all – it is also clear that something had been changing, over the course of several decades, among the artisan journeymen and others in a similar social position. The typical journeyman was not tolerant, not conversant with religion, not especially modern. But it was typical of the time that tolerant, religiously aware, modern people could actually be found among the journeymen, or those close to them. And this was in tune with a steadily progressive devel-opment among those in power towards increased tolerance for people's divergent views. Finally, it is clear that the population – and particularly the urban population – had been growing more law-abiding over the course of several centuries, and by the mid eighteenth century, there was very little in the way of homicide or manslaughter in Stockholm.

The artisan uprising threatened a sort of royalist anarchy within police restrictions. This historically distinctive 'gestalt' gave the journeymen the chance to discharge pent-up frustrations, especially as this could be done without fear of reprisals. At the same time, they could experience a sort of narcissistic gratification precisely by being called to assist the king in his hour of need. *From this perspective* it thus mattered little whether the expressed goal of the action was achieved. Had it not been possible to coerce the nobility, the journeymen would nevertheless have reaped emotional rewards for their industrious clamour on 27 April. Here is a timeless theme, which modifies the goal-rational image held by social history research of the pre-industrial mass.

The efforts to mobilise the artisan journeymen formed one part of the authorities' strategy to obtain funds for the war. On the other hand, these importunate efforts were of strategic importance to the gratification of the journeymen's narcissistic needs. But they themselves acted without strategy, in a double sense. In the first place, they lacked a plan for how the goal of their action was to be achieved. Secondly, their participation had no long-term objective. It is very unclear whether the journeymen themselves wanted to fight the war they clamoured for, although that must presumably have been the consequence of a successful action. As to the concrete causes of the war, they had, at best, a very vague notion of them. Not even a man as well-read as Hjerpe could find any really good reasons for it. The only thing he could think of was that Gustavus III was looking for a fight with Russia in order to flush the traitors out of the Swedish army! Indeed, a far-fetched and weak hypothesis. For the workers of the city, the war could be perceived more as a tempting fantasy, the focus of desires for revenge for any number of economic, social and 'mental' grievances.

This certainly does not mean that the artisan journeymen were, at this point, generally incapable of acting strategically. On the contrary, recent research has demonstrated how journeymen – in their struggle for their immediate economic interests and to defend their honour and status – were capable of behaving rationally, at an early stage, when it came to adapting their means to a given end. They could organise themselves horizontally and await the most suitable opportunity to pick a fight. But at the same time, the artisans embodied the illusion of the strong and mutual love between the king and his subjects, against the aristocrats and other villains. It was an illusion that dated far back in time, and which would come to survive Enlightenment, whatever else this movement managed to achieve.

*

From an actual event I then turned to the insidious changes in the cultural frames of reference. The study reported in Chapter 3 has made plain a number of different circumstances, but one is common and of particular interest: the popularisation of the culture of letters and secularisation in eighteenth-century Stockholm.

That the culture of letters became increasingly profane is not to say that people in general turned away from God. Certainly, the shift in the cultural frames of reference would appear also to have left a number of traces among the burghers and humble folk. But at the same time, it was only now, towards the end of the century, that the Christian culture of letters achieved truly broad dissemination *in written form*, now that the educated élite, under the influence of Enlightenment, had begun to turn away from the eternal evangelical truths.

It has been said by several scholars that the bringing of literacy to the people of Europe by the powers-that-be was a form of Christian acculturation. The day that the farm-hand and the journeyman also learned to decipher the written word, paganism and other wayward thoughts would eventually disappear by themselves. What has emerged in studies conducted by myself and others would seem to fit with this. For on the surface, the acculturation process would seem to have been successful, indeed perhaps particularly successful in Sweden: most people learned to read well and came to have at least some of the decreed writings among their possessions.

Perhaps the authorities knew where they wanted to lead the people. But at the same time, the acculturation process had consequences which cannot have been intended, consequences which in one way came to confirm the fears of Voltaire and others of an overly generous popular Enlightenment.

I am convinced that the religious revival movements of the eighteenth and early nineteenth centuries can be viewed as one of the unforeseen effects of this process. Putting it in somewhat speculative, generalising terms, one could say that most of these revival movements distinguished themselves more through an orthodox than a heterodox attitude. It was because of this that they came to irritate the high priesthood which laid claim to the right of interpreting the established doctrines. The awakened did not, in general, dismiss the Bible as the ultimate source of truth. On the contrary, it was precisely the *letter* of the Scriptures which they turned against those whom they believed threatened the living faith: against the 'spiritually dead' priesthood and against the educated élite which was charmed by science and wandered further and further away from the readiness for spiritual experience which alone was the basis for enduring faith. The literalism in northern Sweden which took off towards the end of the eighteenth century is an excellent example of an ideal type of this process.

The question is now whether, because this revival was bound to the holy word, that constraint could be placed in the context of the contemporary spread of literacy to broad strata of the population. In time, the broad swathe cut by the spread of literacy came to alter fundamentally people's relationship to the printed word. When reading became a private matter and an act which took place in silence, a space was also created for an inner dialogue. The interpretation of the holy *canon* could now be more personal and the absolute truth of the word reduced to a relative one. But at the beginning, the congregation approached the laboriously read text as it had recently approached the spoken word; now as then, what mattered was to impress these incontrovertible truths on the soul. The difference was, however, rather significant: now, each and every one could compare the fruits of his reading with the preaching of the clergyman. And here, right here, was perhaps the origin of the orthodox revival. To be sure, the acculturation process led to many people seeing the light, but in so doing they had also procured themselves a weapon which could be turned against the very powers who had effected their education. A conservative and popular revival thus also came to challenge an authority which was incorporating the notions of Enlightenment in its world view. One could thus, perhaps, say that the representatives of the popular revival *rejected* the notions of Enlightenment, and did so regardless of some of the most prominent representatives of those thoughts having been fearful of spreading them to ordinary people.

*

The hypothesis is, then, that people actively appropriated the culture of letters, in their own way, and in a manner that could not be predicted; they were, indeed, exposed to the texts, but they mastered them just as much as demands were placed on them. In order to come closer to the act of reading – this active appropriation process – and at the same time get an idea of Enlightenment's influence on ordinary people, I took it upon myself to seek reflections of Enlightenment thinking in the writings of Johan Hjerpe and Jacques-Louis Ménétra, the two petty bourgeois in eighteenth- and early nineteenth-century Europe, the one from Stockholm and the other from Paris (Chapter 5).

The two men were compared with each other, with the central themes of Enlightenment, and with the self-reflective cultural relativism which, then, was a common, main theme in the spiritual renewal towards which the encyclopaedic philosophers worked. In general, both men displayed a sort of religious tolerance. Ménétra was an outright enemy of the priesthood and Christian faith, and spoke of the need for tolerance of Jews and others. Hjerpe was, on the contrary, a good Christian, and indeed evinced a certain harshness in his judgement of zealots at home, but at the same time refrained entirely from expressing judgemental views on Jews, Moslems and other exotic believers from foreign parts of the world. He was also very well versed both in the international politics and world history of his times. Even so, he placed neither his own time nor Europe and Sweden above the past nor above the contemporary world beyond the West. It is striking how, in this context, there is an utter lack of Eurocentric disparagement in the face of foreign (and, with time, colonised) cultures. Hjerpe's way of describing Selim II of Turkey or Indian emperors was the same as the way he described power struggles in Europe. This can also be related to the virtually complete absence of a cumulative perspective on the evolution of society, an absence which is conspicuous in the writings of both Hjerpe and Ménétra. Unlike Hjerpe, Ménétra had nothing at all to say about the outside world, but was entirely preoccupied by events in his immediate proximity.

Some of Hjerpe's and Ménétra's lines of thought are reminiscent of the enlightened public debate, although the cumulative perspective was as lacking in both of these men as it was present in the public debate. The similarities one finds were, however, I am convinced, not related to each other through influences from above. It was more a question of a sort of 'convergence': Enlightenment reached a tolerance on matters of faith which many people had never managed to 'overstep'.

Nevertheless, at least one significant and profound difference between the different cultural spheres remained: with their secularising critique of religion, the Enlightenment philosophers developed a self-reflective cultural relativism, which was not intrinsic to the rehabilitation of old pagan values in the popular cultural sphere. Such a relativism is not to be found in Hjerpe or Ménétra either – a failing they had in common, although both these men were very unlike each other and although both differed from their social equals in their educated or half-educated ability to articulate their own ideas in writing. And relativism was, as I see it, a more fundamental change in mentality than secularisation, even if the Enlightenment philosophers themselves did not manage to maintain such a stance more than temporarily.

*

Each of the concrete expositions presented earlier was accompanied by a theoretical discussion. The first of these – the one about how we think – was so concentrated that it cannot be further summarised (Chapter 2). But it is easy to go back and skim through the theses. The two others will be touched on briefly here.

The common denominator in Chapters 4 and 6 was that mentality research benefits from the use of both quantitative and qualitative methods; the one method need not – or rather, *should not* – pre-empt the other. It may seem unnecessary to argue for something which appears so self-evident. But because both approaches have been questioned, neither of them is obvious any more, neither on their own nor together.

If a thousand people change their habits in the same way, one after the other, most of them probably share at least some motives with others, even if they also each give their own explanation as to why they exchanged an old way of life for a new one. It could be that individual motives were as effective as general ones in bringing about the change. On the other hand, it would be odd were no general thought whatsoever to have occurred to those who suddenly began to act in the same way. Thus, the occurrence of general patterns in changes in human habits probably betrays the fact that at least some import in the change is common. Without denying the variety of motives, it is precisely this which a quantitatively oriented researcher into mentalities is looking for.

This was the argument in favour of intensive analytical work into the legacies of individual people.

Only through penetrating analyses of individuals is it possible to create really comprehensive and nuanced models of a more quantitative documentation of the mind of the masses. And vice versa, biographical studies can be a wholesome corrective for overly synthetic analyses of the mind. Similar psychological or ideological traits found in many can be assumed to have had varying meanings to the different individuals who are studied. Perhaps no individual suits the synthesis which has been formulated, and the study of individuals becomes a test of this.

Naturally, every addition of biographical material on new, comparable individuals would yield more certain and representative knowledge, and what is found in the many is more interesting than what is found in the few. The text-analytical interpretation I have made of Hjerpe (and Ménétra) can be seen as a model for the continued analysis of other petit bourgeois from eighteenth-century Europe. Even in itself, however, it testifies to the complications in the transferral of thoughts from one person to another, but also gives an intimation of the very thing to which Giovanni Levi referred as the main question in historical biography: the possibilities for varying moral choice. Perhaps one could also say, in closing, that Enlightenment dramatically enhanced those possibilities.

Bibliography

Unpublished sources

Eskilstuna stadsarkiv (ESA)
Handlingar rörande Christian Johansén:
   vol. 1: dagböcker och räkenskapsböcker 1765–77
   vol. 4: diverse handlingar
   vol. 5: om swedenborgianismen

Evangeliska brödraförsamlingens arkiv i Stockholm (EBAS)
Personalkataloger:
   catalog över Ev Brödrasocieteten i Stockholm 1761–1770
   catalog över Ev Brödrasocieteten i Stockholm för 1780- och 1790-talet
Levnadslopp, vol. 91:
   syster Arnelles levnadslopp

Göteborgs landsarkiv (GLA)
Skånings häradsrätts arkiv:
   bouppteckningar
Synnerby församling:
   dödböcker
   flyttningslängder
   husförhörslängder

Kungliga biblioteket (KB)
Brev från C. C. Gjörwell 27/4, 1/5, 9/6 och 14/6 1789
J. Hjerpe, Kong residensestaden Stockholms historiska merckwärdigheter 1252–1792
Skråarkiv:
   Bokbindareämbetet:
      huvudräkenskaper 1729–1822
      protokoll 1783–1847
      verifikationer 1653–1791
   Guldsmedsämbetet:
      räkningar 1743–1800
   Strödda handlingar till hantverksskrånas historia
Svensk bibliografi 1700–1829 (SB17)

Linköpings stiftsbibliotek (LSB)
J. Hjerpe, Berättelse om en lustresa sommartiden 1809
Samlingsbok av Johan Hjerpe ... för diktavskrifter o d

Nordiska museets arkiv (NordMA)
Skråarkiv:
   Repslagaregesällskapet:
      lådräkning 1688–1809

protokoll 1688–1809
Skomakaregesällskapet:
protokoll 1780–1813
Snörmakaregesällskapet:
handlingar 1752–1797
verifikationer 1748–1883
Tenngjutaregesällskapet:
lådräkning 1687–1854
protokoll 1687–1854

Riksarkivet (RA)
Acta Ecclesiastica:
religionsmål
Gjörwell, C. C., Ödmjukt svar . . .
Börstorpssamlingen:
brev från Isak Askegren till Fredrik Sparre 23/7 1790
brev från F. U. von Rosen till Fredrik Sparre 5/8 1788
Länsräkenskaperna:
mantals- och taxeringslängder för Skaraborgs län, Skånings härad, Skara fögderi
Montgomerys samling:
Fredrik Wilhelm von Ehrenheim, Anteckningar och tankar, Vol. 1
Riksdagsacta:
borgarståndets protokoll vid riksdagen 1789
konceptprotokoll över plenum hos adeln 27/4 1789
prästeståndets protokoll vid riksdagen 1789
Sjöholmssamlingen:
Nordins arkiv:
brev från C. G. Nordin till J. M. Nordin, 4/8 1788

Stockholms stadsarkiv (SSA)
Församlingsarkiv:
Jakob och Johannes församling:
dödboksregister
Nicolai församling:
födelse- och dopböcker
husförhörslängder
Hall- och manufakturrättens arkiv:
fabriksberättelser
kommerskollegii privilegier
matrikel över ledamöter och fabriksidkare
Handelskollegiet:
förteckning på judar 1806–1837
Justitiekollegium:
bouppteckningar
Rådhusrättens arkiv:
Södra förstadens kämnärsrätt:
kriminalmålsprotokoll 1780

Skråarkiv:
Bleckslagareämbetet:
protokoll 1739–1790

Garvareämbetet:
 protokoll 1758–1835
Kammakareämbetet:
 diverse handlingar
Skräddareämbetet:
 protokoll 1777–1787
 konceptprotokoll
Synåls- och knappmakareämbetet:
 protokoll 1744–1796 resp 1703–1822
Sämsk- och handskmakareämbetet:
 protokoll 1775–1845
Stockholms bokauktionskammare:
 inlagor
 protokoll
 register över inlagor och protokoll
Överståthållarämbetet för uppbördsärenden:
 mantalslängder
 taxeringslängder
Överståthållarämbetets arkiv:
 Äldre poliskammaren 1789:
 diarier
Polissekreteraren:
 protokoll och registratur
 en odaterad kungörelse

Uppsala universitetsbibliotek (UUB)
Brev från Axel von Axelsson till Gustav III 1774, 'Projekt till polis i Stockholm'
Brev från Henrik Liljensparre till Gustav III, 19/5 1787, 7/6 1787, 17/9 1787, 27/4 1788, 22/7 1788, 2/8 1788, 5/8 1788, 6/12 1788, 21/1 1789, 27/1 1789, 27/4 1789, 6/8 1790, 9/9 1790, 21/12 1790, 3/2 1792, F 504
Brev från Erik Ruuth till Gustav III, september 1788
Johan Hjerpes journal
Merckwärdige händelser för alla årets dagar ... samlade av J. Hjerpe

Published sources

Allmänna journalen.
Anmärkningar vid den gamla Folks-maximen: 'Det är bättre att tro för mycket än för litet' helgade åt UPlysningens vänner, Jönköping, 1802.
Barfod, J. C., *Dagens märkvärdigheter 1 (1799–1800)*, Stockholm, 1963–1967.
Bauer, J. C., *Adertonde århundradets märkwärdigaste händelser*, Stockholm, 1814.
Baur, S., *Märkvärdigheter utur äldre och sednare tiders Mennisko- Folkslags- och Sede-Historie*, Stockholm, 1824.
Becker, C. F., *Handbok för fruntimmer i äldre och nyare historien 1–10*, Stockholm, 1804–1814.
Björnståhl, J. J., *Resa till Frankrike*, Stockholm, 1780–1784.
Bokauktionskataloger för Sverige 1825, KB.
Botin, A. af, *Utkast till svenska folkets historia 1–6*, Stockholm, 1763–1765.
Dagligt Allehanda.
Dalin, O. von, *Svea Rikes historia: ifrån dess begynnelse til wåra dagar 1–3*, Stockholm, 1760–1765.

Dialogues: English and Swedish, Göteborg, 1813.

Eckerlund, J. F., *Tal om Upplysningens förmånliga följder, i anledning af reformationsseclet*, Kalmar, 1806.

Encyklopédie ou dictionnaire raisonné des sciences . . . , vol. 7 esp. 28, Bern/Lausanne, 1778, resp. 1780.

Förteckning på Johan Hjerpes boksamling, Skara, 1825.

Gjörwell, C. C., *Anteckningar* . . . , *Samlingar utg. för de skånska landskapens historiska och arkeologiska förening 3* (ed. M. Weibull), Lund, 1875.

Gömdt är icke glömdt: Historiska bidrag 12, Linköping, 1846.

Hamilton, A. L., 'Anekdoter til svenska historien under Gustaf III:s regering', *Svenska memoarer och brev 4* (ed. O. Levertin), Stockholm, 1901.

Hammarsköld, L., 'Teleologiska betraktelser öfver verlds-historien', *Hermes 2* (1821).

Hedvig Elisabeth Charlottas dagbok 3, Stockholm, 1907.

Historisk almanacka, Stockholm, 1750–1754, resp. 1780–1784.

Hochschild, R. F., *Memoarer 1*, Stockholm, 1908.

Kant, I., 'Svar på frågan: Vad är upplysning?', in *Vad är upplysning?*

Lagerbring, S., *Mindre sammandrag af Swea Rikes historia*, Stockholm, 1775.

Lagerbring, S., *Sammandrag av Svea rikes historia*, 2: dra upplagan, Stockholm, 1779–1804.

Ménétra, J.-L., *Journal de ma vie: compagnon vitrier au 18ᵉ siècle* (ed. D. Roche), Paris, 1982.

Ménétra, J.-L., *Journal of my life* (ed. D. Roche), New York, 1986.

Nordin, C. G., 'Dagboksanteckningar för åren 1786–1792', in *Historiska handlingar 6*, Stockholm, 1868.

Öberg, P. J., *Minnen från gesällåren* . . . , Landskrona, 1873.

Offentliga trycket: 1787 och 1788 års förordningar.

Om tolerancen, Stockholm, 1809.

Protocoller hos högloflige ridderskapet och adeln wid riksdagen i Stockholm år 1789, Stockholm 1809.

Prästeståndets risdagsprotokoll 1734 (ed. A. NorbergA), Stockholm, 1978.

Prästeståndets risdagsprotokoll 1778–1779 (ed. S. Lundhem), Stockholm, 1990.

Rosén von Rosenstein, N., *Samlade skrifter 3*, Stockholm, 1838.

Schröderheim, E., 'Skrifter till konung Gustaf III:s historia' respektive 'Urval ur Schröderheims brefväxling till Gustav III 17/9 1788', *Från Tredje Gustafs dagar 1*, Lund, 1892.

Stockholms Posttidningar.

Stockholms Posten.

Thorild, T., 'Om upplysningens princip . . .', Thorild, T, *Samlade skrifter 3* (*Svenska författare 15*), Stockholm, 1944.

Voltaire, *Dictionnaire philosophique*, Paris, 1954 (1764).

Voltaire, *Philosophical dictionary*, London, 1988 (1764).

Voltaire, *Traktat om tolransen*, Stockholm, 1964 (1763).

Wallqvist, O., 'Berättelse om riksdagen 1789.' *Historiska handlingar 5:6*, Stockholm, 1866.

[Wargentin, P.], *Stockholms stads (historiska) calendar, 1761–1777.*

Warmholtz, C. G., *Bibliotheca historica Sveo-Gothica 3* och *5*, Stockholm, 1787 and 1790.

Literature

Åberg, Å., *Västerås mellan Kellgren och Onkel Adam: studier i provinsens litterära villkor och system*, Västerås, 1987.

Adlerbeth, G. G., *Historiska anteckningar 1*, Stockholm, 1892.

Adorno, T. and Horkheimer, M. *The dialectics of Enlightenment*, New York, 1973.

Ahlberger, C., *Vävarfolket: hemindustrin i Mark 1790–1850*, Göteborg, 1988.

Åhlén, B., *Ord mot ordningen: farliga skrifter, bokbål och kättarprocesser i svensk censurhistoria*, Stockholm, 1986.

Åkerberg, H., *Hermeneutik och pedagogisk psykologi: premisser för tolkning och förståelse inom beteendevetenskap*, Stockholm, 1986.

Ambjörnsson, R., *Den skötsamme arbetaren: idéer och ideal i ett norrländskt sågverkssamhälle 1880–1930*, Stockholm, 1988.

Ambrosiani, G., *Från det svenska skråämbetets dagar*, Stockholm, 1920.

Andersson, H. O. and Bedoire, F., *Stockholms byggnader: en bok om arkitektur och byggnader i Stockholm*, Stockholm, 1974.

Ankarcrona, A., *Bud på böcker: bokauktioner i Stockholm 1782–1801*, Stockholm, 1989.

Anners, E., *Humanitet och rationalism: studier i upplysningstidens strafflagsreformer med hänsyn till Gustav III:s reformlagstiftning*, Stockholm, 1965.

Arvidson, S., *Thorild och den franska revolutionen*, Stockholm, 1938.

Asplund, J., *Det sociala livets elementära former*, Göteborg, 1987.

Asplund, J., *Sociala egenskapsrymder: En introduktion i formaliseringsteknik för sociologer*, Uppsala, 1968.

Bachtin, M., *Rabelais and His World*, Cambridge (Mass.), 1968.

Barton, A. H., *Scandinavia in the revolutionary era 1760–1815*, Minneapolis, 1986.

Beik, W., 'Popular culture and elite repression in early modern Europe', *Journal of interdisciplinary history* 11 (1980).

Benedict, P., 'Bibliothèques protestantes et catholiques à Metz au xviie siècle', *Annales ESC* 40 (1985).

Berg, G., 'Behövlingen i Enköpings snickaregesällskap', *Fataburen*, (1936).

Bergfelt, B., *Utländska nyheter från Paris: två stockholmstidningars bevakning av franska revolutionen under perioden 1788–1793*, Department of Economic History, Stockholm University, 1989.

Biersack, A., 'Local knowledge, local history: Geertz and beyond', in *The new cultural history*.

Biografiskt lexikon över namnkunnige svenska män 20 (om Olof Wallqvist), Uppsala, 1852.

Boberg, S., *Kunglig krigspropaganda*, Göteborg, 1967.

Boëthius, B., 'Adam de Broën', *Svenskt biografiskt lexikon 10*, Stockholm, 1931.

Boëthius, B., *Magistraten och borgerskapet i Stockholm 1719–1815*, Stockholm, 1943.

Bollerup, E., 'Om franska inflytelser på svensk historieskrivning under frihetstiden', *Scandia* 34 (1968).

Bollerup, E., 'Lagerbrings Svea Rikes historia: tillkomst, utgivning, mottagande', *Scandia* 36 (1970).

Booth, A., Popular loyalism and public violence in the north-west of England, 1790–1800, *Social history* 8 (1983).

Braudel, F., 'History and the social sciences: the *Longue Durée*', Braudel, F., *On history*, Chicago, 1980.

Breisach, E., *Historiography: ancient, medieval & modern*, Chicago and London, 1983.

Bring, S., *Bibliografisk handbok till Sveriges historia*, Stockholm, 1934.

Burke, P., 'Popular culture between history and ethnology', *Ethnologia Europæa* 14, (1982).

Burke, P., *The historical anthropology of early modern Italy: essays on perception and communication*, Cambridge (Mass.), 1987.

Burke, P., *The French historical revolution: The Annales School 1929–89*, Cambridge and Oxford, 1990.

Burke, P., *Popular Culture in Early Modern Europe*, Aldershot, 1994.

Carlsson, A., *Böcker i bohuslänka bouppteckningar 1752–1808*, Göteborg, 1972.

Carlsson, S., *Svensk historia 2*, Stockholm, 1970.

Chartier, R., 'Intellectual history or sociocultural history? The French trajectories', *Modern European intellectual history* (eds D. LaCapra and S. L. Kaplan), Ithaca and London, 1982.

Chartier, R., 'Texts, symbols, and Frenchness', *Journal of modern history* 57 (1985).

Chartier, R., 'Les pratiques de l'écrit', *Histoire de la vie privée: de la Renaissance au Lumières* (ed. R. Chartier), Paris, 1986.

Chartier, R., 'Texts, printings, readings', in *The new cultural history*.

Chartier, R., *Cultural history: between practices and representations*, Cambridge and Oxford, 1988.

Chartier, R., *The culture of print: power and uses of print in early modern Europe*, Cambridge, 1989.

Chartier, R., *The cultural origins of the French revolution*, Durham and London, 1991.

Christiansen, P. O., 'Construction of the past: from "Montaillou" to "The name of the rose"', *Ethnologia Europæa* 18 (1988).

Colley, L., 'Whose nation? Class and national consciousness in Britain 1750–1830', *Past and Present* 113 (1986).

Coutau-Bégarie, H., *Le phenomène 'Nouvelle histoire'*, Paris, 1983.

Darnton, R., *The Literary Underground of the Old Regime*, Cambridge (Mass.) and London, 1982.

Darnton, R., *The Great Cat Massacre and other Episodes in French Cultural History*, New York, 1984.

Darnton, R., 'The symbolic element in history', *Journal of modern history* 58 (1986).

Darnton, R., *The Forbidden Best-Sellers of Pre-Revolutionary France*, New York and London, 1995.

Davis, N., *The Return of Martin Guerre*, London and Cambridge (Mass.), 1983.

Davis, N., *Society and culture in early modern France*, Cambridge and Oxford, 1987.

Davis, N., 'Anthropology and history in the 1980s', *Journal of interdisciplinary history* 12 (1981).

Delumeau, J., *La péché et la peur: la culpabilisation en Occident*, Paris, 1983.

Delumeau, J., *Sin and fear: the emergence of a Western guilt culture 13th–18th centuries*, New York, 1990.

Dreyfus, H. L. and Rabinow, P., 'What is maturity? Habermas and Foucault on "What is Enlightenment?"', *Foucault: a critical reader* (ed. D. Couzens Hoy), New York, 1989.

Edgren, L., *Lärling, gesäll, mästare: hantverk och hantverkare i Malmö 1750–1847*, Lund, 1987.

Ehn, B. and Löfgren, O., *Kulturanalys: ett etnologiskt perspektiv*, Lund, 1982.

Eisenstein, E. L., 'Some conjectures about the impact of printing on Western society and thought: a preliminary report', in *Literacy and social development in the West*.

Ek, S., *Skämtare och allvarsmän i Stockholms Postens första årgångar: studier i tidningens prosainlägg och Kellgrens utveckling 1778–81*, Malmö, 1952.

Elias, N., *The civilizing process 1–2*, New York, 1978–1982.

Elster, J., *Vestenskapliga förklaringar*, Göteborg, 1988.

Erikson, E. H., *Identity and the life cycle*, New York, 1959.

Erikson, E. H., *Identity, Youth and Crisis*, New York, 1968.

Eriksson, N., *Dalin–Botin–Lagerbring: historieskrivning och historieforskning i Sverige 1747–1787*, Göteborg, 1973.

Farge, A., *Livets sköra tråd: våld, makt och solidaritet i 1700-talets Paris*, Stockholm, 1989.

Febvre, L., *The problem of unbelief in the sixteenth century: the religion of Rabelais*, Cambridge (Mass.) and London, 1982.

Fernandez, J., 'Historians tell tale: of Cartesian cats and gallic cockfights', *Journal of modern history*, vol. 60 (1988).

Florén, A. and Persson, M., 'Mentalitetshistoria och mentalitetsbegreppet', *Lychnos*, 1985.

Floto, I., *Historie: Nyere og nyeste tid*, Copenhagen, 1985.

Fogelstrom, P.-A., 'Häxorna i Katarina', *Historia Kring Stockholm*, Stockholm, 1985.

Forser, T., *Bööks trettiotal; en studie i ideologi, Stockholm 1976*.

Foucault, M., 'What is Enlightenment?', in *The Foucault reader* (ed. P. Rabinow), Harmondsworth, 1984.

Foucault, M., *Discipline and punishment: the birth of the prison*, New York, 1979.

Foucault, M., *The history of sexuality: an introduction*, Harmondsworth, 1978.

Foucault, *Madness and civilization: a history of insanity in the age of reason*. London, 1965.

Frängsmyr, T., *Framsteg eller förfall: framtidsbilder och utopier i västerländsk tanketradition*, Stockholm, 1981.

Frängsmyr, T., 'Den svenska upplysningen: fanns den?', *Artes* no. 1 (1987).

Freud, S., *The ego and the id*, London, 1975.

Freud, S., *Group psychology and the analysis of the ego*, London, 1975.

Freud, S., *The unconscious*, London, 1975.

Freud, S., *Introductory lectures on psychoanalysis*, London, 1976.

Freud, S., *New introductory lectures on psychoanalysis*, London, 1979.

Furbank, P. N., 'Nothing Sacred', *New York Review of Books*, number 10, 8/6, 1995.

Furet, F. and Ozouf, J., 'Three centuries of cultural cross-fertilization: France', in *Literacy and social development in the West*.

Gadd, C.-J., *Järn och potatis: jordbruk, teknik och social omvandling i Skaraborgs län 1750–1860*, Göteborg, 1983.

Gardella, P., *Innocent ecstasy: how Christianity gave America an ethic of sexual pleasure*, New York and Oxford, 1985.

Gay, P., 'Editor's introduction' to Voltaire, *Philosophical dictionary*.

Gay, P., *The Enlightenment: an interpretation 1*, London, 1967.

Gay, P., *The Enlightenment: an interpretation 2*, New York, 1969.

Gay, P., *Freud for historians*, New York, 1985.

Giddens, A., *The constitution of society*, Cambridge and Oxford, 1986.

Ginzburg, C., *The cheese and the worms: the cosmos of a sixteenth-century miller*, London and Henley, 1980.

Ginzburg, C., *The night battles: witchcraft & agrarian cults in the sixteenth & seventeenth centuries*, London, Melbourne and Henley, 1983.

Ginzburg, C., *Ledtrådar: essäer om konst, förbjuden kunskap och dold historia*, Stockholm, 1989.

Ginzburg, C., 'Représentation: Le mot, l'idée, la chose', *Annales ESC* 46:6 (1991).

Griessinger, A., *Das symbolische Kapital der Ehre: Streikbewegungen und kollektives Bewusstsein deutscher Handwerksgesellen in 18. Jahrhundert*, Frankfurt, Berlin and Vienna, 1981.

Grönros, H., *Boken i Finland: bokbeståndet hos borgerskap, hantverkare och lägre sociala gruppen Finlands städer enlight städernas bouppteckningar 1656–1809*, Helsingfors, 1996.

Habermas, J., *Communication and the evolution of society*, London, 1979.

Habermas, J., *The theory of communicative action 1: reason and the rationalization of society*, Boston, 1984.

Habermas, J., 'Mit dem Pfeil ins Herz der Gegenwart', taz 7/7 (1984).

Hagen, R., 'Historien om mentaliteterna', *Häften för kritiska studier* no. 1 (1984).

Häll, J., *I Swedenborgs labyrint: Studier i de gustavianska swedenborgarnas liv och tänkande*, Stockholm, 1995.

Hallendorff, C., 'Hedvig Elisabeth Charlotta', *Svenskt biografiskt lexikon 8*, Stockholm, 1929.

Hamberg, E. M., *Studies in the prevalence of religious beliefs and religious practice in contemporary Sweden*, Uppsala, 1990.

Hansson, S., *Skråtidens gesäller*, Stockholm, 1930.

Heckscher, E. F., *Sveriges ekonomiska historia från Gustav Vasa*, Stockholm, 1949.

Hedman, R., 'Massan vid det s k fersenska upploppet', *Historisk tidskrift* 89 (1969).

Hennings, B., *Gustav III*, Stockholm, 1990.

Henningsen, G., *The witches' advocate: Basque witchcraft and the Spanish Inquisition (1609–1614)*, Reno, 1980.

Hertzberg, A., *The French Enlightenment and the jews*, New York, 1990.

Hessler, C. A., '"Aristokratfördömandet": en riktning i svensk historieskrivning', *Scandia* 15 (1943).

Hexter, J. H., 'Fernand Braudel and the Monde Braudellien . . .', *Journal of modern history* 44 (1972).

Hobsbawm, E. J., *Primitive rebels*, Manchester, 1974 (1959).

Hobsbawm, E. J., 'The revival of narrative: some comments', *Past & Present* 86 (1980).

Högberg, S., *Stockholms historia* 2, Stockholm, 1981.

Holmberg, Å., 'Att omvärdera omvärlden – synen på exotiska folk i svenska historieböcker', in *Vetenskap och omvärdering: till Curt Weibull på hundraårsdagen 19 augusti 1986* (eds G. Dahlström, P. Hallberg and Å. Holmberg,). Göteborg, 1986.

Holmberg, Å., *Världen bortom västerlandet: svensk syn på fjärran länder och folk från 1700-talet till första världskriget*, Göteborg, 1988.

Holmberg, O., *Wälmenta anmärkningar . . .*, Uppsala, 1791.

Holmberg, O., *Orsakerna till förtwiflan och sjelfmord*, Uppsala, 1789.

Holmgren, J., *Norrlandsläseriet: studier till dess förhistoria och historia fram till år 1830*, Lund, 1948.

Holton, R. J., 'The crowd in history: Some problems of theory and method', *Social history* 3 (1978).

Horstbøll, H., 'Cosmology and Economics: discontinuity and continuity in economic conceptions on the market for popular prints in Denmark during the seventeenth and eighteenth centuries', *Scandinavian economic history review* 37 (1989).

Horstbøll, H., 'Tingenes natur er ikke en roman: om historieskrivningens tider og rum', *Den jyske historiker* 50 (1990).

Houston, R. A., *Literacy in early modern Europe*, London and New York, 1988.

Hunt, L., 'French history in the last twenty years: the rise and fall of the *Annales* paradigm', *Journal of contemporary history* 21 (1986).

Hunt, L., *The family romance of the French revolution*, Berkely, 1992.

Iggers, G., *New directions in European historiography*, Middleton, 1975.

International handbook of historical studies (eds G. Iggers and H. T. Parker), Westport and London, 1980.

Jägerskiöld, O., 'Rutger Fredrik Hochschild', *Svenskt biografiskt lexikon 19*, Stockholm, 1971–73.

Jarrick, A., 'Freud och historien', *Scandia* 48 (1982).

Jarrick, A., *Psykologisk socialhistoria*, Stockholm, 1985.

Jarrick, A., 'Mentalitetshistoria – parismode eller seriös forskning?', in *Från vida fält: festskrift till Rolf Adamson 25/10 1987* (eds U. Jonsson and J. Söderberg), Stockholm, 1987.

Jarrick, A., *Den himmelske älskaren: herrnhutisk väckelse, vantro och sekularisering i 1700-talets Sverige*, Stockholm, 1987.

Jarrick, A., 'Världen går framåt, tycker jag', *Häften för kritiska studier* no. 3 (1989).

Jarrick, A., 'Framstegstanken i den historiska texten: några uppslag om fiktion och forskning', *Bonniers litterära magasin* no. 4 (1989).

Jarrick, A., 'Ur det förflutnas djup – om psykoanalys och historieforskning', *Psykoanalys och kultur* (eds H. Reiland and F. Ylander), Stockholm, 1991.

Jarrick, A., 'Visst fanns det en upplysning i Sverige!', *Opplysning i Norden* (ed. H. Uecker), Frankfurt am Main, 1998.

Jarrick, A. and Josephson, O., *Från tanke till text: Språkhandbok för uppsatsskrivande studenter*, Lund, 1988.

Jarrick, A. and Söderberg, J., 'Aktörsstrukturalismen: ett nytt hugg på humanvetenskapens gordiska knut', *Historisk tidskrift* 111 (1991).

Jarrick, A. and Söderberg, J., *Empirisk civiliseringsforskning*, research report to the conference *Civiliseringsteori och historisk forskning*, Department of Economic History, Stockholm university, 1991.

Jarrick, A. and Söderberg, J., 'Spontaneous processes of civilization: the Swedish case', *Ethnologia Europæa* 23:1 (1993).

Jay, P., 'What's the use? Criticial theory and the study of the autobiography', *Biography* 10 (1987).

Jersild, M., *Skillingtryck: studier i svensk folklig vissång före 1800*, Stockholm, 1975.

Johannesson, L., ' "Schene Rariteten": antisemitisk bildagitation i svensk rabulistpress 1845–1860', in *Judiskt liv i Norden*.

Johansson, E., *The history of literacy in Sweden: in comparison with some other countries*, Umeå, 1977.

Jonsson, G., *N M Lindh i Örebro: 1798–1829 sedd genom Sveriges bibliografi 1700–1829*, report, Kungliga biblioteket, Stockholm, 1989.

Jonsson, K., 'Mellan den sociala determinismens Scylla och den psykologiska reduktionismens Charybdis: problem i den idéhistoriska biografins genre', *Liv och text*, Idéhistoriska skrifter, Umeå, 1985.

Jonsson, U., *Mortality patterns in 18th century Stockholm in a European perspective*, Stockholm, 1984.

Jonsson, U., 'Annales-traditionen: ett paradigm i upplösning eller förnyelse?', *Historisk tidskrift* 111 (1991).

Jörberg, L., *A history of prices in Sweden 1732–1914*, Lund, 1972.

Judiskt liv i Norden (eds G. Broberg, H. Runblom and M. Tydén), Uppsala, 1988.

Karlbom, R., *Hungerupplopp och strejker 1793–1867: en studie i den svenska arbetarrörelsens uppkomst*, Lund, 1967.

Keesing, R. M., 'Theories of culture', *Annual review of anthropology* 3 (1974).

Kiernan, V. G., *The lords of the human kind: black man, yellow man, and white man in an age of empire*, Boston and Toronto, 1969.

Klaits, J., *Servants of Satan: The age of the witch hunts*, Indiana, 1985.

Kohut, H., *The search for the self: selected writings of Heinz Kohut 1950–1978 1*, New York, 1978.

Korpi, W., *Arbetarklassen i välfärdskapitalismen: arbete, fackförening och politik i Sverige*, Stockholm, 1978.

Kuuse, J., *Från redskap till maskiner: mekaniseringsspridning och kommersialisering inom svenskt jordbruk 1860–1910*, Göteborg, 1970.

LaCapra, D., *Rethinking intellectual history: texts, contexts, language*, Ithaca and London, 1983.

LaCapra, D., 'Chartier, Darnton, and the great symbol massacre', *Journal of modern history*, vol. 60 (1988).

La Fontaine, J. S., *Initiation: ritual drama and secret knowledge across the world*, New York and other places, 1995.

Lamm, M., *Upplysningstidens romantik II*, Enskede, 1963.

[The] Leader: psychohistorical essays (eds C. B. Strozier and D. Offer), New York and London, 1985.

Le Goff, J., 'Mentalities: a history of ambiguities', in *Constructing the past. Essays in historical methodology* (eds J. Le Goff and P. Nora), Stockholm, 1978.

Le Roy Ladurie, E., *The peasants of Languedoc*, Urbana, Chicago and London, 1974.

Le Roy Ladurie, E., *Montaillou: en fransk by 1294–1324*, Stockholm, 1980.

Lenhammar, H., *Tolerans och bekännelsetvång: studier i den svenska swedenborgianismen 1765–1795*, Uppsala, 1966.

Less, G., *Om Sjelfmord*, Stockholm, 1788.

Levack, P., *The witch-hunt in early modern Europe*, London and New York, 1987.

Levi, G., 'Les usages de la biographie', *Annales ESC* 44 (1989).

Lévi-Strauss, C., *Det vilda tänkandet*, Lund, 1987.

Lewis, G. 'The white terror of 1815 in the department of the Gard: counterrevolution, continuity and the individual', *Past & Present* 58 (1973).

Lext, G., *Bok och samhälle i Göteborg 1720–1809*, Göteborg, 1950.

Liedman, S.-E., *Den synliga handen: Anders Berch och ekonomiämnena vid 1700-talets svenska universitet*, Stockholm, 1986.

Liljedahl, R., 'En gustaviansk handelsbetjänt', *Svenska Dagbladet* 20/9 1944.

Liljedahl, R., 'En märklig auktion i Skara', *Skara tidning* 24/1 1973.

Liljedahl, R., 'Samtal med en 1700-talsmänniska', *Helsingborgs dagblad* 1/6 1974.

Liljedahl, R., 'Att umgås med en 1700-talsmänniska', *Norrköpings tidningar – Östergötlands tidningar*, 23/1 1975.

Lindberg, S. G., '500 år av svensk bokproduktion – och biblioteken', *Biblis* (1983).

Lindroth, S., *Vetenskapsakademins historia I:2*, Uppsala, 1967.

Lindroth, S., *Svensk lärdomshistoria: frihetstiden*, Stockholm, 1978.

Lindroth, S., *Svensk lärdomshistoria: gustavianska tiden*, Stockholm, 1989.

Literacy and social development in the West: a reader (ed. H. J. Graff), Cambridge, 1981.

Löfgren, O., 'Mentalitetshistoria och kulturanalys', *Häften för kritiska studier*, no. 4 1984.

Löfgren, O., 'Mentalitet: några reflektioner kring ett problematiskt begrepp', *'Mentaliteter': Meddelanden från Stiftelsen för Åbo akademi forskningsinstitut* no. 118 (ed. P. Sällström), Åbo, 1986.

Löfgren, O., 'På jakt efter den borgerliga kulturen', *Mentalitetsforandringer: studier i historisk metode* 19 (eds. C. Kvium and B. Wåhlin), Aarhus, 1987.

Lönnroth, A., Interview with E Le Roy Ladurie, *Svenska Dagbladet* 19 December 1989.

Lönnroth, E., *Den stora rollen: kung Gustaf III spelad av honom själv*, Stockholm, 1986.

Lönnroth, E., 'Det biografiska synsättet', *Historisk tidskrift* 106 (1986).

Lönnroth, E., 'Europa, Norden och judarna', in *Judiskt liv i Norden*.

Lunden, K., ' "Postmodernistisk" historie, eller systemhistorie', *Historisk tidskrift* (norsk) 68 (1989).

McManners, J., *Death and the Enlightenment: changing attitudes among Christians and unbelievers in eighteenth-century France*, Oxford, 1981.

Magnusson, L., *Den bråkiga kulturen: förläggare & smideshantverkare i Eskilstuna 1800–1850*, Stockholm, 1988.

Mazlish, B., *The riddle of history*, New York and London, 1966.

McCloskey, D. N., 'The achievements of the cliometric school', *The journal of economic history* 38 (1978).

Med tryckpress och giljotin: en utställning om franska revolutionen, Uppsala universitetsbibliotek, Uppsala, 1989.

Merton, R. K., 'The unanticipated consequences of purposive social action', *American sociological review* 1 (1936).

Moore, Jr, B., *Injustice: the social bases of obedience and revolt*, London, 1978.

Moscovici, S., *The age of the crowd: a historical treatise on Mass Psychology*, Cambridge (Mass.) and other places, 1985.

Muchembled, R., *Popular culture and elite culture in France 1400–1750*, Baton Rouge and London, 1985.

Näslund, L., *Studier om importen av utländsk politisk litteratur under frihetstiden*, unpublished thesis, Stockholm, 1971.

Nerman, T., *Crusenstolpes kravaller*, Stockholm, 1938.

[The] new cultural history (ed. L. Hunt), Berkeley, Los Angeles and London, 1989.

Nilsson, Å., 'Elis Schröderheim', Svenska män och kvinnor 6, Stockholm, 1949.

Nordin, S., Från tradition till apokalyps: historieskrivning och civilisationskritik i det moderna Europa, Stockholm, Lund and Stehag, 1989.

North, D. C., 'Comment', The journal of economic history 38 (1978).

Nye, R. A., The origins of crowd psychology: Gustave Le Bon and the crisis of mass democracy in the Third republic, London and Beverly Hills, 1975.

Nyman, M., Press mot friheten: opinionsbildning i de svenska tidningarna och åsiktsbrytningar om minoriteter 1772–1786, Uppsala, 1987.

Nyman, M., 'News from France in a Swedish provincial paper during the years before the French revolution', Lychnos (1989).

Nyman, M. Upplysningens spegel. Götheborgs Allehanda om Frankrike och världen 1774–1789, Stockholm, 1994.

Nyrop, C., Haandwærksskik i Danmark, Copenhagen, 1903.

Nyrop, C., Nogle gewohnheiter, Cophenhagen, 1904.

O'Brien, P., 'Michel Foucault's history of culture', in The new cultural history.

Odén, B., Lauritz Weibull och forskarsamhället, Lund, 1975.

Ödman, P.-J., Konformismens triumf: utvecklingslinjer i svensk 1600-talspedagogik, Stockholm, 1987.

Ödman, P.-J., Tid av frihet, tid av tvång: utvecklingslinjer i svensk 1700-talspedagogik, Stockholm, 1990.

Ong, W. J., Orality and literacy: the technologizing of the word, London and New York, 1982.

Ozouf, M., Festivals and the French revolution, Cambridge (Mass.) and London, 1988.

Pardailhé-Galabrun, A., La naissance de l'intime: 3 000 foyers parisiens XVIIᵉ–XVIIIᵉ siècles, Paris, 1988.

Paz, O., Sor Juana or the traps of faith, Cambridge (Mass.), 1988.

Peterson, B., 'Vad läste sundsvallsbon på 1840-talet?', Historia nu: 18 umeåforskare om det förflutna (eds A. Brändström et al.), Umeå, 1988.

Peterson, G., Jordbrukets omvandling i västra Östergötland 1810–1890, Stockholm, 1989.

Piaget, J., Language and Thought of the Child, London, 1960.

Piaget, J., Play, dreams and imitation in childhood, New York, 1962.

Piaget, J., Structuralism, London, 1971.

Qvarsell, R., Kulturmiljö och idéspridning: idédebatt, bokspridning och sällskapsliv kring 1800-talets mitt, Stockholm, 1988.

Qvist, G., 'Om bouppteckningar och deras bokbeståndsuppgifter som historiskt källmaterial', Historisk tidskrift 93 (1973).

Reuterswärd, E., 'Kungörandet av Gustav III:s ryska krig 1788–1790', in Över gränser: festskrift till Birgitta Odén (eds. I. Norrlid et al.), Lund, 1987.

Richards, R. J., Darwin and the emergence of evolutionary theories of mind and behavior, Chicago and London, 1987.

Richters, A., 'Modernity-postmodernity controversies: Habermas and Foucault', Theory, culture & society 5 (1988).

Ricoeur, P., Hermeneutics & the human sciences, Cambridge and Paris, 1987.

Roche, D., 'La violence vue d'en bas: réflexions sur les moyens de la politique en période révolutionnaire' Annales ESC 44 (1989).

Rudé, G., 'The London "mob" of the eighteenth century', The historical journal 2 (1959).

Rudé, G., The crowd in history 1730–1848, New York, London and Sydney, 1964.

Sahlberg, G., 'Henric Liljensparre', Svenskt biografiskt lexikon 23, Stockholm, 1980–81.

Sahlin, G., Författarrollens förändring och det litterära systemet 1770–1795, Stockholm, 1989.

Sahlins, M., Kapten Cooks död, Stockholm, 1988.

Sanders, H., *Den gudelige vækkelse på Langeland 1837–39: en vurdering af dens samspil med lokal-samfundet*, unpublished thesis 'speciale', Copenhagen, 1987.

Sanders, H., *Svensk forskning om den religiöse väkkelse 1800–1850 problematiseret af dansk forskning om samme emne*, research report, department of history, Stockholm university, 1988.

Schlumbohm, J., ' "Traditional" collectivity and "modern" individuality: some questions and suggestions . . .', *Social history* 5:1 (1980),

Schmitt, J.-C., *The holy greyhound. Guinefort, healer of children since the thirteenth century*, Cambridge, 1983.

Seaver, P. S., *Wallington's world: a puritan artisan in seventeenth-century London*, Stanford, 1985.

Segerstedt, T. T., *Nils von Rosenstein: samhällets människa*, Stockholm, 1981.

Silvén, E. and Söderlind, I., *Ett annat Sverige: dokument om folkets kamp 1200–1720*, Stockholm, 1980.

Soboul, A., *The Parisian sans-culottes and the French revolution 1793–1794*, Oxford, 1964.

Söderberg, J., 'Den stagnerande staden: Stockholms tillväxtproblem 1760–1850 i ett jämförande europeiskt perspektiv', *Historisk tidskrift* 105 (1985).

Söderberg, J., 'Real wage trends in urban Europe, 1730–1850: Stockholm in a comparative perspective', *Social history* 12 (1987).

Söderberg, J., 'Makrohistoria och lokalhistoria', *Lokalt, regionalt, centralt: analysnivåer i historisk forskning* (ed. I. Hammarström), Stockholm, 1988.

Söderberg, J., Jonsson, U. and Persson, C., *Stagnating metropolis: economy and demography in Stockholm 1750–1850*.

Söderlund, E., *Hantverkarna 2*, Stockholm, 1949.

Söderlund, E., *Stockholms hantverkarklass 1720–1772*, Stockholm, 1943.

Spufford, M., 'First steps in literacy: the reading and writing experiences of the humblest seventeenth-century spiritual autobiographies', in *Literacy and social development in the West*.

Staf, N., *Polisväsendet i Stockholm 1776–1850*, Uppsala, 1950.

Statistisk årsbok för Stockholms stad 1905, Stockholm, 1905.

Stone, L., 'The revival of narrative: reflections on a new old history' *Past & Present* 85 (1979).

Svenska män och kvinnor 6, Stockholm, 1949.

Svensson, J., *Kommunikationshistoria: om kommunikationsmiljön i Sverige under fem sekler*, Lund, 1988.

Svensson, S., 'Erik Ruuth', *Svenska män och kvinnor 6*, Stockholm, 1949.

Sveriges riksdag I:6 (ed. N. Edén), Stockholm, 1934.

Thomas, K., *Man and the natural world: changing attitudes in England 1500–1800*, London, 1983.

Thompson, E. P., *The making of the English working class*, Harmondsworth, 1977.

Thompson, E. P., 'The moral economy of the English crowd in the eighteenth century', *Past & Present* 60 (1971).

Tilly, C., *The contentious French*, Cambridge (Mass.) and London, 1986.

Torstendahl, R., 'Leopold von Rankes historiografiska betydelse', in Torstendahl, R. and Nybom, T., *Historievetenskap som teori, praktik, ideologi*, Stockholm, 1988.

Turner, J., *Without God, without creed: the origins of unbelief in America*, Baltimore and London, 1985.

Upmark, G., 'En gesällbok från 1700-talet', *Fataburen* (1990).

Vad är upplysning? (ed. B. Östling), Stockholm and Stehag, 1989.

Valentin, H., *Judarna i Sverige*, Stockholm, 1964.

Vovelle, M., 'Ideologies and mentalities', *Culture, ideology and politics* (eds Raphael Samuel and Gareth Stedman Jones), London, 1982.

Vovelle, M., 'Le tournant des mentalités en France 1750–1789: la "sensibilité" pré-révolutionnaire', *Social history* no. 2 (1977).

Vovelle, M., *La mort et l'Occident de 1300 à nos jours*, Paris, 1983.

Vovelle, M., *La mentalité révolutionnaire: société et mentalité sous la révolution française*, Paris, 1985.

Vucinich, A., *Social thought in Tsarist Russia*, Chicago, 1976.

Vyverberg, H., *Historical pessimism in the French Enlightenment*, Cambridge (Mass.), 1958.

Wallace, E. R., *Historigraphy and causation in psychoanalysis: an essay on psychoanalytic and historical epistemology*, Hillsdale (New Jersey) and London, 1985.

Wentworth, S., *Marginalizing history: a critique of the cliometric program in economic history*, Uppsala, 1984.

Wessel, N., *Svenska typografernas historia*, Stockholm and Oskarshamn, 1916.

Will, D., 'Psychoanalysis and the new philosophy of science', *International review of psychoanalysis* 13 (1986).

Williams, D. E., 'Morals, markets and the English crowd in 1706', *Past & Present* 104 (1984).

Winberg, C., 'Några anteckningar om historisk antropologi', *Historisk tidskrift* 108 (1988).

Woods, Jr, R. L., 'Individuals in a rioting crowd: a new approach', *The journal of interdisciplinary history* 14:1 (1983).

Wrong, D. H., *Skeptical sociology*, New York, 1976.

Zitomersky, J., 'The jewish population in Sweden 1780–1980: an ethno-demographic study', in *Judiskt liv i Norden*.

Index of Names